# The Horseshoe Colonel

*The Untold Story of Colonel John Williams,
Andrew Jackson's Greatest Rival*

By Alexander Fyffe Brandau III

© 2018 by Alexander F. Brandau III

I send you here a little book, For you to look upon,

Where you may see a Hero's face when he is past and gone.

- John Williams in *The Political Mirror*

*Colonel and Senator John Williams*
*1778-1837*
Courtesy of East Tennessee Historical Society

General Richard G. Dunlap to Jackson

Knoxville, Tennessee, July 2, 1823

Your nomination to the presidency, has been of subsequent origin and in fact was viewed of minor importance, to the warding off, those deadly blows which were aim(ed) at your standing: and now can be use(d) as a means by which, pay can be had for former injuries. "A change how sad!" Though not to me, its truly melancholly notwithstanding. "Anguish rends the heart" but still your friends feel a soothing comfort.

To be or not to be, is the awful struggle with the colo, and not to be, is what I'm for. Things seemed to have been, under the guidance of heaven, going on smoothly, for the defeat of the horse shoe Colo.- . . . . .

Your friend,

I do not request an answer.
N.B. I have not shewn this letter to any person.

R.G.D.[1]

*Letter from General Richard G. Dunlap to General Andrew Jackson*

# Foreword
# The Beginning

This story started for me when I was four. My paternal grandmother's second husband had died unexpectedly. I had barely begun my participation in this life-changing event the night before the funeral.

Grandmother Linda had bad asthma. My older brother says she "never took a good breath in her life." For one who had started so high in society in the small town that remains Knoxville, Tennessee, she had lived a tough life. Her domineering father was a judge; he disapproved of her first husband, who had given her two young boys, so the judge made life so miserable for my grandfather that he, Alex, stole company money from his family and disappeared overnight. Four generations later, we're still trying to get over that!

She had found her second husband twelve years after the first one abandoned her, and though he was a simple man, he loved her and gave her much joy. He loved we three grandchildren too and was a farmer and security guard at a large aluminum plant. The Great War had ended six years earlier, and though our parents had divorced, my grandmother and her second husband, Reuben, were still our grandparents who visited often, loved us much, and brought us candy and treats.

When they raised me up at the funeral home to look into Reuben's casket, my four-year-old brain didn't understand death. I asked why he wouldn't wake up and play with me, and that inadvertently stabbed the adults in the heart. When we left the funeral home we had to stop at a Rexall Drug Store to get my grandmother some Felsol powders for her asthma. I'd heard that store mentioned on the radio, and as my dad left the car to run the errand for his mom, I chimed in, "Be sure to tell them Amos and Andy sent ya!"

That kind of made up for my previous faux pas, and we all laughed and went home.

I didn't get to go to the funeral the next day, but everyone came home to our house afterward and it was decided I would get to go home with Grandma to their farm just outside Knoxville. She drove a pink 1948 Plymouth; I say drove, but she barely knew how. So she planned our route so that it went completely over dirt roads, and being virtually unaware of what was going on I happily settled into the front seat. Even at four, I knew she was driving way too slowly—like fifteen mph slowly. Pretty soon I had to wet and told her so; she replied by telling me to just hold it.

A couple more dirt roads later I reminded my grandmother of my urgent need, but she was concentrating on getting us and that car home; I guess she'd hardly ever driven and she was being exceptionally careful. I was becoming exceptionally in distress. She told me we were close and to pull my pants down and "pinch it." I stood up in the front seat and did that and was exceedingly miserable. About that time we pulled into her driveway and the old Plymouth hit a bump that sent me a little into the air, and I let go. I peed all over that car—hit the windshield and everything and was just traumatized that I had done that. She never said a word. Just cleaned up me and the car and got us into the house and settled.

Her old farmhouse was like a lot of rural homes in east Tennessee in 1951: it just had rudimentary plumbing and electricity. There was a cistern that I was never to go near, but I did, and she had a pump in the kitchen sink where we got water. Being a city kid, I had never seen that, and thought it pretty exciting; I wished I had one too and volunteered to pump it any time she needed it.

The bedroom had a single strand of black electrical wire with only a bulb and socket on the end. She had cried off and on and told me earlier that her husband used to go to bed before her and warm up her side of the bed, then move when she showed up. When we retired for the evening I did that too, and she literally cried herself to sleep.

The next day I was introduced to the rooster who "owned" the yard. He didn't like me—she had to swat him with the broom a couple of times to get him to leave me alone, and even then I eyed him warily. She cried off and on, and at my age I didn't quite understand all that, so she began at lunch the next day telling me stories. Stories of how she had grown up a judge's daughter, and that she and her brother were dressed up at my age and paraded at a popular social event then known as cake-walking. I guess if you did it correctly you won a cake, and she said they never failed to win one.

She began telling me stories about her great-grandfather, Colonel John Williams, and I was at the perfect age to soak it all up. She lived with us for a while later on and she, as family historian, would repeat too many times those same stories. She had received those stories verbally from her mother and wanted them to be passed along to the future.

A few years later, while studying my first history course in fifth grade, I asked her if our family had anything to do with Andrew Jackson. She replied, while looking out the window, "You mean Stonewall Jackson!"

"No," I persisted, "I mean Andrew Jackson!" She continued to stare out the window and again mentioned Stonewall Jackson. I became frustrated and stated, "No! I mean Andrew Jackson, Old Hickory, seventh president of the United States." She looked at me with a glimmer of anger in her eyes and said, "Never heard of him," and averted her gaze back to the window.

*Joseph Williams Sneed and sister Linda Lanier Sneed*
Copyright: Alex F. Brandau III personal property

*Sonny (Alex III) Brandau, David Patterson, and Linda Wolfenbarger (my grandmother)*

I knew then that something was drastically wrong. When she died in 1972, she willed to me the family treasure she and her ancestors had worked so long to preserve: the Flag of the 39th Infantry.

*Flag of the 39th Infantry*
Copyright: Alex F. Brandau III personal property

When I married and began my own family in 1974, I took seriously the obligation of preserving this flag. In the spring of 1976, I attended an event at Travellers Rest, the home of Judge John Overton. I asked at a book vendor's stall if they had anything about Colonel John Williams, and was told that Mr. Williams, an Overton descendant, might know more about him, and that they'd have him find me. When he did, he asked why I was interested, and I told him of the flag and of my descent from Colonel Williams.

Williams replied, "I will tell you that it all goes back to that petition signed by the officers of the 39th before the Battle of Horseshoe Bend. I'll also tell you that John Williams was a gentleman and Andrew Jackson was a scoundrel." He and I became friends that day and continued to be so until his death. We were cousins through Overton's wife, who was a sister of Colonel John Williams' wife, Melinda White.

I began to research the flag and Colonel John Williams in 1975 and I have yet to stop; every question I answer raises two more! I did not begin this project to perpetuate the feud between the two men, and I had no intention of writing anything unfavorable about Andrew Jackson. But when I would interview historians, invariably they would make excuses about Old Hickory that I found curious. "Well, Jackson had his eccentricities." He surely did.

After I had the Flag of the 39th preserved at the Museum of Early Southern Decorative Art, I took it to a public appraisal event sponsored by the new Tennessee State Museum. They were in awe of it, but laughed when I stated, as I had been told, that Sam Houston carried it in the battle. I asked why they had laughed and they replied, "Well, objects acquire legends just like people do; somebody says something and it gets passed down through time. We'd need to see some documentation of that claim." I found six written references, and it was displayed in the Houston exhibit at the Tennessee State Library for many years.

What I found through the many years of research was that many inaccuracies had survived through time regarding all three men and the Battle of the Horseshoe. To be accurate, some things cannot be proven without any doubt. But this is my attempt to tell an old story from a different point of view.

I ended the feud with the Jackson family and mean them no harm. I hope you can too.

- - - ! ! !

I use that subject divider because John Williams did too. His great-great-grandson, Tom (TN), did also!

This story is written primarily from three sources, though many others are cited. The three sources are:

### Woodward's Reminiscences,
by Thomas S. Woodward, 1859

Colonel Woodward was a young man of mixed descent—including some Indian blood—who fought on the side of the white settlers. He spent several campaigns with General Jackson and wrote his remembrances late in his life. He contradicts several "popular" stories of the Indian Wars and clarifies the Indian society.

### Andrew Jackson and Early Tennessee History,
by S. G. Heiskell, 1920

Heiskell was a mayor of Knoxville. This book was described to me by Charles Elder, a lifelong Tennessee historian and bookseller, as being "the best Tennessee history book ever written." According to Elder, the book was not successful. The article on Colonel Williams stresses his heroism at the Battle of Horseshoe Bend and mentions the Flag of the 39th.

**The East Tennessee Historical Society's Publications, No. 30–1958: "Colonel John Williams"**
by Leota Maiden Driver

Supported by descendants of Colonel Williams, a celebration was given in Knoxville in 1958 honoring the accomplishments of the colonel. A portrait by Eleanor McAdoo Wiley was donated to the State of Tennessee and hangs on Capitol Hill in Nashville in the Secretary of State's office. The book gives the most accurate account of the feud between Jackson and Williams and of Williams' military and senatorial deeds.

Except for the last one, these references are written in the language of their times. I have transcribed many portions of those books in the language in which they were written on purpose; they are quaint and truthful to their times, and they reflect truths about the story before it became legend.

They will require of the reader patience and their own interpretation. On some subjects I will leave conclusions vague, so that the reader can infer what they wish into this version of the story.

I have additionally chosen to give strong consideration to the point of view of the Native Americans. In some cases, said version simply does not exist; the Creek Nation doesn't even mention the Battle of Tohopeka on their website. But I am, again, quoting the oldest sources known.

Because they were in conflict, Jackson saw Williams as the cause of almost all of his problems. Jackson's supporters saw to it that Williams was written out of history.

This book will seek to correct that injustice. John Williams was a "Renaissance man" of his times. Without John Williams there would have been no Jackson.

**Lastly, please don't throw rocks at me and say I am continuing the feud. I'm NOT! I'm a Democrat.**

**Alex III**

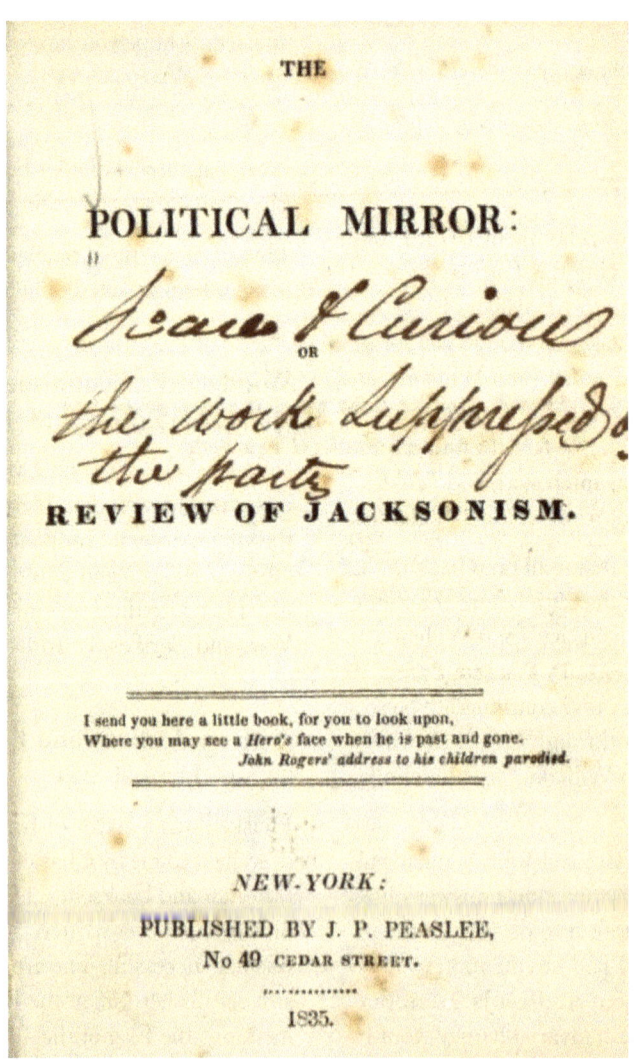

*Written anonymously by Col. John Williams in 1835*

# Chapter 1
# Williams and Jackson Family Histories

**Make no mistake, our Williams ancestors KNEW Andrew Jackson. In the frontier that was western North Carolina, this description was given of Andrew Jackson after he had left the area: "He was the most roaring, rollicking, game cocking, card playing, mischievous fellow that ever lived in Salisbury."**[3]

Even when Jackson ran for president in 1824, the people of that region were both shocked and astounded. His character was widely known during his youth there.

John Williams said of Jackson, "He is the most cunning man" he ever knew and that Jackson "never settled upon the ruination of any man that he did not succeed."[4]

This is how he tried to ruin us.

There once was a man known as "the Horseshoe Colonel." It was a name applied to Williams by his enemies, for he never used it himself, nor was it used in common reference by people of the day.

It referred to his heroism at the Battle of the Horseshoe, March 27, 1814. While this battle is little-known in American history, the events that transpired there changed forever the course of human events in the southeastern United States and consequently the entire world. The battle is little-known because it was overshadowed by Andrew Jackson's later and more famous victory at New Orleans. It was quite possibly overlooked because it was a slaughter.

Besides being Andrew Jackson's first significant military victory, the Battle of Tohopeka, as the Creeks called it, was nearly the end of the Creek Nation. Over eight hundred corpses lay dead at the end of the battle and the entire central region of the southeast became open for settlement as a result of it. The implications of that one day pale in comparison to the effect it had on the course of the United States—for out of the ashes of battle emerged a new hero, a new direction for the United States, the death of the social system that had held since medieval times, and one of the darkest chapters of American history.

---!!!

Andrew Jackson was born to poor Scottish immigrants. His father died shortly before Andrew's birth on March 15, 1767. He had only two brothers, Hugh and Robert. Andrew was named for his father.

Andrew's mother, Elizabeth, was said to be a weaver. Their father had perished only two years into the New World after toiling at manual labor in North Carolina. Andrew claimed South Carolina as his birthplace, and it remains somewhat in dispute where he actually entered this world. He grew up wild and free in the community of Waxhaw and was thirteen when, during the American Revolution, the English Army attacked his neighborhood.

Up until that time he had not been known for scholarly pursuits, preferring instead the more banal pursuits of frontier America. There were two social classes for white males in those days, and he was not born to nobility, but rather was forced to observe the conduct of gentlemen from the outside looking in.

His oldest brother, Hugh, had died in a battle at Stono some months before the English invasion of Waxhaw.[5] Thus when faced with impending doom from the redcoats, Andrew and his older brother, Robert, fought in different units in a vain attempt against the most powerful army of its time.

---

3 Barrett, John Spencer, The Life of Andrew Jackson, Archon Books, 1911, p. 1
4 Letter from John William to George Mason
3 Barrett, John Spencer, The Life of Andrew Jackson, Archon Books, 1967, p. 10

Andrew was captured, along with his brother. While in confinement, Jackson's biographers wrote, he was ordered by an English officer to blacken the officer's boots. When he insolently refused the officer, he received a sword blow that was partially deflected by his arm, and he was scarred on the arm and face for the rest of his life. That story was never corroborated by anyone and is likely untrue. Currier and Ives published a picture of it much later that has become accepted history for a long time.

Brother Robert died from illness a short while after the brothers were released in an exchange of prisoners. Captured soldiers from the region were held in Charleston as prisoners. Hearing of a smallpox epidemic amongst the prisoners, Elizabeth, his mother, accompanied the women who went to minister to the prisoners. She caught the fever herself and died a short time later. Thus, at thirteen, Andrew became an orphan without any family in America to guide him.

Andy entered his thirteenth year a tall, lean, remarkably agile, freckle-faced boy with bright blue eyes, a shock of tousled hair that was almost red and a temper in keeping with his hair color. He would fight at the drop of a hat, by that means mitigating a misfortune that would have ruined the prestige of an ordinary boy. Andy had a habit of 'slobbering' which he was unable to control until almost grown, but a jest at this circumstance spelled combat, whatever the odds.

When the war ended a year later, it found the fourteen-year-old Andrew incapable of taking care of himself. He tried leatherworking and teaching. Jackson received a sizable inheritance from a relative in Scotland and instead frequented the horse race tracks of Charleston, where his bravado and wagering earned him gentlemen friends whose manners he copied.

Determined to make something of himself, he sought education on his own. In 1784, he removed himself to study law in Salisbury, North Carolina, under local lawyer Spruce Macay. This instruction was limited and drawn out. Within three years he finished his law course and was authorized to practice law by two judges of Surrey County:

*"Story" told by Jackson and Reid*

Samuel Ashe and John Williams. He was twenty years old, had few clients and no backers, was raw-cultured according to gentlemanly standards, and showed neither great aptitude for law nor outstanding gentlemanly traits.

It was during these years that Jackson met Judge Williams' cousin, Colonel Joseph Williams. Colonel Williams and his wife, Rebekah, were leading citizens of western North Carolina. They knew Andrew Jackson all too well in his early years. He once brought a prostitute to their community party; she fell into a mud hole, and young Andrew was too drunk to pull her out. It was left to host Joseph and other male attendees to get her out and send the inebriated couple on their way. [6]

- - - ! ! !

Joseph Williams' father had died young, and he lived for a few years with his Uncle John. Life amongst the Williamses in the New World was difficult, but it would have been so in Wales too, had his grandfather not emigrated from there around 1669.

Original immigrant John Williams had been called "the Wealthy Welshman." He and his wife, Mary, settled in Hanover County, Virginia, built a house named Studley and reared their eight children there. Their previous home had been in Llangollen, Wales.

Their fifth child, Nathaniel, believed that his children should learn a trade as well as a profession in case of adversity. Nathaniel lived fifty-one years, and his and Elizabeth's fourth child, Joseph, was only fifteen when Nathaniel died. Three years later, Joseph moved to North Carolina, where he clerked in a store owned by his uncle, another John. Joseph was trained as a carpenter, but being literate, he was quickly elected clerk of the Surrey County Court. [7]

Joseph married Rebekah Lanier of nearby Richmond on September 16, 1772. The Laniers were Huguenots who had escaped France, where they had been musicians in the French court for several generations. They came seeking religious freedom following the Verdict of Nantes; they were aristocrats. They had some opposition to young Joseph because he worked with his hands, but love prevailed and the young couple lived in a cabin called The Sink House on the banks of the Yadkin River. There they prospered and began rearing children in the wilds of frontier North Carolina in 1772.

*Quoting a newspaper article from 1903:*

*"In 1772 before that war, they managed to build what would become their permanent home, named Panther Creek because James had shot a panther near there. The house was exceptional in every way. Frame houses were rare in those times and two-story ones were even fewer. They needed two stories for their large family and the house was planned that way to accommodate the large pipe organ that extended into the uppermost attic. Two fireplaces at either end of the house could roast a whole animal. Formal gardens of boxwoods surrounded the drive and theirs was a manor of wealth, affluence, and warmth."* [8]

The Cherokee Indians did not welcome the incursion of European settlers in their territory, so they went on the warpath. Joseph Williams organized the Surrey settlers into a militia to fight back and later became a colonel in the British Army. He captured and destroyed five Cherokee villages and drove them back to the Tennessee River as part of a tri-colony campaign (Virginia, North Carolina, and South Carolina). The Indians sued for peace and accepted a treaty (the Treaty of the Watauga). The result was not only to leave the Yadkin valley settlers in peace, but to open up Tennessee and beyond for settlement.

While on this expedition against the Overhill Cherokee, Joseph Williams went across the mountains and into what would become east Tennessee, going downriver to the junction of the French Broad and Holston Rivers. From a boat in the river he observed a flat plain atop a sharply rising hill and was said to have stood in the boat and exclaimed, "A great city shall rise here someday." The "perfectly defensive" site would become Knoxville, Tennessee, and three of his sons would immigrate there.

Unfortunately, there was to be no early peace for Joseph and Rebekah. In Philadelphia, the Continental Congress published a Declaration of Independence from Great Britain. They set up a revolutionary government under the Articles of Confederation, raised an army, and commissioned George Washington of Virginia as commander-in-chief. Provisional governments were established in the thirteen colonies. Joseph Williams was a Whig, as the revolutionists termed themselves. He resigned his commission in the British Army and served as the delegate from Surrey County elected to the Hillsborough Convention to set up a provisional government for North Carolina. He was also commissioned a major in the state militia, and he was soon promoted to lieutenant colonel. [9]

6 Brumfield to Brandau, personal conversation, 2012
7 Williams, Nicolas Lanier, *Brief on the Williams Family* ms, "Panther creek," Surrey County, NC, 1879
8 Davis, Mrs. Haynie, "Panther creek," *N.C. Booklet*, v. III., Raleigh, NC, Uzell and Co., 1903, p. 12
9 Williams, Lewis, Joseph L., Rebecca, and Lewis L., *Williams: 300 Years of Leadership in America*, Panther Creek Publishing, 1997

*Colonel Joseph Williams*
*Family Portrait owned by Clarke Williams*

Williams fleeing from Lord Cornwallis' Army with son, Nathaniel and se...
From Forsyth, A County on the March by Adelaide L. Fries et al. Sketches by Joe King
Copyright © 1949 by the University of North Carolina Press. Used by permission of the publisher

Colonel Williams fought several battles with the Tories, to whom he was exceedingly obnoxious.

Three of his neighbors ventured to Fayetteville and entered into a plot with other Tories to kill the Colonel, then returned home to carry out their plan. A runner sent by Colonel Collier, who had learned of the plot, advised Colonel Williams and Williams quickly joined up with Collier and they arrested the three conspirators. Two of the three were taken a short distance and shot, but one was spared at the insistence of the Colonel since the man was from Williams' home county. [10]

"The British Army swept south into North Carolina late in the Revolutionary War. While Colonel Williams was away at war, Rebekah Williams, who had three sons, took charge at home and managed all things well. Before leaving for the war, Colonel Williams had laid in all kinds of supplies for his family. In February 1881, news came of the approach of the army of Lord Cornwallis. Mrs. Williams had an infant, her fourth son, Nathaniel, who was only two weeks old. As the British Army approached, she took her children and an old Negro woman and sought refuge in a cave, where she remained until the army had crossed the river at the Shallow Ford of the Yadkin River. When the English had gone, she returned home to find that all of her supplies had been either taken or destroyed by the enemy. They were not as ruthless as many other invaders because her home and Negro quarters were not burned." [11]

---

10 Williams, NL, op cit, p 28
11 Davis, Mrs. Haynie, "Panther creek," *N.C. Booklet*, v. III., Raleigh, NC, Uzell and Co., 1903, p. 12

Surveying the damage, Rebekah placed her two older sons with neighbors and, with two-week-old Nathaniel in her arms and three-year-old John behind her, mounted a horse and sought help at her family's plantation in Granville County, North Carolina. Since much of the territory through the mountains consisted of forests and was swarming with Indians and Tories, she made the trip unharmed, but her infant son was forever afflicted by the exposure. The soft bones in his head never closed and he lived the remaining twenty-two years of his life in her constant care and slept in a trundle bed at her side.

John became Rebekah's consistent traveling companion, and he later accompanied her on a mission to locate the children of cousins who had immigrated to Tennessee. Word had reached them that their cousins had become ill and died. Their trip extended through frontier Knoxville into present-day Jackson, Tennessee, but the orphaned children were never found. [12]

While in Knoxville, John and Rebekah almost certainly stayed in White's Fort. There, John's good looks and education would have made a large impression on the young settlement, especially on James and Mary White's youngest daughter, Melinda.

- - - !!!

A local North Carolina historian asserted that Andrew Jackson left North Carolina for the wilderness that became Tennessee in 1788; he was twenty-one years old and it was much alleged that he left owing debts. [13]

On his ride over the mountains to the lands the Cherokee called Tenasi, Jackson encountered a sizable group of travelers in the forest. There being some safety in numbers, this group stayed together for some time. One evening as they settled in late from the day's ride, their early hours in camp were interrupted by late arrivals that had seen and heard Indians all that day.

Jackson told the story of how he had heard suspicious noises and persuaded his party to leave the site in the darkness. The remaining party caught up with him the next day and said they were attacked after the Jackson group's departure. Such travel in those days was a life-and-death matter, and apparently Jackson had mastered many of the frontier skills necessary to survive. [14]

*A different version of that legend was told in 1912:*

    Mr. James [Parton] was a most industrious biographer, a most amusing writer, and a most amusingly incredulous man. If a story about one of his heroes tickled his fancy, he couldn't help believing it to save his life. Therefore, he straight way put it into his book.

That Andrew Jackson could travel one hundred and eighty-three miles in the wilderness without having "adventures" appeared unnatural to biographical and historical writers of the Peter Parley school and therefore we learn from Parton that the guard which had been sent from Nashville to watch over the lives of the emigrants was totally unfit for the business, and that had not Andrew Jackson and his cob pipe been along, the Indians would have surprised and butchered the whites.

Remember that we have been told by Parton that Jackson and McNairy waited several weeks at Jonesboro for the assembling immigrants and for the guard from Nashville. Remember that the immigrants did assemble in due course and that the guard did arrive. Remember that the party numbered about one hundred, and that the military escort must have consisted of backwoodsmen familiar with Indian ways, Indian fighting and all necessary woodcraft. Remember that this guard from Nashville came from the dark and bloody ground of constant and bloody antagonism between the white intruders and the Red Men who believed that the Great Spirit had given them the land. Remember that it was the special duty of this Indian-fighting escort to protect the men, women and children of the immigrant train from surprise, ambuscade and attack. Remember that at night, in the midst of the unbroken forest, the danger would be greatest and the guard most vigilant. Remember all these things, and then smile as you read the story, which Parton repeats, of the child-like manner of which the trained and trusted backwoodsmen from Nashville had all become negligent, and how the young lawyer, Andrew Jackson, who happened to be "sitting with his back against a tree smoking a corncob pipe an hour after his companions had gone to sleep" called the attention of the young clerk of the court, Thomas Searcy, to the suspicious hoots of the owls which hoots the young lawyer from North Carolina knew must be made by Indians and not by owls! The trained and trusted backwoods Indian fighters had not suspected that these owls were other than owls! How mean and cheap those trusted and trained Indian fighters from Nashville must have felt as the young lawyer from old North Carolina aroused them to a sense of the perils from which they were

---

[12] Joseph Lanier Williams, Lewisville, NC
[13] Brumfield, Lewis to Brandau, personal conversation, 2012
[14] Parton, *Life of Andrew Jackson*, New York: Mason Publishing, 1860

encompassed! According to this marvelous yarn which Parton swallows without the wink of an eye, the Andrew Jackson band rose up and marched away from there unmolested whereas a party of hunters who came up to the same camp, during the same night, and laid them down to sleep in the same place were remorselessly butchered by the same Indians who had been hooting those owl-hoots at the Jackson band.

*Heiskell's response to this was:*

"What an credulous Parton! In such haste was he to make a wonderful figure of the raw young lawyer from Salisbury, North Carolina, that the best borderers that Tennessee could select were made to neglect the simplest duties and get caught napping in the stupidest fashion at the very time when such a thing was the least likely to have happened.

"That there may have been a narrow escape for the immigrants from some night-attack; but it is simply incredible that a guard, picked by pioneers of the times of Robertson and Donelson and Sevier, for the very purpose of watching over the safety of the inexperienced and helpless immigrants, should have gone to sleep in the depths of the wilderness with Red Men all about them, or should have been so unskilled as not to detect so common an Indian signal as the imitation of the owl-hoot. The unsuspicious, indiscriminate and comprehensively incredulous Parton is so sure of his ground that he actually gives his readers the exact time which elapsed between the flight of the Jackson band and the coming of the hunters that were butchered. It was one hour.

"Thus we have one band of white borderers who wait to be led out of the Indian ambuscade by a young attorney, and a second band of white borderers who come upon the deserted campfires, one hour later, and who see no "signs" which are sufficient to arouse suspicion and excite watchfulness. The second band white borderers—men who live among continual dangers who carry their lives in their hands, and to whom the reading of the "signs" in the woods is the necessary condition of life in the savage wilds lie down around the abandoned camp-fires of Jackson's band without so much as posting a picket, fall into the arms of sleep and of death.

"The credulous Parton! Of all things which would have put the second band of white borderers upon instant notice that danger lurked along the trail, it was the abandoned camp which must have shown, even to the untrained eye of an immigrant, that it had been suddenly and recently." [15]

15 Watson, Thomas E. *Watson's Magazine*, Volume 5, 1905

There was great expansion west as immigration increased the size of the new country and the new arrivals pushed civilization westward. The trip across the Appalachian Mountains was treacherous, but possible if one exercised caution and chose travel dates correctly. Most people knew how to live off the land; they could hunt or gather edible plants as game and food was abundant.

Young Andrew Jackson settled in the young settlement begun by James Robertson and John Donelson. They had traveled by boat, one group going against the current of the Cumberland River from near its confluence with the Ohio River, as well as an expedition that came down the Tennessee River. They settled the city high on another flat-planed bluff and called it Nashboro in 1799. The settlement was under almost constant threat of Indian attack, but it was much safer than the frontier. It had a stockade log fence.

Colonel Joseph Williams had been a land speculator; as a veteran of the Revolutionary War, he was rewarded with land grants. To get people to settle upon them, he would give away parcels of land in desirable locations. Once established, adjoining tracts could be sold for profit. Hard currency was in short supply, so many commodities were bartered and, as such, pioneers accumulated debt from one individual to another that sometimes was paid in notes, land, or barter.

Knoxville and Nashville were in competition with each other from the time Knoxville was established in 1791. Knoxville was a second stop for those coming across the mountains, and outgrew Greeneville and other eastern Tennessee communities only because it had water transportation.

HOW KNOXVILLE STARTED—How'd you like to have lived in Knoxville when it was no more than James White's Fort, built about 1785? Gen. White, Knoxville's founder, first built his cabin, shown at lower left, and later erected three other cabins to house visitors. He built the stockade as defense against possible Indian attacks. Today the City Association of Women's Clubs is heading a movement to restore the cabin and fort on on E. Main Ave. site adjacent to the James White Memorial Auditorium. Betty Mitchell, Knoxville artist, did this sketch.

*Used with permission of James White Fort*

Knoxville was a planned settlement. Streets and tracts were drawn out in north-south and east-west directions from the very first. Outside of what became the main business district, cow paths and wagon trails became major arteries that meandered across the hilly countryside of east Tennessee. Knoxville was in a valley between two mountain ranges, and the climate there was pleasingly temperate. The Cherokee had known that it was a great place in which to live for a very long time.

The Cherokee had settled the valley of Tenasi by displacing an older tribe of mound-builders. The land was fertile, the abundant streams were full of fish, and edible fruits and berries grew in abundance. Usually settlers from North Carolina would approach White's Fort from the east, and most would wait for winter to be over before attempting a mountain crossing. Wild strawberries grew in the fields of rich-soiled valleys and were so prolific that travelers' horses' forelegs would be completely red-stained by riding through them in the spring. Many farmers settled near those plentiful Strawberry Plains.

Outside of the United States, there was much ado in the European world at this time. Mozart and Haydn were writing and performing classical music. A young Beethoven was presented at court as a child prodigy, even though they lied about his age.

In 1787, the United States Constitution was adopted. In 1789, a young Tecumseh visited Cherokee Chief Dragging Canoe's settlement on the Tennessee River. He returned north to the Indiana territory in 1790. In December 1791, the Bill of Rights was ratified.

In February 1792, the United States Postal Service was established; in June, Kentucky became the fifteenth state; and in December, President George Washington was reelected to a second term. On March 2, 1793, Sam Houston was born. In 1794, the United States Navy was established. And in 1796, Tennessee became the sixteenth state.

When the Whites settled their fort, mysterious, dark figures still roamed the riverbank across the Tennessee River. In the ensuing years, the Cherokee would become increasingly domesticated and civilized to the point that they wore pants, farmed, and read Bibles. Intermarriage between the Cherokees and white trappers and settlers was common.

---!!!

John Williams' second generation of Americans had seen the founding fathers glorified, praised, and made wealthy by the Revolution; lithographs of Washington hung in many homes. There was a proven method of profit and fame to be won in war, and these boisterous young Americans knew about it. When war again threatened with France, young John Williams entered the Army in April 1799 and was promoted to captain. His father being a military veteran, he was simply following in his father's footsteps.

The founding settlers in the New World brought the progenitor system with them from Europe. In that system, derived during the Chivalric Age, the oldest male children inherited everything. Second and third sons were encouraged to enter the religious orders or the military, and daughters were to be provided for by their husbands. Many of the original immigrants to what became the United States did so because they had nothing to lose, and, moving westward to the New World, colonies continued to be the land of opportunity.

The Williamses educated most of their children at the nearby Moravian (German) Academy in old Salem, North Carolina. Affluent pioneer families continued to send their children there for many years, and it proved a fertile ground for the mating game. There is some hint that young, lawyer-educated John suffered a bout of unrequited love, for when he chose to move to Knoxville in 1803, he was as yet unmarried. Surely by then he was a mature, educated man, having led other men in the Regular Army.

He spent some time with his brother William setting up a farm in the Strawberry Plains community before embarking upon his legal career. John Williams filed the brand used on Williams' cattle and other livestock and is said to have helped erect a water-powered mill for grain grinding. In 1803, he was accepted as a member of the Knoxville and Tennessee Bar. Governor John Sevier's farm was nearby, and it is possible young John not only knew him, but also clerked and refined his law career with him.

At that time, judges and lawyers traveled from one community to another by means of circuits, just like preachers did. So, all those who were practicing would travel together and set up court and make their living going from one small town to another. Andrew Jackson and John Williams were acquainted as grown men in that way. They had some regular correspondence, and once Williams remarked politely to Jackson that he was sorely missed.

Jackson, still living in Nashville, had been a man of some prominence in 1796, when the State of Tennessee was admitted to the United States. He had been elected congressman from his district and had prospered as a politician and a lawyer. Yet he remained a prisoner of his passions. Thomas Jefferson said of him that at this time he "never saw a man who would become so aroused by his emotions that he could not express himself for his own anger." [16]

When Andrew Jackson first moved west to Tennessee, he immediately founded a profitable law business; the town had only one other lawyer, who had been retained by several debtors. Jackson was a welcome prosecutor to the creditors, and in eight years' practice he became wealthy by way of land holdings. He met and was befriended by Federal Judge John Overton, who in North Carolina had been a best friend to Robert Overton Williams, John Williams' brother.

--- !!!

In 1805, John Williams chose the Whites' sixteen-year-old Melinda as his wife. The Whites at first protested because of the eleven years' difference in their ages, but he persisted: "it is Melinda that I love and I will have no other." [17] The young couple might have honeymooned in New Orleans because Williams paused while there to send market pricing and current news by letter to Jackson in 1805. [18]

John Overton was a federal judge, and in an early letter, Williams suggested the national government should do something "to make use of the energy potential of the abundant streams of east Tennessee." [19] Franklin Delano Roosevelt would do so in the 1930s in the form of the Tennessee Valley Authority.

--- !!!

At that time, one's *honor* was of the utmost importance among gentlemen. You could beat your wife since she was legally considered chattel—barely more than property; you could get as drunk as you wished since no laws forbade that; you could kill Indians all night and day since that wasn't against the law; but if you offended another man's honor, a strict code of social mores came into play.

The means of settling these conflicts had followed these new Americans from Europe. The gentleman offended would challenge the other to a duel, demanding satisfaction and qualified seconds, and a few witnesses would attest to the event afterward. The gentleman challenged selected the weapon of his choice, and the distinct probability was that one or both would leave the grounds dead or wounded. Because of that, most gentlemen chose their words carefully.

Dueling, however, was becoming illegal and was losing social favor. When Vice President Aaron Burr killed Secretary of the Treasury Alexander Hamilton, much outrage ensued and a great debate occurred within the aristocracy of gentlemen. When Burr left Washington and tried to lead ex-patriots to another country, he was arrested. Jackson befriended Burr on his journey through Nashville. He was roundly criticized for it but was never brought to any charges that he had aided Burr. During that time, Williams wrote that he had defended Jackson amongst their peers.

"Panther Creek" built by Col. Joseph Williams in Surry County, North Carolina about 1766

*used by permission of Joseph Lanier Williams*

16 Daniel Webster's Interview with Jefferson, 1824
17 Family story from Linda Lanier Sneed Brandau Wolfenbarger
18 Williams to Andrew Jackson, Sept. 9, 1805, The Jackson Papers
19 Maiden, Leota Driver, *"Col. John Williams,"* East Tennessee Historical Society publication, No. 30, 1958, pp. 6-46

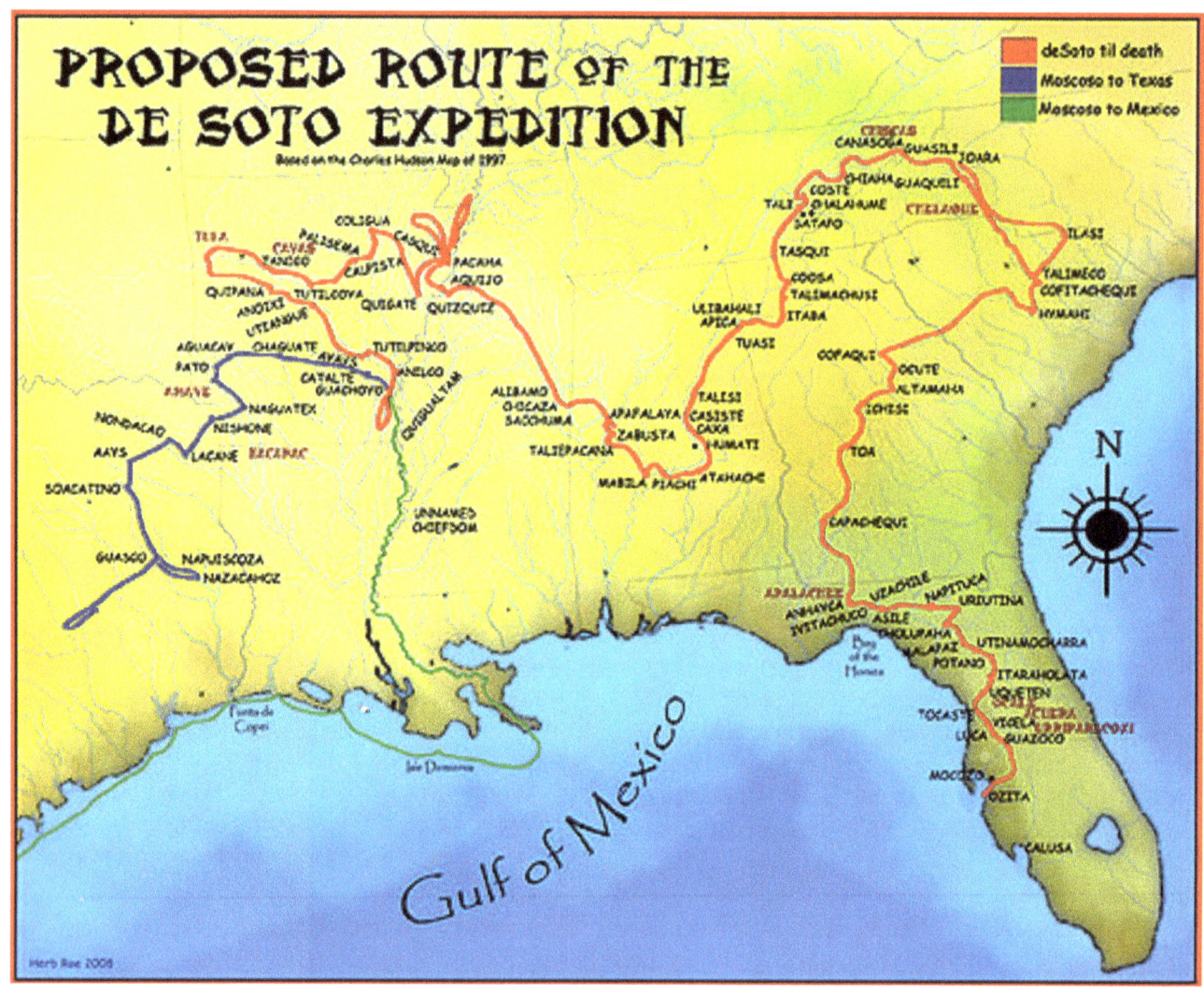

*Wikipedia*

# Chapter 2
# History of Native Americans

**One cannot mention the histories of Jackson and Williams without considering the histories of Native Americans because they quickly became a major factor in these times.**

When Christopher Columbus "discovered" the New World in 1492, it changed the "civilized" world and began one of the greatest episodes of genocide ever. The indigenous people of North and South America were regarded as less than human, souls to be converted, and "savages" to be conquered.

Many years later a man of mixed blood, General Thomas S. Woodward, participated in the Indian Wars in the Southeastern United States. He had the unique perspective of knowing how misunderstood the Native Americans were. As he described in his memoirs, written shortly before the Civil War, the Indian way of thinking, living, and writing had not been accurately portrayed. He had participated in those Indian Wars on the white side since he was mostly of white blood. He began their story with the invasion of the Southeast by Spanish explorers Cortez and De Soto:

"When Hernando Cortez began his exploits in the New World, his object was gold. The people he first encountered in Mexico were somewhat civilized and very timid and after subduing them and taking possession of the City of Mexico he then commenced extending his conquests or robberies up the Gulf Coast as far as what is now Texas. There he encountered the Muscogees, Alabamas and other tribes.

"In order to hold on to what he had taken and subdued of the timid ones, he found it necessary to kill or drive these more war-like tribes from the country, which with the great advantage of firearms he succeeded in doing. The Muscogees and their confederates crossed the Mississippi River and called a halt at Baton Rouge. The Nitches settled where Natchez is now. The Choctaws settled the country on Yazoo, Pearl, Leaf, Chickaswaha, and as far as the Tolmbecba rivers. The Chickasaws settled at Memphis. The Creeks settled on the Alabama and its tributaries. [20]

"In May 1539, John Ferdinand Soto, called by most persons Hernando de Soto, landed nine ships with over 620 men and 220 surviving horses at present day Shaw's Point, in Bradenton, Florida. He named it Espíritu Santo after the Holy Spirit." [21]

- - - ! ! !

As Colonel Woodward describes:

"His army was composed of one thousand men, some on horseback and some on foot, with greyhounds as fleet as the wind, bloodhounds large and ferocious, and in addition of all these were lots of Catholic priests, clergymen, and monks. This was certainly a very imposing show, and was a show very well calculated and no doubt did impose on the unoffending natives, and the tons of iron, handcuffs, chains, neck collars and the like were things well calculated to inspire the natives with very exalted notions of the Christianity they were soon to be taught."

"It is equally shameful as true that other Christian nations

---

20 Woodward, Thomas S., *Woodward's Reminiscences*, Alabama Book Store and Birmingham Book Exchange, Tuscaloosa and Birmingham, Alabama, 1939, p. 18
21 Woodward, Thomas S., p. 30-31

have followed the example of Spain with the natives of this and other countries; wherever the Bible (which was seldom applied correctly) failed, the musket and bayonet were resorted to. The hogs and cattle were next; the introduction of these animals was the only philanthropic movement during the expedition.

De Soto, no other man, nor any set of men could have reduced the Indians to such abject slavery. There is not one Indian male or female but would have put an end to their existence, rather than to submit to such treatment. Even as late as 1836-37, several Indian women, rather than risk their children under the control of the Emigrating Indian Agent, would put them to death (some of them old enough to walk).

You may take almost any other that we read of and train them to be slaves, or yet make them perform those menial offices that slaves do; but such is never the case with an Indian. Harsh words or blows never can control an Indian."

That the Creeks, Alabamas, and others ever were or considered themselves subjects of the great Mexican Empire, is doubted. [22]

De Soto marched his expedition from present-day Florida into Georgia, South Carolina, North Carolina, and Tennessee, then back into Georgia, Alabama, Mississippi, Arkansas, Louisiana, and eastern Texas.

> "One of the severest battles Soto had with the Indians, was fought with the Creeks at what is now known as Cuwally. To spell it as the Indians pronounced it would be Thelawalla, which signifies rolling bullet. The Indians say it was there that a spent ball was seen rolling on the ground, and from that the place took its name." [23]

> The Creeks themselves said that there was once among them a giant Chief, Tistanooga Lusta, or Black Warrior, who fought with Soto. The Alabama Indians too were known in later days to be the most bitter enemies (except the Nitches) that the French had. Even the Chattahoochee Indians, who were Muscogees, would show many places where Soto, or Desoto, had camped. There is a place on the Appalachicola that is yet known as one of Soto's camps. The Indians call it Spanny Wakka—that is "the Spaniards lay there." [24]

It was only twenty years after Cortez conquered Mexico that Soto commenced his march from Tampa Bay. Early histories suggest Soto passed through Alabama before the Muscogees reached that country. The Indians say they were there and fought him: and the number of copper shields, with a small brass swivel (which an old man by the name of Tooley worked up into bells), would go to show and prove that the Indians were correct. [25]

Soto died in what is called Natchidotches parish in the last fort he built, called the Azadyze, and according to the Indians and oldest Spanish settlers he was buried there. Indians are very particular in their relations of circumstances and events, and not half so apt to embellish as the whites, and the march of Soto through their country, and his fights with them, were affairs not likely to be forgotten by them, and would be handed down for a generation or two, at least very correct, no doubt. [26]

- - - ! ! !

"When other conquering nations explored the new continent, the French and English concentrated on what became the then-Southwest colonial territories. The Indians that originally inhabited from the middle parts of the Carolinas (particularly South Carolina) and Georgia to the seaboard were known as Yamacraws or Yamasees, Oconees, Ogcheeses, and Sowanokees or People of the Glades. The Sowanokees are known as the Shawnees. And these Indians the Creeks found to be their equals as warriors; but when the whites began to approach them from the east, and the Creeks already very close on the west, the Shawnees fell back upon the north and northwest. Tecumseh was of that stock." [27]

When white settlements extended into the western Carolinas and Georgia, they were met by the Cherokee and Creek tribes. The indigenous Cherokee made most of their villages along the banks of the Little Tennessee River. This stream began in the mountains of Georgia, wound east back into North Carolina, and then cascaded out of the mountain heights into east Tennessee. It was very cold water, but it was easily navigated by carved-tree canoes. Their way of life had first been challenged by English soldiers from South Carolina in 1756.

It was the first colonial attempt on the western side of the Appalachian Mountains by the southern colonies and was some twenty years before the Declaration of

---

22 Woodward, Thomas S., *Woodward's Reminiscences*, Alabama Book Store and Birmingham Book Exchange, Tuscaloosa and Birmingham, Alabama, 1939, pp. 30-31
23 Woodward, Thomas S., *Woodward's Reminiscences*, , pp. 14-15
24 Woodward, Thomas S., *Woodward's Reminiscences*, pp. 16-17
25 Woodward, Thomas S p. 23
26 Woodward, Thomas S p. 26
27 Woodward, Thomas S., *Woodward's Reminiscences*, p. 18

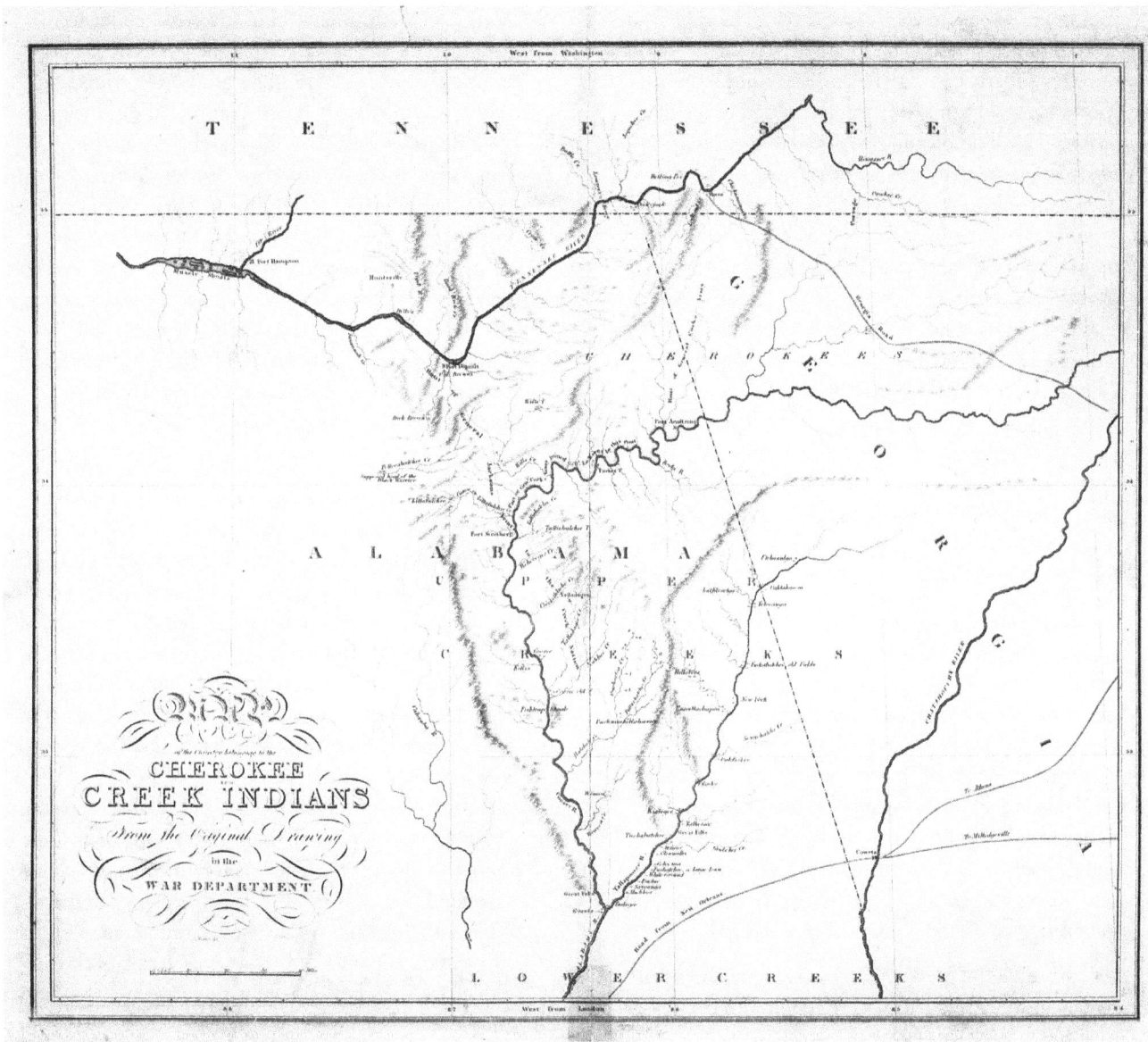

*1815 map*

Independence. The Cherokee had ceded a large portion of their territory to what became Kentucky, Virginia, North Carolina, South Carolina, Georgia, and a small portion of east Tennessee.

S. G. Heiskell writes an excellent account of the threat Native Americans posed to new settlements west of the Appalachians. Though wordy, he sometimes catches the spirit of east Tennessee like no other. The British Army's first expedition into the wilds of extreme western North Carolina tells how yet *another* tribe reacted to the European invaders. Here follows Heiskell's narrative:

> "In that same year (1756) after laborious preparations and in consequence of donations by Prince George himself, and by the colonies of Virginia and South Carolina, Ft. Loudon was erected on the southern bank of the Tennessee River in what is now Monroe County, near the point where the Tellico river runs into the Little Tennessee, more than thirty miles Southwest of Knoxville. It was built by General Andrew Lewis, the chief engineer of the British troops, under the direction of the Earl of Loudon. This was the first Anglo-American settlement in Tennessee.
>
> "The expedition consisted of one hundred regular soldiers of the king and one hundred provincial troops, together with about forty artisans, mechanics and farmers, and they carried some two score horses and a number of hunting dogs. On a rocky ledge,

jutting into the river the fort was built. The ridge was cleared of heavy timber and the fort was securely built of heavy square logs with blockhouses and bastions. The walls were trunks of trees imbedded in the earth touching each other, and sharpened at the top; it was made so secure that with ample provisions the garrison could endure a long siege by many time their number. Ten cannon and two guns were mounted upon the ramparts, or platforms. These cannon were probably brought over the mountain on pack horses, as no wagon road had ever been cut through that wilderness. The fort was five hundred miles from Charleston and was in a place to which it was utterly impracticable to convey necessary supplies. The Indians were invited to the fort for a while. A settlement grew around the fort with the arrival of traders and hunters. They began to cultivate the land. Thus they lived and maintained this lone outpost for four years until 1760.

"At first, their relations with the Cherokee were cordial, but they quickly soured. The soldiers, making incursions into the woods to secure fresh provisions, were attacked by them and some of them were killed. Constant danger threatened the garrison. The settlers were drawn into the fort and communication with the settlements across the mountains, from which they derived their supplies, was cut off. Parties of the young warriors rushed down upon the frontier settlements and word of the massacre became general knowledge along the borders of the Carolinas.

"All this time the garrison of Fort Loudon had been besieged, so that now they were reduced to the dreadful alternative of perishing by hunger or submitting to the mercy of the enraged Cherokees. The two hundred miles between it and Fort Prince George were so beset with dangers and so difficult was it to march an army through the barren wilderness, that no further attempt at relief was made. The garrison was near starvation. For a month they lived on the flesh of lean horses and dogs and a small supply of Indian beans, procured stealthily for them by some friendly Cherokee women. Blockaded and beleaguered night and day by the enemy, with starvation staring them in the face, they threatened to leave the fort and die, if necessary, by the hands of the savages. Then Captain Stuart, resourceful and brave, summoned a council of war. They agreed to ask for the best terms possible and leave the fort. Stuart slipped down to the consecrated city of Chota, where no Indian dared molest him. He obtained terms of capitulation, which were: 'that the garrison of Fort Loudon march out with their arms and drums, each soldier having as much powder and balls as the officer shall think necessary for the march, and all the baggage they choose to carry; that the garrison be permitted to march to Virginia or to Fort Prince George; that the Indians provide for the garrison as many horses as they conveniently can for their march, agreeing with the officers and soldiers for payment; that the fort, great guns (cannon), powder, ball and spare arms, be delivered to the Indians without fraud or further delay, on the day appointed for the marching of the troops.

"In pursuance of these stipulations, on August 7, 1760, the white people, after throwing their cannon into the river, with their small arms and ammunition, except what was necessary for hunting, broke up the fort and commenced the march into the settlements in South Carolina. That day they marched fifteen miles toward Fort Prince George. At night they encamped near Taligua, an Indian town, where their Indian attendants all suspiciously deserted them. A guard was placed around the camp. At break of day, the treachery was revealed. A soldier came running in and told them that he saw a vast number of Indians, armed and painted creeping toward them. They had hardly time to form and meet the attack before the savages poured in among them a heavy fire, accompanied by hideous yells. The thousands of savages were too many for the two scant companies of half-starved regulars and a motley following of settlers, with wives and children."[28]

The majority of the entourage were killed, but some women and children were assimilated into the Cherokee tribes and culture.

### - - - ! ! !

English officer Lieutenant Henry Timberlake had been among the first Caucasians to explore the valley of the Cherokee in 1761. There had been Ft. Loudon and the inevitable trading with trappers and wanderers, but Timberlake was the first to document their culture.

Timberlake was a Virginian by birth, whose father, dying when he was a minor, left him some means, but not enough for his support without an income from employment. He had always wished to be a soldier and saw his first service in 1756. In 1759 he served in a campaign under General Stanwix, and saw various

---

28 Heiskell, S. G., *Andrew Jackson and Early Tennessee History*, Ambrose Printing Company, Nashville, TN, 1920, pp. 277-280

military service from that time until the spring of 1761, when he entered on a campaign under Colonel Stephen against the Cherokees.[29]

At Long Island, the British began erecting a fort and were soon visited by four hundred Cherokee (known as Overhill Cherokee) and their "king," Kanagatucko, who wanted peace with the English. They offered to accompany him on a river trip to their villages on the Little Tennessee because they feared for his safety from northern tribes of Indians without their knowledge and protection. He followed them downriver "in a canoe with a sergeant (named Sumpter), an interpreter, a servant, and about ten days' provisions and about twenty-odd pounds in goods to buy horses for their return."[30] This being late November, their heavily loaded canoe often ran aground in the shallow waters, and a trip that would have taken six days in spring took twenty-two instead. They often portaged the canoe and supplies, and Timberlake thought his trek to be 250 miles (though it was but 140 miles). Quite by accident, they lost both rifles taken along, the latter instance of which was quite amusing:

> "When seeing a large bear coming down to the water-side, Sumpter, to whom this remaining gun belonged, took it to shoot; but not being conveniently seated he laid it on the edge of the canoe, while he rose to fix himself to more advantage; but the canoe giving a heel, let the gun tumble overboard. It was irreparably gone, for the water here was so deep that we could not touch the bottom with our longest pole. We were now in despair. I even deliberated whether it was not better to throw ourselves overboard, as drowning at once seemed preferable to a lingering death." [31]

"Entering the Tennessee River we began to experience the difference between going with the stream, and struggling against it, and between easy paddles, and the long poles with which we were constrained to slave, to keep peace with the Indians, who would otherwise have laughed at us. When we encamped about ten miles up the river, my hands were so galled that the blood trickled from them, and when we set out next morning I was scarce able to handle a pole.

"Within four or five miles of the nation, the Slave Catcher sent his wife forward by land partly to prepare a dinner, and partly to let me have her place in his canoe, seeing me in pain, and unaccustomed to such hard labor, which seat I kept till about two o'clock, when we arrived at his house, opposite of the mouth of Telliquo River, completing a twenty-two days' course of continual fatigues, hardships, and anxieties." [32]

The Cherokee thought him dead behind them, as the same trip took them ten days less; and they were preparing to let his servant, who had accompanied them, return to advise the English of his demise. There he was feasted and treated kindly. He visited the site of the former Ft. Loudon and noticed they still had drums of the late unfortunate Captain Damere. Everywhere he went he was met by half-naked, feather-wielding, drum-playing, and pipe-smoking Indians. He complained he had been offered 170-180 peace pipes, which he dared not decline, and that it made him so sick he dared not stir for several hours. He even encountered survivors of the Ft. Loudon defeat, meeting one "Mary Hughes who told him she had been prisoner there near a twelve month, and that there still remained near thirty white prisoners more, in a very miserable condition for want of clothes, the winter being particularly severe; and their misery was not a little heightened by the usage they received from the Indians."[33] He gave her some shirts and blankets that she distributed amongst the prisoners.

He described the Cherokee thusly:

> "[They] are of a middle stature, of an olive color, tho' generally painted, and their skins stained with gun powder pricked into it in very pretty figures. The hair of their head is shaved, tho' many of the old people have it plucked out by the roots, except a patch on the hinder part of the head about twice the bigness of a crown-piece which is ornamented with beads, feathers, wampum, stained deer hair and such like baubles. The ears are slit and stretched to an enormous size, putting the person who undergoes the operation to incredible pain, being unable to lie on either side for near forty days. To remedy this, they generally slit but one at a time; so soon as the patient can bear it, they are wound round with wire to expand them, and are adorned with silver pendants and rings which they likewise wear at the nose. This custom does not belong originally to the Cherokees, but taken by them from the Shawnees, or other northern nations.
>
> "The women wear the hair of their head, which is so long that it generally reaches to the middle of their

---

29 Heiskell S. G., *Andrew Jackson and Early Tennessee History* p. 282
30 Heiskell, S. G.,, p. 283
31 Heiskell S. G., , p. 284
32 Heiskell, S. G., , p. 284
33 Heiskell, S. G., , p. 288

legs, and sometimes to the ground club'd, and ornamented with ribbons of various colors; but, except their eyebrows pluck it from all the other parts of the body. The rest of their dress is now become very much like the European, and, indeed, that of the men is greatly altered. The old people still remember and praise the ancient days, when they had but little dress, except a bit of skin about their middles, moccasins, a mantle of buffalo skins for the winter, and a lighter one of feathers for the summer. The women, particularly the half-breed, are remarkably well featured; and both men and women are straight and well-built, with small hands and feet." [34]

Lieutenant Timberlake spent the winter, a total of seventy-eight days, with the Cherokee in Tanasi and returned to his unit the following spring of 1762. His return took only nine days. He accompanied three Cherokee Indians to London later that year and published his memoirs there in 1765. He lived in England the remainder of his life.

Thus were the Native Americans of the then-Southwest exposed to white settlement and "civilization." When Governor William Blount met the Cherokee at the future site of Knoxville on July 2, 1791 (thirty-one years later), it was said that he was met by blue-eyed, English-speaking Cherokee. The assembled whites and Cherokee agreed upon the Treaty of the Holston that made significant laws and a second significant cessation of land.

"The Creeks and Alabama tribes were organized in families—that is Bears, Wolves, Panthers, Foxes and many others. In addition, the Wind family was allowed more authority than any other family in the nation. There was nothing in their laws to prevent blood cousins from marrying, but marriage was never allowed in the same family—a man of the Bear family could marry a woman of the Fox family, or any other family he pleased, and the children would be called Fox. The children took the mother's family name." [35]

*The Memoirs of Lt. Henry Timberlake (1765)*
Thepublicdomainview.org

34 Heiskell S. G, p. 288
35 Woodward, Thomas S., p. 19

# Chapter 3
# Cultural Change, Tecumseh, and Becoming the Volunteer State

Being a lawyer in a territory becoming a state was a good thing in the 1790s and 1800s. There were several major settlements in Tennessee at that time, with Western Tennessee holding a majority over Knoxville (Nashville had earlier been called Mero). A rivalry began and bad blood began to develop between Eastern and Western Tennessee.

In the new country that their fathers wrought, the gentlemen of the turn of the 19th century in the United States adhered to specific rules. These rules were a continuation of the chivalric code of the medieval knights in Europe. One clearly had a choice of becoming a civilized being or a ruffian, and that usually was decided by birth, not ability.

Women of those times had little respect and virtually no legal rights. They were, in fact, considered chattel. They and their property belonged to their husbands. Wealthy men of the day would build homes for their daughters in hopes that they would at least have a place to live. Since the gentlemen of the day were expected to provide for their wives and children, this often was a source of wounded pride for some men.

Men were expected to respect the femininity of their ladies and to treat them with grace, dignity, and good manners. Ladies were expected to be obedient to their husbands, to rear their children, to manage their homes, and to keep their opinions to themselves. Not all women would do this, but for the most part this was their accepted lot in life.

Men were expected to put their best foot forward every day; they were the true representatives of their families and their families' honor every time they appeared in public. Honor was the all-important word—one's honor was to be preserved at all costs!

When Tennessee became a state in 1796, John Sevier was elected its first governor, and held the office through two reelections to enjoy three two-year terms, the maximum number of consecutive terms allowed by the Tennessee Constitution of 1796. Upon his relinquishment of that post, he sought the semi-elective position of major-general of volunteer forces for all of Tennessee. The vote was a tie, broken in favor of Sevier's rival, Andrew Jackson, by the new governor, Archibald Roane, who was a personal friend of Jackson's. In that same year, Sevier would be reelected to the governor's chair, defeating Roane, and held it for six more years. Partially because of the unusually short length of his first term due to the time of the admission of the state to the Union, Sevier served as governor of Tennessee longer than any other person except for William Carroll. [36]

> The importance of honor is illustrated by Jackson's challenge to Charles Dickinson, a rising young aristocrat who resided in Maryland and was a member of a prominent family in Nashville, in 1806. The circumstances connected with the famous duel between Andrew Jackson of Tennessee and Charles Dickinson of Caroline County, Maryland, are herewith given as gleaned from several apparently reliable sources.

[36] http://en.wikipedia.org/wiki/John_Sevier

In 1806, Jackson was living on a farm along the Cumberland River in Tennessee, about ten miles from Nashville. He had a passion for fine horses, and breeding them became a principal branch of his farming business, using the best stock imported from Virginia and North Carolina. More for the purpose of exhibiting his stock and recommending it to purchasers, than to indulge in the practices common at such places, he brought out his favorite horses to the racecourses of the day and competed in many races in challenging fields of excellent horses.

Jackson owned a favorite horse, Truxton, which he was challenged to run against a horse owned by a Mr. Erwin and his son-in-law, Charles Dickinson. The stakes were to be two thousand dollars on a side, in cash notes, with a forfeiture of eight hundred dollars. The bet was accepted, and a list of notes made out; but when the time for running arrived, Erwin and Dickinson chose to pay the forfeit. Erwin offered sundry notes not due, withholding the list that was in the hands of Dickinson. Jackson refused to receive them, and demanded the list, claiming the right to select from the notes described upon it. The list was produced, a selection made, and the affair satisfactorily adjusted. Afterwards a rumor reached Dickinson that Jackson charged Erwin with producing a list of notes different from the true ones. Jackson instantly proposed to call him in; but Dickinson declined. Here the affair ought to have ended, but there were those who desired to produce a duel between Jackson and Dickinson. Jackson was brave and reckless, a trader in slaves and blooded horses, and reputed to be the best shot in the country. Exasperation was produced; publication followed publication; insults were given and retorted; until, at length, General Jackson was informed that a paper, more severe than its predecessors, was in the hands of the printer, and that Dickinson was about to leave the state. He flew to Nashville, and demanded a sight of it in the printer's hands. It was insulting in the highest degree, contained a direct imputation of cowardice, and concluded with a notice that the author would leave for Maryland within the coming week. A stern challenge, demanding immediate satisfaction, was the consequence.

The challenge was given on the 23rd of May and Dickinson's publication appeared the next morning. Jackson pressed for an instant meeting; but it was postponed, at the request of the other party, until May 30th, at which time it was to take place at Harrison's Mills, on Red River, within the limits of Kentucky. Dickinson occupied the intermediate time in practicing.

*Artist's depiction of Jackson and Dickinson Duel*

Jackson went upon the ground firmly impressed with the conviction that his life was eagerly sought, and in the expectation of losing it, but with a determination which such a conviction naturally inspired in a bosom that never knew fear. As Dickinson rode out to the place with a party of friends, he fired at a string supporting an apple and cut the cord in two. It had been agreed that the two men should use pistols and stand eight paces apart facing the same direction and that at the word they should turn towards each other and fire as they chose.

"Later, however, Jackson and his second, Dr. John Overton, decided it best and agreed that Dickinson shoot first. When all was ready and Overton gave the word, Dickinson fired and Jackson was seen to press his hand lightly over his chest while the dust flew from his clothes. Dickinson at first thought he had missed his man and was seized with terror. Jackson now had his adversary at his mercy and slowly pulled the trigger. There was no explosion; the pistol stopped at half cock which by the rules was not considered a shot. [37]

"Jackson was given a second shot. With Jackson appearing not to be injured, the gentlemanly thing to do would have been to have fired into the air and spared Dickinson's life. Witnesses were said to have pleaded with Jackson to do so. He re-cocked the pistol and fired into his chest, and Dickinson suffered in great agony while thinking he had missed his shot.

"Jackson, with his friend and surgeon, left the ground, and had traveled about twenty miles towards home when his attendant first discovered that the general was wounded, by seeing the oozing through his clothes. On examination, it was found that Dickinson's ball had buried itself in his breast, and shattered two of his ribs near their articulation with his breastbone. It was some weeks before he was able to attend to business. Dickinson was taken to a neighboring house, where he survived but a few hours." [38]  Other sources say he lingered a painful death the next afternoon.

Jackson carried that ball in his chest the rest of his life. It caused him pain and suffering for forty more years. [39]

The code for dueling was coming under challenge of its own in the years following the American Revolution. Some states, including Tennessee, were outlawing duels, and they were considered unnecessary by many gentlemen. This is why the Jackson–Dickinson duel was held in Kentucky. It was during a time of growing social change as well as changing customs for the country. Sentiment in Nashville turned against Andrew Jackson. It was rumored by some of his enemies that he had lined his coat with newspapers to slow the ball and spare his life. He remained at the Hermitage and continued his military and legal duties while struggling to recover from his wounds.

Current Dickinson descendants claim that the entire affair was merely that Jackson wanted to kill Dickinson, who had married the daughter of his rival, and he did! Dickinson was not as portrayed. He was young and not a crack shot as described by the lie, and had not previously dueled. It was a ruse of manipulation and cost Dickinson his life. John Williams' sister, Fanny, was in the household, and gentlemen of the household were appalled. Jackson had three strikes against him in this affair: one, he cheated by lining his coat with newspaper; two, he took a second shot when the honorable thing to do was fire high; and three, he lied about Dickinson and got away with it. So much for the chivalric code.

Tennessee was yet a wild and rugged state by the early 1800s. The civilized settlements all competed for incoming immigrants to increase their wealth, industry, and governmental influence. Since representation was determined by population, the early settlements were pitted against each other virtually from their founding.

Knoxville and upper East Tennessee benefitted most from immigrants crossing the Appalachian Mountains to settle in the valleys across the mountains, which were very similar to the land they had just left. Most of these new Tennesseans had relatives remaining in North Carolina and, though difficult, it was simply a trip across the mountains to return home for supplies. Travel there was still dangerous because of Indians and highwaymen. Sometimes men left and never returned.

Nashville, being in the middle of the new state, was more accessible from the northern territories of Ohio, Kentucky, and Pennsylvania. Offering access by river, it was somewhat easier to reach and was available to more people moving west. Thus, it grew faster than its eastern neighbors. With significant cultural differences among the immigrants, there also developed political differences and rivalries

- - - ! ! !

---

37 http://www.rootsweb.ancestry.com/~mdcaroli/Duel.htm
38 http://www.rootsweb.ancestry.com/~mdcaroli/Duel.htm
39 Remini, Robert V., The Life of Andrew Jackson, New York: Penguin, 1990, p. 54

There was a short interlude in the country's history where peace ruled in the very young United States. Noah Webster published his *Compendium of the English Language* in 1806. In the year before, the *Claremont* was the first reliable steamboat in New York. John Williams became adjutant general of the state militia and became a trustee of East Tennessee College. During this time of his life, he and Andrew Jackson rode the law circuit and exchanged letters. Jackson stayed in Nashville. Williams was gaining legal experience, but Jackson was not. Williams advised him of actions within the courts, and both men speculated on the always-imminent war and what size military units should be raised to fight in it. In 1809, James Madison was sworn into office as president.

John and Melinda Williams continued to live and love in Knoxville. In 1810, Melinda lost two infant girls, Rebekah and Fanny, who was born on Rebekah's birthdate. Fanny lived only one month. Williams and Jackson remained friendly, for on December 15th of that year, Williams sold three slaves to Jackson for $850. He never did so again.

Williams would become an early advocate of stopping slave trading several years before abolition became popular.

---!!!

*Tecomseh on Twitter.com*

In 1809, Tecumseh began promoting his confederacy of tribes. He became the first American Indian to stand up to the officials of the new United States. He swore to unite the tribes in open revolt against the white people. He swore to give up no more land. At that time, there were a few tribes still east of the Mississippi and their lands were coveted.

Tecumseh had started Prophet's Town in what would become Indiana. His brother, blind in one eye from a childhood hunting accident, began declaring himself a prophet. Said prophets were believed to have magical and mystical powers. From his teachings and ceremonies, the town and confederacy grew, and that provided a basis of tribal agreements. Though he preached war with the whites, Tecumseh also called for the end of inter-Indian tribal warfare and advocated an end to the practice of slaughtering women and children.

When war with England threatened again in 1810, British agents regularly landed guns and supplies at various places within the Gulf Coast and gave them to the Creeks and Seminoles for use against the American settlements. These two tribes quickly learned they could raid settlements and escape into Florida, where they could not be followed nor attacked for fear of reprisals from the Spanish government.

The conditions and events that led up to the Creek Indian War began before the start of the War of 1812. In the early 1800s, the loosely confederated tribes of the Creek Nation numbered somewhere between 18,000 to 24,000 persons and primarily inhabited present-day Alabama, Mississippi, and western Georgia. Their territory was generally bounded by the Tennessee River on the north, the Gulf of Mexico on the south, the Oconee River in Georgia on the east, and the Tombigbee River on the west, and comprised about 300 square miles.

In the years following the American Revolution, the United States, Great Britain, Spain, and France all sought alliances with the Creeks as they attempted to diminish the others' influence in the region. The Creeks had signed four treaties with the new American government by 1805, but the continual international intrigue in the Alabama backwoods and the animosity between England and America would spark the Creek War as an extension of the War of 1812.

A visit of this noted chief, Tecumseh, to the Creek Indians has been named as one of the causes leading to the Creek War. When this visit to the southern tribes occurred, it was a question of much interest shortly after the Creek War. The Creeks were known to be easily influenced by spiritual leaders, and the appearance of a comet and the New Madrid fault earthquake were largely felt to have influenced the Creek sentiment.

"In the spring of 1811 Tecumseh, leaving his affairs in the hands of his brother, the Prophet, went to the South preaching his crusade…. The fall of 1812 again found Tecumseh, accompanied by the Prophet and a retinue of thirty warriors, haranguing the Creeks in the midnight council, and this time with prodigious effect." [40]

The Public Broadcasting Service produced and aired a series of programs in 2009 regarding the American Indians' plight. The series was called We Shall Remain, and they intimated that Tecumseh was the first Native American to unite tribes and to speak as one for all tribes. One historian on that program, Dave Edmonds, put Tecumseh's actions into modern terms:

> "What Tecumseh is fighting for is the ability of Indian people east of the Mississippi to hold onto their homelands. Their lands are under siege in the period after the American Revolution. The white frontier is moving into the Ohio Valley. It's also moving onto the Gulf Plains in the South. And Tecumseh says, 'This has got to stop. We have to stand and all realize that we're in this together.'

> "I think Tecumseh is one of those people that, if he were alive today and would walk into a room, people would stop talking and just stare at him. Tribal people back in the first part of the 19th century would say, 'Tecumseh is a man of very, very strong medicine.' There was this aura around him of leadership and respect, that even people who opposed him—even his enemies—admired him.

> "His genius was in inspiring people. And he was a very inspirational man that was able to bring out the very best in those people who supported him, and to see beyond any particular tribal affiliation, and to realize that this was a struggle that was of greater magnitude. I also think that there was a spiritual component to this—that he believed that he was appointed by the powers in the universe to really bring people together and to make this stand. And to retain what was left of the Indian homeland. This was his life. This was what he had been born to do." [41]

General Woodward gave secondhand testimony from many Indians who had seen Tecumseh during that visit.

"He [Tecumseh] was at this time one of the most splendid specimens of his tribe—celebrated for their physical proportions and fine forms. He is described as having been tall, athletic, and manly, dignified and graceful—the beau ideal of an Indian chieftain." [42]

Before Tecumseh's visit, a white man came from Pensacola and made a visit to the Creek chief called Big Warrior at Tuckabatchee. Woodward's informer was William Weatherford, himself a noted Indian leader of mixed blood. They were beside a campfire on the west bank of a stream called the Pinchgong. Weatherford thought the Pensacola man was Scotch, so he is sometimes called "the Scotch emissary." He held many conferences with Big Warrior "through a negro interpreter." Shortly after the disappearance of this man the oldest son of Big Warrior, Tuskanea or Tuskahenaha, "took a trip to the Wabash and visited several tribes." He brought back some Shawnee women whom General Woodward saw. Weatherford further related that not long after the return of Tuskanea, Tecumseh with a prophet called Seekaboo and with other stranger Indians appeared at the town of Tuckabatchee. "A talk was put out" by Big Warrior. This Weatherford and another Creek of mixed blood called Sam Moniac, the original name having been McNac, attended. "No white man was allowed to be present." [43]

Weatherford also reports, through General Woodward:

> "Tecumseh stated the object of his mission; that if it could be effected, the Creeks could recover all the country that the whites had taken from them; and that the British would protect them in their rights." [44]

Moniac objected to Tecumseh's speech. He said the talk was a bad one, and he said that Tecumseh "had better leave the nation." The interpreter was Seekaboo, "who spoke English." Weatherford told the interpreter to tell Tecumseh that the whites and Indians were at peace, that the Creeks were doing well, that it would be bad policy for them to take either side if the Americans and English went to war, and if they did unite with either side they "had better join the Americans."

Claiborne, Woodward's historian contemporary, says of Tecumseh, "entering the Creek territory he harangued the warriors at Autauga and Coosanda and the Hickory Ground. Wherever he went crowds attended, painted for war, and dancing the war dance."

41 Edmonds, David, historian, *We Shall Remain*, PBS, 2009
42 Ellis, Edward Sylvester, *Indian Wars of the United States: From the First Settlement at Jamestown, in 1607, to the Close of the Great Uprising of 1890-91*, New York: Cassell Publishing, 1892, p. 66
43 See note
44 Halbert, Henry Sale, and Timothy Horton Ball, *The Creek War of 1813 and 1814*, Chicago & Montgomery, AL: Donohue & Henneberry & White & Woodruff & Fowler, 1895, p. 68

Woodward adds:

> "In October the annual grand council of the nation, in pursuance of immemorial usage, assembled at the ancient town of Tookabatcha. These councils were always attended by the United States Agent, by all the traders, by many strangers, and by the warriors and their families. On this occasion the fame of Tecumseh's visit, and his expected address, had assembled some five thousand persons at Tookabatcha.

> "Each morning a Shawnee warrior announced that his chief would speak at noon, and each noon the speech was put off till the next day, until Colonel Hawkins, the United States Indian agent, left the town. The next noon after the Agent's departure, amid imposing ceremonies, Tecumseh made his appearance and delivered his speech. The assembly continued till midnight. There later was much debate over what Tecumseh had actually said."

Different written accounts blamed the British for telling Tecumseh of the coming appearance of a comet as well as the occurrence of a large earthquake near the same time and that Tecumseh predicted such events. It was said he would cause the earth to quake when he stomped his foot, but that was a total lie and there was no way the British could have known of these incidents ahead of time. Tecumseh's talk was tarnished by the Americans of his time.

Halbert and Ball continue,

> "With that brilliant comet, its tail according to Milne '132,000,000 miles long,' shining over them night after night all through September, and being nearest the earth October 15th it is unreasonable to suppose Tecumseh to have said to those Creek warriors, "Soon shall you see my arm of fire stretched athwart the sky." Tecumseh had too much good sense to say that. Nor is it probable that he claimed to be able to shake the earth. The Claiborne speech is not given here, for it does no credit to Tecumseh. It rests on no authority.

> "The Tecumseh visit to the Southwest resulted in little compliance. Only the Creeks seemed incited to unite against the Americans, but the seeds of division were sown; much of the tribe was divided about what course to follow. The appearance of the comet and timely earthquake did much to arouse the minds of many Creeks." [45]

About this time, or a little after, a chief, Tustanuggachee or Little Warrior, and a Coowersortda Indian, known as Captain Isaacs, who had gone north-west with Tecumseh, were returning to the Creek nation, and learned from some Chickasaws that the Creeks had gone to war. Relying on this information, Little Warrior's party did some mischief on the frontier of Tennessee as well as killing a few persons. On their return to the nation they found that war had not actually broken out. [46]

They had made a huge mistake.

Tecumseh had returned to his settlement of Prophets Town to learn that his brother, left in charge during his absence, had disobeyed him and had lost a battle to Territorial Governor William Henry Harrison at Tippecanoe. (Harrison was forever after known by the nickname "Tippecanoe," and its use as a campaign slogan helped him win his election to the presidency in 1840.) Tecumseh was furious with his brother, but the official War of 1812 intensified for the Shawnee. They faced more battles with the Americans while supposedly partnered with the British.

> On August 16th, at the Battle of Detroit, Tecumseh convinced the American defenders inside the fort that they were facing an army many times greater than their own, parading his small host of warriors again and again through a clearing in the forest. Before the British and Indian attack had even begun, a white flag appeared above the ramparts of the fort, and the American army marched out and surrendered their weapons. It was one of the most humiliating defeats ever suffered by an American army. [47]

- - - ! ! !

"On June 19, 1812 the United States House of Representatives voted 71 to 44 to authorize the president to take possession of the two Floridas. It was, however, not successful in the Senate. The fear was that Great Britain would by some amicable agreement with Spain take over Florida, forestalling this country." [48] The War of 1812 had officially begun.

---

45 Halbert, Henry Sale and Timothy Horton Ball,.*The Creek War of 1813 and 1814.* Chicago & Montgomery, AL: Donohue & Henneberry & White & Woodruff & Fowler, 1895, p. 440
46 Woodward, Thomas S., , pp. 35-36
47 *We Shall Remain*, PBS, 2009
48 Williams, "A Forgotten Campaign," *Tennessee Historical Magazine*, Vol. VIII, January 1925, No 4, p. 268

At that time, there were two forms of troops: regular U.S. Army soldiers who were professionally trained, uniformed, and painfully aware of the chain of command and of their lawful duty to obey commands, and state militias. In Tennessee, those militia were under the command of the governor; the Regular Army units were commanded by the President and the Secretary of War, followed by the generals commanding the seven military districts. There was much ambiguity in the ranks about who outranked whom between the two forms of troops.

Knoxville attorney and Regular Army veteran John Williams published an "Address to the People of East Tennessee" in both Knoxville and Nashville newspapers on November 10, 1812:

> "The latest newspaper accounts show a want of troops in East Florida to check the hostile Indians. 'Tis shameful that Georgia alone should bear this burden. All those who have enrolled themselves with me, are directed to parade, at Knoxville, on Tuesday the first day of December next, prepared with a supply of provisions to take them to the point of destination.
>
> "The patriotic freemen of Tennessee, who have not enrolled themselves, are requested on that day, to come well mounted, and prepare to march to Saint Johns, where the troops of the United States are stationed, and where the Indians are said to be assembled in such numbers as to threaten the destruction of our troops.… War now rages in our land—A deranged Monarch, venal Prince, and a corrupt Ministry, have driven us to assert our rights, at the point of the bayonet. They have enlisted under their banners the savages, those hell hounds fitted only for deeds of ferocity, who seek victory by the indiscriminate slaughter of all ages and sexes.
>
> "Our females and property are in a place of security—our brethren in a sister state need our aid, will it be withheld!… Let us march to their relief—let us give decided evidence that while others talk we are prepared to act—Let us go to the scene of action, and there present ourselves ready to share with our brethren the dangers and glories of the field— Let us not wait the slow formality of being dragged from home by compulsory orders—Freemen ought to risk something—Let us go on our own expenses in the first instance—If we can thus be useful to our country, we will be more than compensated." [49]

Williams called for every man to assemble at his home "mounted on a strong horse, armed with a musket or rifle, with a brace of pistols, a tomahawk and a butcher's knife—dressed in black hat, black hunting shirt or roundabout and pantaloons" for an expedition into the wilds of the Southern frontier controlled by the Creeks and the Seminoles.

To understand the purpose of Colonel Williams in projecting for this expedition, it is necessary to look at recent and current happenings on the southern frontiers of Georgia and East Florida along the St. Marys River, which was the boundary between the American state and the Spanish province.

The Seminole Indians, who derived from the lower Creek Indians and who on separating from the Creeks had moved down into Florida, were under Spanish influence and were at this period giving much trouble to the inhabitants of South Georgia. Georgians in considerable numbers had settled across the St. Marys river. When war was imminent, these Georgians in Florida intended immediately to make "a vigorous effort to possess themselves of the Province and to deliver it to the United States." [50]

General Jackson asked his men to assemble to meet at Nashville, on November, 27, 1812. [51] He had promised 2,500 men to President Madison, but they were not called to service earlier because Madison did not need them—his attention was elsewhere. "Madison wanted men of proved ability, men who had attained military stature in the Revolutionary War. Secretary of War Eustis, an old soldier of Seventy-Six himself, concurred in this policy. Furthermore, Eustis could not see the temperamental Jackson, who had called the secretary 'an old granny,' as the man for an important command." [52]

In October, Madison wrote Tennessee Governor Willie Blount in Nashville that he wanted 1,500 Tennesseans to go to New Orleans to reinforce General Wilkinson. Jackson's lack of mention was conspicuous by its absence. However, Governor Blount gave him the order and General Jackson issued the order to assemble in Nashville on December 10, 1812; the men were to wear dark blue or brown uniforms—only officers were to be uniformed in US Army ones. Eighteen hundred men showed up on that bitterly cold day; they camped on the hills just outside Nashville and slept 25-30 in a tent with little but body warmth to sustain them. The final count was 2,070 when the militia loaded up on boats to many hurrahs by

---

49 *Clarion*, November 23, 1812
50 Williams, p. 268
51 *Tennessee Gazette*, Nov. 12, 1812
52 Patrick, p. 238

the Nashville citizens to descend the Cumberland River, the Ohio River, and the Mississippi River to reach New Orleans 1,300 miles away.

On December 1, 1812, in Knoxville, 164 men assembled on what became the campus of the University of Tennessee. The men could have stayed in better accommodations, but were said to have preferred the camp-like conditions that they knew awaited them. On December 3, Colonel Williams wrote to President Madison, informing him of the volunteers' intent to reinforce the Georgians against the Creeks and Seminoles. By the next day when they left, Knoxville citizens had contributed over $300 toward their campaign. The volunteers rode to Asheville, North Carolina, for there was no road going south in those days. "There a Mrs. Erwin had beeves butchered and barbequed for the hungry men. She and another patriotic woman of North Carolina collected and presented the volunteers with $100 for their expenses." [53]

By December 11, Williams' force had grown to 200 men, and he wrote Georgia Governor Mitchell of his intentions; it was said that Asheville at that time was very cold. On the 15th, the *Nashville Clarion* reported on the expedition and stated that they were the "finest looking body of men ever assembled in this sector." General Cocke, general of the East Tennessee Militia, himself enrolled in this group as a private and followed Colonel Williams.

By the 19th of December, 240 men reached Washington, Georgia. While providing needed relief, their appearance put Georgia's governor into an embarrassing predicament. "He could not welcome the Tennesseans whole-heartedly, for their expedition implied the failure of Georgians as Indian fighters and an official could not admit such a damaging fact. On the other hand, Mitchell could not ask the Tennesseans to return home and let his people subdue the Indians, for that would be inhospitable. Moreover, the futile efforts of the past months contradicted any claim of military prowess which Georgians might advance."

General Pinckney commanded the Sixth Military District from Milledgeville, and General Flournoy at St. Marys sent the volunteers to Camp Pinckney. Flournoy would later command the Seventh Military District at New Orleans.

By the time their letters would have been received in Washington, the volunteers had progressed into the southern part of Georgia near St. Marys.

Williams had alerted the Secretary of War of his actions. Because everything was horseback-delivered, the secretary was merely advised of their actions and had no opportunity to direct them. But at one point, Governor Mitchell of Georgia wrote: "What am I to do with the Tennessee Volunteers?" It was the first time the two words were ever used together and capitalized. The nickname stuck and the unit became known as such.

> The Governor of Georgia was having trouble with the militia of Savannah, the chief city of his state, where some of the leading officers had declined to obey orders that would cause them to march beyond the borders of Georgia; and the Governor had threatened to reduce them to the ranks. The contrast of this action with that of the Tennessee Volunteers was too marked for complacency on the part of Georgia's Governor.
>
> That Georgians generally welcomed the relief (coming without money and without price) is perhaps shown by the action of their General Assembly, which on December 28th sent a resolution requesting that a road be opened between East Tennessee and Georgia through the country of the Upper Cherokees to Georgia's senators in Congress. Aid from the people of the East Tennessee Valley had so often in the past been proffered or given to Georgians in the years of the existence of Franklin state and of the Southwest Territory that Georgia's legislature thought it wise to have a more direct connection with such a source of succor in case of need. [54]

When the new year began in 1813, the *Augusta Chronicle* published that General Flournoy was going to use the Volunteers against the Seminoles. A few days later, General Pinckney once again asked President Madison for guidance, only to be ignored. Pinckney then asked the Secretary of War for military advice. Neither official replied. Quietly near the end of January, while the Volunteers waited anxiously for action, the Congress authorized the formation of a new regiment of US infantry to be formed: the 39th.

On February 7, 1813, the returning Creek warriors, being misinformed that the Creeks had gone to war, attacked and killed several Tennessee border families. Only a Mrs. Crawley was spared; she was to be rescued and gave a horrendous account of her experience. On February 10, General Pinckney advised Secretary

---

53 *Clarion*, Jan. 5, 1813
54 Williams, *"A Forgotten Campaign,"* p. 272

Armstrong that the Tennessee Volunteers had now 250 men.

During that month of delay, the rabid Tennesseans were bitterly resentful. Some went into St. Marys and presented their case to General Flournoy; others castigated Benjamin Hawkins for his interference. One volunteer wrote Tennessee Governor Blount that the volunteers had been stopped by the "Chief of the Creek nation, to wit, Benjamin Hawkins." That Volunteer went on to say that their group "would plant the American eagle on the walls of St. Augustine before we return." Given his writing style and bravado, this sounds like none other than Colonel Williams. (One wonders if they had an American eagle standard begun, but not completed, until the 39th Infantry left Knoxville.)

Benjamin Hawkins was negotiating with the Seminole Indians and requesting General Pinckney not to punish them. Lacking a response from President Madison and Secretary Armstrong, General Pinckney could do nothing but allow the Volunteers to proceed.

> This was the wish of Madison and Monroe, for their silence had a purpose. By striking the Seminoles, the danger of attack on Pinckney's forces, or Jackson's, when they should enter east Florida, would be eliminated. It is evident, therefore, that the Madison administration purposely refrained from answering Benjamin Hawkins or issuing General Pinckney orders. Long after the Volunteers should have proceeded on their mission, the Secretary of War informed Pinckney: "When the mounted volunteers under Colonel Williams shall have performed the duty which you have assigned them against the Indians, you will consult your own judgment, and either continue them in service with the Regular Troops assembling at St. Marys, or dismiss them, as the good of the service may require." The unquenchable thirst of the Madison administration for the Floridas had blinded it to right: Indians suing for peace would be given the sword because their destruction was part of a plan of conquest. [55]

"A part of the hostility toward the Seminoles was due to the fact that they received and harbored large numbers of runaway slaves. General Flournoy's orders to the troops stated: Every Negro found in arms will be put to death without mercy." [56]

> Earlier, a tribe called the Yemasses had migrated to middle and eastern portions of Florida; they had "dark skins, thick lips, and flat feet." A war of extermination was waged by the Creeks against the Yemasses, and finally, at Tallahassee, the last of the warriors were killed—but about a thousand of the young Creek warriors took sweethearts among the Yemassee girls, and saved them from death. According to a law among Creeks, these were required to remain out of the nation a year for purification. Before the end of the year, the young warriors concluded to make wives of the Yemasses girls and set up a nation for themselves, which they did. The Creeks called these warriors *Seminoles*— meaning *wild*, wild man, crazy, mad-man. These Seminoles were afterwards joined by the outlaws and runaways from all other nations, and soon became a formidable nation. [57]

Finally, on February 3rd, the Volunteers left Camp Pinckney and arrived in Payne's Town, home of King Payne of the Seminoles, six days later. Their first fight with the Seminoles caught the Indians by surprise, and they killed fifteen, wounded seven, and burned the town. Advancing before the Regular Army troops, they reached Bow Leg's Town, home of King Payne's brother. It had been abandoned, so there were no casualties, but it was destroyed and the force returned to Payne's Town the next day and camped.

> "Here they were attacked by two hundred Indians, who had collected, purposing a surprise. The action continued for an hour and a half when a charge by the whites dispersed the savages with a very considerable loss. Chief Bow Legs fell wounded before the Tennesseans. In all engagements, thirty-eight Indians were killed, many wounded, seven taken as prisoners; four hundred horses and about the same number of cattle were taken. It was estimated that 386 Indian huts and houses were destroyed.

> "The losses of the Tennessee Volunteers were: one killed and seven wounded. The volunteers celebrated their victory. They described how the Indians had taken the bodies of Newnan's unfortunate soldiers, cut off their heads, and nailed them on trees in the Indian villages. An elderly Volunteer named Wildear displayed his son's scalp, which he found in an Indian hut." [58]

---

[55] Patrick, *Florida Fiasco*, p. 230
[56] Williams, *"A Forgotten Campaign,"* p. 273
[57] Woodward, Thomas S. p. 130
[58] Patrick, p. 245

Meanwhile, Jackson's force had survived a torturous winter river trip and arrived at Natchez on February 16. There Jackson received orders from General Wilkinson at New Orleans telling him to stay at Natchez, as New Orleans hadn't the means to support them. They marched through Natchez and set up camp outside the city. There they stayed for over a month, wallowing in a quagmire while Jackson awaited orders to invade Florida. Finally, new Secretary of War John Armstrong's orders reached Natchez on March 15; to their dismay and utter surprise, Jackson's force was "dismissed from public service." Jackson refused to disband his troops and they set about *walking* back to Nashville—some four hundred-plus miles.

The policy of the Madison administration continued to change; in fear of war with Spain, all American settlers in Florida were ordered to submit to Spain. So, by April, the mission of the Volunteers was over. They received a hero's welcome and banquets in Savannah, Lexington, and Augusta. In Lexington, one of the toasts was, "The Volunteers of Tennessee—an example worthy of imitation to Massachusetts and Connecticut; while others half in their duty, these brave men are foremost in the path of glory." In Augusta the toast was: "Colonel Williams and the brave Volunteers of Tennessee—We admire their patriotism and feel gratitude for their services. Music—Volunteers' March!"

It would seem that the very uniqueness of this expedition, reminiscent of the days of knighthood, would have marked it for historical record. It is without barest mention in any history of Tennessee. It was perhaps without parallel in this country's history, in that the men embodied and volunteered service without any call made by nation, state, or sister-state, and they financed their own equipment and the cost of transportation over many hundreds of miles to the scene of the conflict, not to mention the most uncommon elements that went into the composition of the command.

The victorious volunteers could return home where families and friends would sing their praise. "You have rendered an essential service to the public," Flournoy wrote Colonel Williams, "and merit for yourself and the officers and men under your command, the praise so justly due to brave and patriotic men." [59]

> The job done by the Tennessee Volunteers was a thorough one. Their destructive expedition left the Indians of central Florida facing starvation, forced them toward the west coast, and eliminated them as an enemy in the planned conquest of the Floridas. The first step in the conquest of the Floridas was an established fact. [60]

Jackson's men arrived in Nashville on May 22, 1813, having accomplished nothing except incurring a debt that General Wilkinson wanted General Jackson to pay. That trip is said to have inspired the nickname "Old Hickory" for Jackson. While walking to let a sick soldier ride his horse, it was noticed and complimented among his men that he was "tougher than Old Hickory." Though it was seldom used until 1824 when Jackson ran for president, that nickname stuck. No one ever claimed to have given him that name, though.

In August 1813, Georgia's militia was rendezvousing for an expedition against the Upper Creeks, and an express was sent to Governor Willie Blount of Tennessee for the aid of 1,500 men. The reply was that "5,000 can be as easily obtained as 1,500." A tradition of service had begun that culminated in the nickname "Volunteers" applying to the entire State of Tennessee and later to its university. That nickname also stuck. It had begun with John Williams and his Tennessee Volunteers. Williams wrote to Jackson that "our state has accrued a reputation for volunteerism."

On August 30, 1813, the Creeks attacked and massacred over 400 men women and children at Ft. Mims. The frontier became a wildfire of fear as panic sprang up across Tennessee.

---

59 Patrick, p. 234
60 Patrick, p. 236

## Muster Roll of the Field and Staff Officers of the East Tennessee Volunteers in the service of the United States, commanded by Colonel John Williams December 1, 1812–March 25, 1813

**1. John Williams, Colonel, December 1, 1812**

**2. John Cocke, Major, January 1, 1813, appointed Major January 16, 1813**

**3. James King, surgeon, December 1, 1812**

**4. Richard Meredith, 1st Lieutenant**

..................................................

### Samuel Bunch *Capt*

*I certify upon honor that the within muster roll exhibits a true statement of the company under my command and the remarks set offside the men's names are accurate and Just to the best of my knowledge.*
*Saml Bunch, Capt of Rifle Company of E.T.V. February 25, 1813*

John Reynolds 1st LT
Ira Green 2nd LT
John Stephens Ensign
Jacob Noe Sgt
John W. Flowers "
Reuben Tipton "
Absalom Hawkins "
Armstrong, William, Pvt
Baldridge, Francis, "
Brown, Joseph "
Blackley, Thomas "
Bean, Bacter "
Branner, Michael "
Bowman, Abraham "
Bayles, Reese "
Bayles, Williams "
Cummins, James "
Conway, William "
Click, George "
Click, Henry "
Cunningham, James "
Cruthchfield, William "
Crocket, William "
Derrik, Michael "
Dokes, Robert "
Findley, James "
Freshour, George "
Freshour, Henry "
Fine, David "
Felby, Williams "
Gideon, Edward "
Green, Arnold "
Green, Joseph "
Gann, Isaac "
Galbreath, Abnear "
Smith, Charles M "
Smith, John "
Skaggs, James "
Simpson, John "
Shough, John "
Trimble, John "
Upton, William "
Worthington, James
Wheeler, John "
Williams, James "
Welch, Daniel "
White, Benj J "
White, Benjamin "
Welles, Jacob "
Worthington, William "
Young, William Sr. "
Young, Williams, Jr "
Aetley, William "
Clyatt, Samuel "
Staffers, James "
Wilder, Thomas "

..................................................

### David C. Vance *Capt*

*I certify upon honor that the within muster roll exhibits a true statement of the company under my command and the remarks set offside the men's names are accurate and Just to the best of my knowledge.*
*D.C. Vance*

Samuel Wilson 1st LT
John K. Smith 2nd LT
James S. Johnson Ensign
Wm K Vance Sgt
Thomas A. Rodgers "
Michael McCain "
Nathl Smith "
Anies, James pvt
Akin, Benjamin "
Acard, John "
Boyd, Michael "
Bishop, Mason "
Brabson, Ephriam "
Cocke, Sterling "
Coates, Cody "
Cain, Hardy "
Derrick, E. William "
Ford, Peter "
Gaines, John S. "
Granturn, Amis "
Goforth, Zachariah "
Hamilton, William "
Howel, John "
Hunter, John "
Hale, Walter "
Holly, Frazier "
Jacobs, Joseph "
Kirkham, William "
Kinchloc, Enock "
Kean, Enoch "
Lyon, Jacob "
Lockey, Thomas "
Lea, Thomas "
Letner, Christian "
McCorkle, Joseph "
McCunce, James "
Martin, Isaac "
Mulvaney, Henry "
Messer, John "
McCoy, Jacob "
McClary, Thomas "
McClary, Thomas "
McDaniel, Jeremiah "
Nail, Mathew "
Parker, James "
Robertson, David "
Ragan, William "
Simpson, John "
Smith, Richard "
Stewart, Robert "

Simmons, John "
Trotter, David "
Tate, David "
Thompson, David "
Whitesides, Thompson "
Woods, M. Richard "
Walker, Elias "
Young, Ewen "
Charlton, John KM "
Cruthfield, Sam'l "
Mason, nat'l "
Mann, Gilbert "
Christopher, John "
Connor, Edward "
Garner, Jeremiah "

..................................................

**Williams Walker** *Capt*

*I certify upon honor that the within muster roll exhibits a true statement of the company under my command and the remarks set offside the men's names are accurate and Just to the best of my knowledge.*
*Williams Walker, Capt*
*1st Company E.T.V.*

Richard Meredith 1st LT
Jack Denton 2nd LT
John Chiles, ensign
Joseph Hart sergeant
John R. Houston "
Thomas H. Miller "
Wm H. Greenway "
Armstrong, Williams Pvt
Ayers, Marshal "

Alston, John W. "
Bartlett, Jessie "
Bennett, James D. "
Bacon, Allen S. "
Campbell, Alexander "
Campbell, Alexander "
Cowan, Andrew "
Crawfird, English "
Collins, Francis "
Davis, Thomas "
Dean, Benjamin "
Douglass, Charles "
Dearmond, Richard "
Eddington, Phillip "
Fornewalt, Jacob"
Gordon, A.W. "
Grady, Bevid "
Graves, Daniel, "
Gerring, Joseph "
Hodge, Charles G. "
Handcock, Robert "
Hindman, James H. "
Jioghes, William "
Jackson, Hazekiah "
Lea, Luke "
Matclock, Henry "
McConnell, James "
Malcolm, William "
Miller, Pleasant M. "
Mynatt, William C. "
McEldry, Samuel "
Mackland, Nathaniel "
Morgan, Gideon "
Mayo, Valentine "
Mayo, William "

Murphy, James "
McConnell, Thomas "
McNair, John "
Nolan, Thomas "
Outlaw, Alex S. "
Parsons, Enoch "
Parsons, Peter "
Page, James "
Pangle, Tracie "
Peterson, Joseph "
Purvis, Williams "
Stephens, Henry "
Smithe, George "
Stout, Benjamin "
Sawyers, William "
Skaggs, Stephen "
Turner, James "
Tipton, Jacob "
Tipton, Abraham "
Williams, Thomas L. "
Waterhouse, Rich "
White, Moses "
Wheeler, Benjamin "
Williams, John "
Wells, Thomas F. "
Tunnel, James "
Cox, Coleman "
Cox, Jacob "
Dell, James "
Vince, Williams "
Hampton, Wade "
Mace, Joseph "
Henry, Newman

**234 members who helped start the term Tennessee Volunteers.**

*I certify that this muster roll is just and true and that the remarks set up opposite the names are accurate and just as Mustered by me.*

*John Williams Colonel*
*East Tennessee Volunteers*

*U.S. Archives*

*Flournoy*
Public Domain

*Thomas Pinckney*
Public Domain

*William Carroll*
Public Domain

*Willie Blount*
Public Domain

*Ellen Berry's Christmas Card '53*
Credit

*Jackson Assassination attempt*
Artist depiction. Public domain

*Annabelle Janes and Linda Carson at Williams House 1920s*
*Used by permission of Charles Higgins., Jr.*

*David Crockett*

*Public Domain*

*"Tennessee Gentleman"*
*portrait of Andrew Jackson by Ralph E. W. Earl*

*Public Domain*

*Defiled $20 as in story by hardware owner in 1978*

# Chapter 4
# The Benton Fiasco, the Creek War, and the Death of Tecumseh

By the end of their journey, the Volunteers were among the few Southerners to have faced enemy fire. The war was being waged in the Northeast, and, to this day, said conflicts outrank everything accomplished south of Kentucky. A leading military collector stated, "Nobody north of Kentucky knows anything about the War of 1812 in the South." However, action was headed toward Tennessee and Jackson's behavior affected much of what happened; some of his behavior was good and some was bad. There has never been any claim that Jackson had military training.

The Tennessee Volunteers returned to Knoxville and were disbanded in March. Colonel Williams was almost immediately commissioned a colonel in the US Army, and was given the task of recruiting an entire regiment of infantry. His sister-in-law, Polly Lawson McClung Williams, his brother Thomas Lanier's wife, set about creating a flag for the newly formed unit. She hand-engraved a copy of the eagle on his commission on blue silk with a golden banner along the outside edge. This flag would prove all-important later as it was used by the ensign to signal commands in the field where, because of noise and smoke, verbal commands were difficult to execute.

When John Williams arrived in Washington, DC, he learned that Andrew Jackson had planted a friend, Thomas Hart Benton, on his staff of the 39th Infantry. While Williams had been wandering the wilderness with his Volunteers, Jackson had written a note of recommendation for Benton and sent him to Washington to secure the second-ranking commission in the unit as lieutenant colonel. It was a small breach of military courtesy, and a small betrayal of Williams' confidence, since they had discussed plans for such a unit.

The United States Army had developed into the country's first bureaucracy in the years since the founding of the country. The need for a standing army had decreased, but had not gone away, and Congress had continued to fund it. It was a select club of aristocracy who ruled as officers, and money could be made supplying it with the tools of its trade. Even George Washington had warned against the power of the military-industrial complex in his Farewell Address.

Williams would have met with Secretary of War John Armstrong, who would have sworn him in as a commissioned officer, gotten him outfitted with the necessary uniforms and tools of his authority, and would have secured the provisions, arms and currency needed to outfit and train the 39th. Like all other officers, Williams personally would have assumed responsibility for all of the cost of such expenditures.

When he returned to Knoxville, Williams' first recruit was a rising young gentleman graduate of the East Tennessee College, Lemuel Montgomery. Major Montgomery was "28 years of age. His eyes were keen and black, his hair was of a dark auburn color, his weight was 175 pounds, his height was six feet and two inches, his form was admirably proportioned, and he was altogether the finest looking man in the army. His mother was related to the Donelsons." [61]

---

[61] Heiskell, p. 497

John Williams then began the grueling process of recruiting new soldiers into the 39th. He would march into a small town on horseback in full dress uniform, amid drums beating and a few uniformed recruits, to draw a crowd. He would then make a stirring speech announcing his recruiting intentions and arousing feelings of patriotism amongst the crowd. Then he would place silver dollars on the drumhead and invite new recruits to join the Army by taking one of the dollars. This must have been an impressive show amidst the locals: silver dollars were in very short supply, and fervor for the war was very high.

Sam Houston was a somewhat rebellious youth. He had lived with the Cherokee on and off while his family lived in Maryville. He had reportedly earned the Cherokee name "The Raven" in their tribe. He had tried to live in the white society, but was not skillful with money and bartering, and had amassed debts he needed to pay. At six-foot-five, he was an impressive physical specimen, was intelligent, and quickly became an elected leader of his peers. His lack of discipline after he transferred into the unit did not impress Colonel Williams.

Colonel Williams trained the 600-plus recruits of the 39th at his cantonment four miles from Knoxville. This was a traditional assembly and meeting ground that he supposedly owned, and it is now the site of the Knoxville Zoo and Chilhowee Park. Having previously been a captain in the Army, he would have followed the military rules of the day to perfection by drilling, disciplining, and teaching the unskilled and undereducated recruits how to fight as an army. By the time he was finished, his men were professional soldiers who followed orders, did their duty impeccably, and made state militias pale by comparison.

On April 13, a party of Creek warriors, led by McIntosh, avenged the killings in Tennessee by the misinformed band led by Little Warrior by executing his entire band of aggressors. Later that month, the nine executioners were killed by a band of Red Sticks, and this set off a civil war within the Creek Nation. Red Sticks burned villages and killed cattle, and the angry Creek faction was generally rebellious against civilization. There was growing unrest and indecision in the Creek towns.

Knowing they could not defend it, the Spanish government surrendered the city of Mobile, Alabama, the back door to New Orleans, to General Wilkinson.

Andrew Jackson remained as commanding general of the West Tennessee Militia based in Nashville. His soldiers were citizens first with short enlistments and less dedication to military training, discipline, and obedience to chain of command and fighting skills. Jackson continued his raucous lifestyle.

Excelling almost exclusively in his role as military commander, Jackson mentored newly returned William Carroll, who was a major in his state militia. Carroll was unpopular with his peers and received several challenges that he quickly dismissed and did not fight. One such challenge came from Jesse Benton, brother of Jackson appointee Thomas Hart Benton.

Carroll accepted this challenge, and, not finding an adequate second for the duel, asked Jackson to assist him. This duel occurred with Benton receiving a grazing wound in the buttock while Carroll lost a thumb. Jesse Benton was publicly humiliated, and his brother, Thomas, returning from Washington, became enraged that Jackson had sided against his brother.

In June, Colonel Williams had been in Nashville, reporting the results of his Tennessee Volunteers campaign to Governor Willie Blount. Apparently, Major Montgomery came with him because his lone entry in *The Jackson Papers* was a one-line sentence to Jackson: "under orders from General Jackson I am ordered to say that Lieutenant Colonel Benton called him a hollow-hearted scoundrel." This was a *second* military indiscretion committed by Jackson upon Colonel Williams; one did *not* give orders to another officer's staff without going through the ranking officer.

Thomas Hart Benton had succeeded while in Washington in getting Jackson's debt with General Wilkinson resolved, but he was incensed at what he perceived as Jackson's treachery. He made incendiary statements that got back to Jackson, who threatened to "horse whip him." [62]

The war of words escalated in Nashville and culminated in an eventful fight at a boardinghouse downtown. The Benton brothers had come armed and intentionally stayed in a boardinghouse not frequented by Jackson. On the morning of September 4, 1813, Jackson, who was forewarned, came to town with his friends, John Coffee and Stockley Hays.

Having noticed the Benton brothers across the street, the Jackson party went to the post office and intentionally walked by the tavern where the Bentons were. As they reached the tavern, Jackson entered, saw Thomas Hart Benton, and, while raising his whip, said, "Now, defend yourself, you damned rascal!"

---

62 Heiskell, p. 466

Thomas Benton tried to arm himself, but was too slow, and Jackson advanced on him down the hallway toward the rear porch on the river side of the building. Jesse Benton emerged from behind Jackson and fired twice at close range at Jackson, hitting him in the shoulder and side. The falling Jackson fired at Thomas, but missed him, and crumpled severely injured to the floor. Thomas Benton fired also, but missed the prostrate form of Jackson, and Jackson was shielded by James Sitler as Jesse lunged forward to finish Jackson.

Jackson's friend, John Coffee, fired two shots over the heads of Jesse Benton and Sitler, at which point Thomas Benton fell down some stairs. Stockley Hays then drew a sword and advanced on Jesse Benton, whose life was saved when the sword broke on Benton's coat button.

Jackson was removed to a room in the Nashville Inn, where he bled profusely and doctors recommended the amputation of his arm. "I'll keep my arm," he was reported to have said, and he carried the ball in his shoulder until it was removed by surgeons many years later while he was in Washington, D.C.

With fall approaching and a major campaign planned against the Creeks, Jackson was severely wounded and Thomas Hart Benton sat out the early part of the war. Jackson lived with the pain and memory of that day for twenty-two years. His only comment was to offer to have the ball returned to Benton when it was removed; Benton politely declined.

- - - ! ! !

Earlier in July 1813, a large party of Red Stick warriors proceeded to Pensacola, Florida, with a British officer at Fort Malden and four hundred dollars to buy munitions. The Spanish governor gave them, in the words of Peter McQueen, a Creek chief, "a small bag of powder for each ten towns, and five bullets to each man." The governor presented this as a "friendly present, for hunting purposes." [63]

But conversely Samuel Moniac, a Creek warrior, testified in August 1813: "High Head told me that, when they went back with their supply, another body of men would go down for another supply of ammunition; and that ten men were to go out of town, and they calculated on *five horse-loads for every town.*" [64] So were parts of the Creek nation given ammunition to use against United States settlements.

US soldiers at Fort Mims, having heard of McQueen's mission, responded by sending a disorganized force, led by Colonel Caller and Captain Dixon Bailey, to intercept McQueen's party. The Americans ambushed the Red Sticks as they bedded down for the evening on the banks of Burnt Corn Creek, in what is now northern Escambia County, Alabama.

The Americans scattered the Red Sticks, who fled to the nearby swamps. Flush with victory, the Americans began looting the Red Sticks' packhorses. From the swamp, the Creeks noticed that the Americans were getting carried away with their looting and had dropped their guard. The Creeks regrouped and launched a surprise attack of their own, which scattered the Americans, and ten to twelve Creeks were killed.

The Red Sticks considered this ambush to be a "declaration of war" by the American settlers. Since the American militia had attacked from Fort Mims, the Red Sticks directed their next offensive at that fort. Many mixed-blood Creek families from the lower towns had fled to Fort Mims at the outbreak of the Creek War, and these refugees were also likely targets of the Red Stick aggression. [65]

Back in Knoxville, where the 39th Infantry remained in their cantonment, Private Sam Houston was rewarded by his fellow soldiers and was elected ensign. The duty of the ensign was "to carry the flag." [66]

In Nashville, Militia General Jackson was suffering mightily from his wound, and on the 25th of August he published General Orders telling his volunteers to remain alert for service. "There is no doubt of the hostility of the Creek Indians; the volunteers are required to be ready to march at a moment's notice." [67] About three days later, Governor Blount wrote the Secretary of War requesting Williams' 39th be sent to aid Jackson in an expedition against the Creeks; it was not received in Washington until September 19, and someone wrote up the side of its cover, "Is this not the unit intended for General Flournoy?" [68]

That was never resolved and "one of the most horrible massacres in frontier history" had occurred. [69]

---

63 Adams, Henry, *History of the United States of America: The Second Administration of James Madison, 1813–1817*. C. Scribner's, 1891, pp. 228–229
64 Modette, *History of the Mississippi Valley, Volume II*, archived from the original on July 7, 2011
65 http://en.wikipedia.org/wiki/Battle_of_Burnt_Corn
66 Lossing, Benson J., *Pictorial Field Book of the War of 1812*, New York: Harper & Brothers Publishers, 1868, p. 779
67 *Nashville Whig*, Aug. 25, 1813
68 Blount to secretary of war, Aug. 28, 1813
69 Holland, James W., *Andrew Jackson and the Creek War*, University of Alabama Press, 1968, p. 243

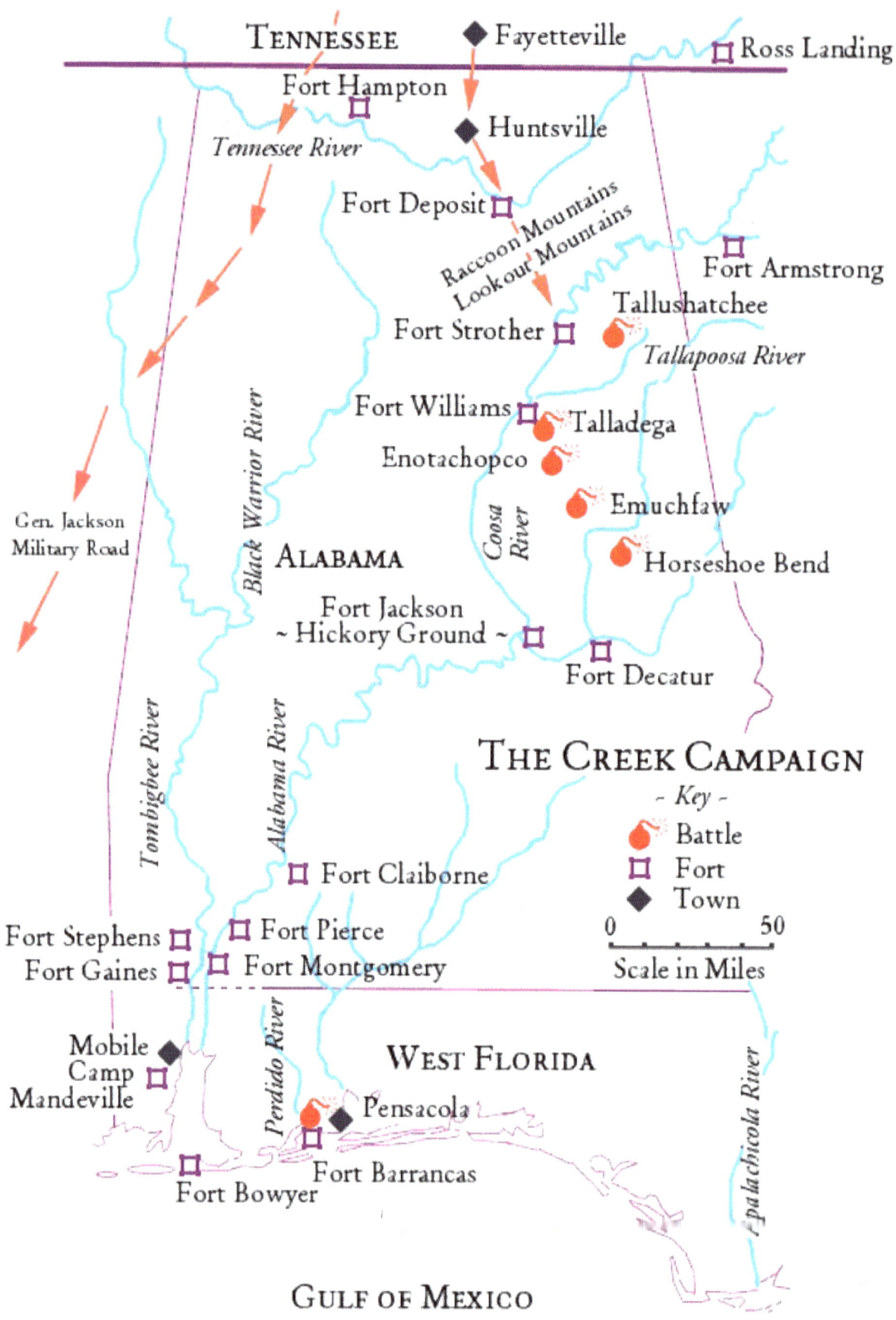

Situated on relatively high ground on the east bank of Tensaw Lake, Fort Mims began as the fortified home and outbuildings of Samuel Mims. The lake was formed from an old channel of the Alabama River and was connected to the river by a navigable passage. The fort consisted of 17 buildings, including one blockhouse and a log palisade. By early August 1813, about 550 settlers and slaves from the surrounding area had crowded into the tiny stockade. A number of friendly Indians and half-breeds had also sought protection within the fort. Before the massacre, the Creek nation had generally peaceful relations with the white settlers, and intermarriage was not uncommon. In fact, many of the settlers who died at Fort Mims were of mixed blood. [70]

Brigadier General Ferdinand L. Claiborne of the Mississippi Territorial Militia was in charge of military affairs in the region and divided his forces to garrison the frontier outposts. He sent Major Daniel Beasley and 170 men of the 1st Mississippi Volunteers to defend the Fort Mims area. Major Beasley posted 120 men, mostly Louisianans, in Fort Mims and scattered the balance among other smaller area posts, including forty soldiers stationed at Fort Pierce located on Pine Log Creek, about two miles south of Fort Mims.

Major Beasley had no military experience and was a lawyer in the territory's Jefferson County when General Claiborne, a close personal friend, used his influence to have him appointed major in the militia in February 1813. Beasley had been at Fort Mims only a few days when General Claiborne inspected the post on August 7, 1813, and recommended that at least two, and possibly three, additional blockhouses be built. "To respect our Enemy, and to prepare in the best possible way to meet him, is the certain means to ensure success," General Claiborne wrote in orders to Beasley after the inspection.

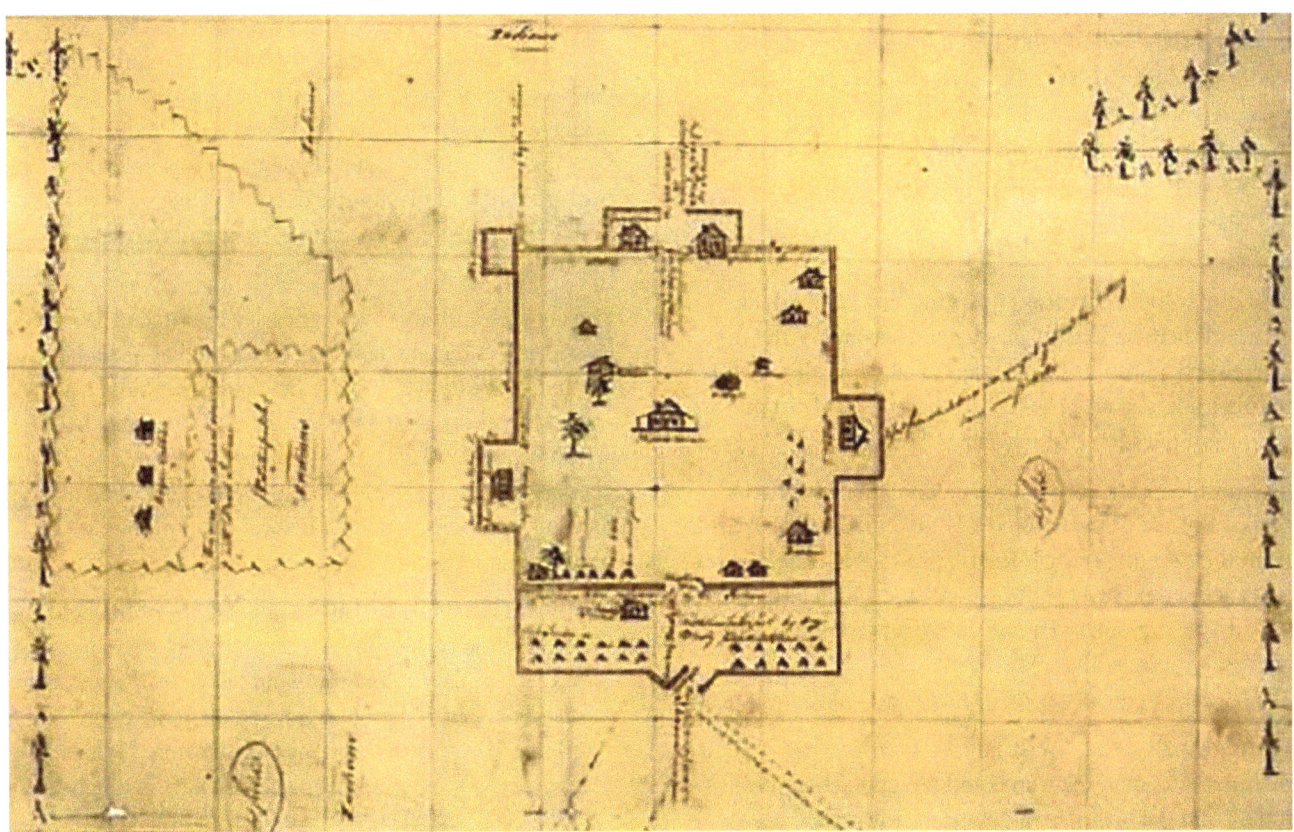

*Map of Fort Mims*

[70] http://www.canerossi.us/ftmims/massacre.htm

However, Major Beasley was slow to strengthen Fort Mims' defenses, apparently believing there was no danger of imminent attack. The defenders did, however, construct a second defensive wall a few yards inside the stockade and facing the main gate on the east side of the fort. "We are perfectly tranquil here," Major Beasley wrote General Claiborne on August 12, 1813, "and are progressing in our works as well as can be expected considering the want of tools. We shall probably finish the stockade tomorrow."

On August 13, 1813, about fifty of Beasley's men at Fort Mims were sent to Mount Vernon, a cantonment on the Mobile River a few miles west of the fort. "It is with regret that I send them as it weakens my command very much," Major Beasley wrote to General Claiborne, who had ordered the movement. Yet the loss of these troops, which left Beasley with only seventy militiamen in addition to the volunteers among the settlers, did not cause the major to hasten work on the fort's defenses.

Adding to Beasley's tranquility were reports—supplied by supposedly friendly Indians and believed by militia leaders, including General Claiborne—that the Creeks were massing for an attack on Fort Easley, located on the Tombigbee River about thirty miles northwest of Fort Mims. Major Beasley's post seemed to be out of immediate danger.

On August 24, 1813, General Claiborne led about eighty men to reinforce Fort Easley, writing that if the Creeks attacked there he would "give a good account of them." Whether the hostile Creeks intentionally misled the militia leaders in order to divert reinforcements from Fort Mims is a question that may never be answered.

The hostile Creek Indians, the faction known as Red Sticks, learned of the weakness of the Fort Mims garrison from their scouts, and gathered 750 to 1,000 warriors for an attack on the pioneer stronghold and Fort Pierce. A mixed-blood prophet, Paddy Welsh, was chosen to lead the assault, but William Weatherford, also known as Chief Red Eagle, was instrumental in planning the attack.

By August 29, 1813, Welsh and Weatherford had hidden their main force in the woods and tall grass about six miles from the unsuspecting outpost, where soldiers and settlers were enjoying a supply of whiskey that had arrived that day. Sometime during the day, two young slaves tending cattle outside the stockade were startled to see war-painted Creeks in the forest near the fort. They hurried back to the fort and informed Major Beasley. He quickly ordered a mounted patrol of about ten men to check out the sighting.

Two of these scouts apparently rode within 300 yards of the Creek attack force without seeing the concealed warriors. Indian accounts stated that two of the militiamen, talking between themselves, passed along a road leading to the fort with the Creeks watching from the brush. Since the patrol reported no Indian activity in the area, Major Beasley ordered the slaves to be whipped for bringing false information and took no other defensive precautions.

By nightfall of August 29, 1813, the Creeks had advanced to within one mile of the unsuspecting fort. During the night, Weatherford and two warriors silently crawled up to the walls and peered through the fort's firing ports (loopholes), which were cut into the palisade timbers about four feet from the ground. The sentries were playing cards, and evidently never saw them.

On the morning of August 30, 1813, few of Fort Mims' defenders stirred in the steaming heat. In the forested shade, the Creeks watched and waited. The fort's main gate, located on the east side of the stockade, had not been closed by the garrison troops and was lodged open by a shifting bank of sand. Some historians believe Weatherford and his night scouts may have piled the dirt to hold the gate ajar. No sentries occupied the blockhouse.

During the morning, Major Beasley dispatched a message to General Claiborne, unaware that he had only a few hours left to live. Beasley described the "false alarm" spread by the slaves. He added that, while he had been initially concerned because other slaves sent to a nearby plantation to gather corn had reported seeing Indians "committing every kind of Havoc," he now doubted the truth of that report. [71]

> "I was much pleased at the appearance of the Soldiers here at the time of the Alarm yesterday when it was expected that the Indians would appear in Sight, the Soldiers very generally appeared anxious to see them," Beasley wrote in his last dispatch. "I have improved the fort at this place and have it much Stronger that when you were here," Beasley continued. With more that a hint of frustration, he noted that his initial force had been so divided among the other outposts that he would be relegated to defense if attacked and "utterly unable to leave the fort and meet any number of the enemy." [72]

---

[71] Halbert & Ball, The Creek War of 1813 and 1814, 1895
[72] http://www.canerossi.us/ftmims/massacre.htm

Before noon, Major Beasley received one last warning, but also ignored it. James Cornells, a scout, galloped into the fort and shouted to Beasley on the parade ground that he had seen hostile Creeks approaching. Beasley told him that he had only seen a few red cattle and mistaken them for Indians. Witnesses stated that Cornells yelled to Beasley that the red cattle would "give him a hell of a kick before night." Beasley ordered Cornells arrested, but the scout galloped away, leaving the outpost and its occupants to their fate.

At noon, a drummer sounded the call to mess, and the soldiers and settlers headed for their midday meal. Some of the girls and young men were dancing, and the soldiers were playing cards as they waited for their food. The rattle of the drum was the Creek's signal to attack, and the death knell for most of the settlers and militia. Hundreds of Red Stick warriors, hidden in a ravine only four hundred yards from the fort, stormed across the open field and crowded through the open gate, their war whoops mingling with scattered musket shots from the soldiers and screams of terror from the pioneer women and children.

Before the attack, the prophet Welsh had performed a magical ceremony to make four braves impervious to bullets. These warriors were to lead the attack through the gate and divert the defenders' attention long enough for other Red Sticks to occupy the stockade's loopholes and fire into the fort from outside the walls. The "bulletproof" braves were the first to rush into the gate, and three were immediately shot down. Despite the failure of the magic, the militiamen were occupied long enough for the Red Sticks to take many of the loopholes and open fire on the whites running for cover inside the fort. Within minutes of the initial attack, the Creeks had also seized the unoccupied blockhouse.

Major Beasley, who according to some accounts was drunk at the time of the attack, drew his sword and vainly fought to close the gate, but was quickly clubbed to death in the Creeks' initial onslaught. Dixon Bailey, a mixed-blood man who had been elected captain of the fort's volunteers, took command and led a group of riflemen who fired at the attackers from the loopholes not occupied by the Indians. Other militiamen set up a hasty defense behind the inner wall and among the fort's buildings. By surprise and sheer numbers, the Indians quickly established a foothold inside the palisade, and slowly pushed all of the frontiersmen back behind the secondary defenses. The militiamen and pioneer riflemen poured fire into the Creeks but were overwhelmed by the sheer numbers of screaming warriors rushing into the stockade.

Despite their manpower advantage, the Red Sticks, most of whom were armed with only tomahawks, clubs, knives, and bows and arrows, suffered heavy losses. Many of the fort's defenders, however, were killed by Indians firing into the fort through loopholes behind the defenders' positions. The Creeks set fire to most of the fort's buildings using flaming arrows. Many settlers, including numerous women and children, were burned alive. The fort's powder magazine, located in one of the cabins, exploded, ignited by the raging flames.

Yet, by 3 p.m., the battle was far from decided. The Creeks were exhausted and many were ready to quit the fight. Most of the surviving settlers and militiamen had sought refuge in a loom house and another log building against the fort's north wall and were grimly holding out. The Creek leaders rallied their braves, who now set these last two structures ablaze. Some settlers died in the flames, but others were forced out and immediately killed by the warriors. Bailey was mortally wounded in these closing moments of the battle. Some settlers, mostly men, were able to hack their way through the northern stockade wall and make their escape. A few found a flatboat and floated down the river to Fort Stoddert, near Mobile.

The Creeks apparently spared most of the slaves to serve them, but this reprieve was to be short-lived. During the Battle of Horseshoe Bend, Alabama, fought on March 27, 1814, the Indians vainly used these slaves as a human shield, but the attacking soldiers under General Jackson quickly killed them. While the slaves were spared during the massacre, the Indians showed no mercy to the whites. By some accounts, the Creeks slaughtered the settlers, including brutalizing women—some of whom were pregnant—and children. Some of the wounded and dead bodies were thrown into fires.

Weatherford apparently was horrified by the gruesome spectacle and vainly tried to stop the slaughter, but the Red Sticks, angered by the deaths of many comrades and in a killing frenzy, could not be stopped. The Creeks also believed a false rumor that British officials in Pensacola offered five dollars for every white scalp. Many of the victims at Fort Mims were scalped before they were killed. However, not all of the Creeks participated in the slaughter. One survivor told of a friendly Creek named Johomobtee, who shot three Red Sticks who were killing women.

Another survivor, as she watched her husband being killed, decided to bravely meet her own fate. Taking two children by their hands, she walked into the middle of the carnage, expecting to die at any moment. She was startled to see a blood-stained Creek calling to her. She recognized him as Dog Warrior, an Indian she had known when he was a child. Dog Warrior led her and the children to safety out of the fort. However, these actions were the exception.

A slave who escaped told authorities he and others including Dixon Bailey's sister were in Mims' house when the hostile Creeks entered. A warrior asked the woman if she was related to anyone in the fort. The woman pointed to the body of her brother and said "I am the sister of that great man you have murdered there," whereupon the warrior knocked her down and mutilated her.

About three miles away, the forty soldiers and about 150 settlers at Fort Pierce listened to the sounds of the chaos through the day and nervously waited for an attack. "The firing and yells of the Indians were heard at this post until after four o'clock in the afternoon when the firing ceased," wrote militiaman Lieutenant Andrew Montgomery, who commanded Fort Pierce. "It was impossible to render them any assistance with my small force."

By 5 p.m., the battle was over, and the Creeks and their captives left the blazing ruins and dead behind.

A soldier who had served under Major General Wayne along the northern frontier was wounded but escaped from the fort and gave an account of the massacre. He ran into the forest and shot a brave who confronted him, then hid beneath the lake bank as darkness settled over the fort. To the soldier's horror, some of the Creeks from the war party camped near his hiding place. The next morning, the Red Sticks threw the bodies of three people into the lake and departed. In the abandoned camp, he said he found a young boy's body sprawled on an animal hide.

The fort's assistant surgeon, Dr. Thomas G. Holmes, escaped from the burning fort and hid in a hole by the roots of a fallen tree. He wandered through the wilderness for nine days before being found by a friendly settler.

The frightened defenders of Fort Pierce remained on the alert through the night of August 30 and saw bands of warriors in the distance, but the expected attack never came. About noon on August 31, Lieutenant Montgomery sent out a mounted patrol that reported that Fort Mims had fallen and the river swamp was full of Indians. Believing he could not defend Fort Pierce with his small force, Montgomery made plans to abandon the outpost. Thwarted in an attempt to find a boat to help evacuate the fort, Montgomery waited until dark and led the militia and refugees out of the fort headed for Mobile, about thirty-five miles to the south. In a grueling march through the wilderness, Montgomery's party reached Mobile early on the morning of September 4 with no losses.

Exact casualty figures will never be known, but most authorities agree that between 250 to 400 settlers and militiamen died at Fort Mims. A settler who returned to the grisly scene four days after the battle to search for his family reportedly saw about "250 dead bodies and the women in a situation shocking to behold or relate." Many accounts state the death toll exceeded five hundred, but this apparently does not take into account the approximately 100 to 175 slaves who were captured by the Creeks; however, among the bodies were the remains of about 20 slaves. Additionally, a few white women and children may have also been taken prisoner.

Militia Major Kennedy commanded a detachment sent to the gruesome site to bury the dead three weeks after the massacre. The soldiers were horrified to find throngs of vultures and wild dogs, which had been attracted to the corpses. Major Kennedy reported he found and buried the bodies of 247 men, women, and children. "Indians, Negroes, white men, women, and children lay in one promiscuous ruin," wrote Kennedy. "All were scalped, and the females of every age, were butchered."

In the charred remains of Mims' house, the soldiers found the bones of many victims. In the woods nearby, the militiamen found the graves of about one hundred Red Sticks. In a letter of September 4 to Territory Governor David Holmes, General Claiborne wrote that about two hundred Creeks were believed to have been killed in the attack. Some historians believe the Creeks may have lost three hundred to four hundred warriors in the fight.

News of the Fort Mims massacre spread quickly, shocking and outraging the American nation. General Claiborne was widely criticized for his handling of the frontier defenses, but Major Beasley's carelessness appears to be more to blame for the Fort Mims massacre. The Creek victory raised the confidence of the Red Stick warriors as much as it panicked settlers along the entire western frontier. [73]

> Many years later, the whites began to settle Alabama. A very poor man by the name of Stoker settled on the Autauga side, opposite Holy Ground. His little boys, while out hunting one day, found the irons of an old trunk and some $100 or $200 in eagle half dollars.

[73] http://www.canerossi.us/ftmims/massacre.htm

This money had been plundered at Ft. Mims, and the plunderer placed it where the boys of Stoker found it and then went back into a fight and was killed. [74]

At that time, the Creeks had about eight thousand warriors, but not all of them were fighting the white man. Two days later, on September 1, a band of Creeks swooped in on the homes of the Kimbell and James families near present-day Whatley, killing about twelve members of the family. Those who survived fled to nearby Fort Sinquefield, which was attacked the next day.

One group of settlers was on the east side of the fort, burying twelve members of the Kimbell and James families who were massacred at their home near Whatley by the Indians the day before, while on the southwest side a group of women were at a spring washing clothes.

"Isham Kimbell and Charles Phillips were sitting at the at the east gate of the fort talking when Phillips commented on a fine bunch of turkeys approaching from the southeast. Isham looked and recognized them as a large party of Indians. When he cried out the warning, the Indians rushed the burial party, which dashed safely into the fort. Then the attackers discovered the women at the spring and turned their attention toward them. Two men guarding the women had run to the fort when they heard the warning, leaving the women unprotected.

"The attack was made by around 100 Red Stick warriors, who faced 25 or more armed men inside Sinquefield (and possibly some friendly Indians). The warriors were dressed for battle with painted faces, turkey feathers in their heads, and some with a cow tail tied on each arm from the shoulder to the wrist.

"Isaac Hayden, who was in the relief column from Fort Madison, saw the plight of the women in danger of being cut off at the spring. Calling the dogs from the fort, he jumped on a nearby horse that had two holstered pistols on its saddle and charged the Muscogee braves. Some of the Indians ran, others were bayed by the dogs. One warrior had his tomahawk drawn ready to strike one of the women when Hayden shot him. This confusion allowed all the women except one to reach safety. Mrs. Sarah Phillips, hampered by pregnancy, fainted and fell before she reached the top of the hill. An Indian buried his tomahawk in her skull. But a black woman named Hester turned a washpot over her head and ran untouched up the hill. The Creeks thought she was crazy, and since they were afraid to kill the insane, she escaped unharmed.

"With Indians in close pursuit, Hayden, the last to return, approached the fort only to find the gate closed. He kept riding, circling the wall. When he reached the gate again, it was cracked open and he slipped through. Just as he got inside, his horse fell dead with a shot through the neck. His clothes were ripped with rifle fire, but his flesh wasn't scratched."

After the short-lived battle, in which one settler was killed in addition to the slain woman, the settlers abandoned the fort for the larger and stronger Fort Madison south of present-day Suggsville.[75]

The massacre at Fort Mims had upset the entire western frontier that was the new state of Tennessee. It being only seventeen years in existence, its rapid growth had attracted a lively group of citizens. Those citizens had elected governors and legislators as well as municipal governments. They were itching for a fight. Emotionally aroused, bombastic statements and boasts were made that were appropriate to the times. The Tennessee legislature voted for the extermination of the Creek tribe. The governor gave Militia General Jackson that task.

By the 14th of that month, the news from the frontier was fearfully charging the Tennessee settlers to action. Andrew Jackson complained of his "indisposition," then five days later he issued a general order for the militia "to rendezvous at Fayetteville on September 24th." [76]

## "GENERAL JACKSON TO THE VOLUNTEERS AT FAYETTEVILLE

"We are about to furnish these savages a lesson of admonition; we are about to teach them that our long forbearance has not proceeded from an insensibility to wrongs, or an inability to redress them. They stand in need of such warning. In proportion as we have borne with their insults, and submitted to their outrages, they have multiplied in number, and increased in atrocity. But the measure of their offenses is at length filled. The blood of our women and children, recently spilt at Ft. Mims, calls for our vengeance; it must not call in vain. Our borders must no longer be disturbed by the warhoop of these savages, and the cries of their suffering victims. The torch that has been lighted up must be made to blaze in the heart of their own country. It is time they should be made to feel the weight of a power, which, because it was merciful, they believed to be impotent." [77]

---!!!

---

75 Cox, Jim, *The Clark County Democrat*, Aug. 28, 2003
76 *Nashville Whig*, Sept. 14, 1813 and Sept. 19, 1813
77 Heiskell, S. G. p. 481

About this same time a British schooner was anchored at Pensacola and loaded with war supplies. The Spanish governor wrote to William Weatherford, offering him support and aid. [78]

As the Tennessee troops began to gather in early October in southern-middle Tennessee, the War of 1812 continued to rage in the north. After losing Detroit, the Americans invaded Canada and attacked the British and Indian forces near present-day Toronto.

> The British-Indian army turned to make a stand at Moraviantown, on the Thames River in Ontario, in 1813. The outcome of the battle seems really to have been a foregone conclusion. By the time the British general Proctor actually stops to turn to fight, he has lost the confidence not only of his Indian allies, but of his own men. When the fighting breaks out, the British resistance is minimal. What resistance is mounted is mounted by Tecumseh and the Indian warriors. [79]

The British simply abandoned the Indians and withdrew, leaving them to fight by themselves.

And in one of the more remarkable speeches given throughout American history, Tecumseh says to the British, "Look. You have somewhere to go. But we are standing here, and we are fighting for our homeland. And if you want to run, you run. But leave us the guns and ammunition, because we will stand and fight." [80]

The PBS series *We Shall Remain* personalized the campaign thusly:

> "And then, finally, at the end, you often tell great leaders in the way they react in adversity. He knew that the British had given way before they engaged themselves. And, yet, there is no question of him retreating—there is no question of him doing the "sensible" thing, which is to fight another day. He has committed himself to this act. He has said he's going to defend this land, and, if necessary, he's going die for this land. And that's what he does. [81]
>
> "And you couldn't think, in some ways, of a more fitting way for Tecumseh to die. He dies in the final battle here for the control of the Great Lakes. And he dies surrounded by his comrades. He dies killed by the Americans. And in the aftermath, his body is mutilated so badly by Harrison's Kentucky militia that the Americans who know him can't really identify him." [82]

The circumstance of the bold stand made by the supposed chief being communicated to Gen. Harrison, he visited the spot where the dead Indian lay; the body was much mangled, and as the general approached the spot a soldier was in the act of taking off a piece of skin from the Indian's thigh. The general ordered the soldier to stop, and said he regretted to know that he had such a man in his camp, and reprimanded him severely. He had some water brought, had the Indian washed and stretched his full length, examined his teeth and pronounced it to be Tecumseh.
One of Tecumseh's legs was a little shorter than the other, and the foot on the short leg a little smaller, and he had a halt in his walk that was perceptible, and he had a tooth, though not decayed, of a bluish cast. [83]

With Tecumseh gone, British support lagging, and patriotic white men responding to the call of battle, it was inevitable that the Indians east of the Mississippi River would be forcefully removed and their properties acquired. The policy of the United States toward the native Indians established by Thomas Jefferson would become reality.

---

77 Heiskell, S. G. p. 481
78 Used by permission of Paul Ghiotto, Sept. 4, 2018
79 Calloway, Colin, historian, *We Shall Remain*, PBS, 2009
80 Edmonds, David, historian, *We Shall Remain*, PBS, 2009
81 Sugden, John, historian, *We Shall Remain*, PBS, 2009
82 Edmonds, David, historian, *We Shall Remain*, PBS, 2009
83 Woodward, Thomas S. *Woodward's Reminiscences* p. 85

# Chapter 5
# The Creek War

This chapter goes deeply into the early military events of the Creek War, a seldom-addressed event. There are many previously printed statements and some never previously shown.

Jackson's prosecution of this war is controversial, yet hardly ever examined. So many characters are involved. I cannot count them all, but they include Andrew Jackson, John Williams, Hugh Lawrence White, Davy Crockett, Governor Willie Blount, General Thomas Lindsay, General Thomas Pinckney, General Thomas Flournoy, and some who are possibly falsely named.

It is important because these events solidified the feud between Jackson and Williams and included a military execution that could have been considered "military murder." [84]

In the fall of 1813, Andrew Jackson was a forty-seven-year-old man who had had various successes and failures in business and government: He was a frontiersman, a patriot at thirteen, and had fallen from public favor; yet he retained command of the Western Militia of Tennessee. It was the one occupation where his nature blossomed.

Prior to his wounding, there had been much written about him, President Madison, and Governor Willie Blount, Secretary of War Armstrong, and the district military commanders of the United States, General Flournoy in New Orleans (District 7) and General Pinckney in Milledgeville, Georgia (District 6).

General Andrew Jackson assumed command of an "army designed to avenge the blood of their countrymen, and to conquer the most warlike tribe of barbarians in the universe." [85] John Coffee reported from Huntsville that he had received reports from Indian runners that hostile Creeks in great numbers intended to attack the frontiers of Tennessee and Georgia simultaneously. [86] That did *not* happen.

> After their successful attack on Ft. Mims, the Creeks scattered in different directions within their nation. The Indians expected after this that the whites would pour into the nation from all quarters. But the movement of the whites were so slow that the Indians grew careless, and a few Indians, with Weatherford and the chief, Hossa Yoholo, made what has been known as the Holy Ground their headquarters. [87]

On the 22nd of October, General Jackson had recovered well enough to establish Ft. Deposit in south-central Alabama, and no hostile Indians were encountered. Jackson's troops began cutting a road toward the Coosa River. The Creeks there withdrew to Tallushatchee. General Coffee's nine hundred men engaged them there on the 3rd of November and killed 186 and took 84 prisoners, and the town was burned. Coffee lost five men. Jackson boasted to Governor Blount, "We have retaliated for the destruction of Ft. Mims." [88]

---

84 Watson, Thomas E., *Watson's Magazine*, Volume 5, 1905
85 Waldo, Samuel Putnam, *Memoirs of Andrew Jackson*, J&W Russell, Hartford, 1820, p. 66
86 Holland, James W., "Andrew Jackson and the Creek War: Victory at the Horseshoe Bend." *Alabama Review*, 1968, 21(4): 243–275
87 Woodward, Thomas S., *Woodward's Reminiscences*, , p. 100
88 Jackson to Blount, Nov. 4, 1813

The legendary confrontation that became known as the "Canoe Fight" took place on November 12, 1813, on the Alabama River during the Creek War of 1813-14. The skirmish gained fame for the novelty of having taken place in canoes, pitting a small band of militia led by Captain Samuel Dale against a larger group of Red Stick Creeks.

Captain Samuel Dale, who was stationed at Fort Madison in present-day Clarke County, volunteered to lead a mission to drive the Indians away so as to bring stability to the area. Dale and his party soon encountered a large party of Red Stick warriors near the mouth of Randon's Creek on the Alabama River.

The ensuing confrontation (observed from both sides of the river by a number of soldiers) was retold in several slightly differing accounts, but the core facts are fairly consistent. Captain Dale and eleven of his men, including Jeremiah Austill and James Smith, had become separated from the main force. Their late morning breakfast on November 12, 1813, was interrupted with a cry that Indians were in the vicinity. When Dale and his small party reached the riverbank, they saw a canoe containing a reputed chief and ten warriors coming down the river. As the canoe approached the bank, its occupants saw Dale's men, and reversed their canoe back into the river. Two warriors then jumped from the canoe into the water, and one was shot by Smith. Dale ordered a large canoe to be brought over from the other side of the river to aid in attacking these Indians. Eight men began to carry out this order but got cold feet when they saw the number of warriors in the canoe and returned to their side of the river.

Dale was determined to engage the Indians. He thus ordered a free African American, known only as Caesar, to paddle a small dugout canoe that would only hold himself, Austill and Smith to meet the Creek canoe now bearing nine warriors. As Caesar paddled the canoe toward their target, Dale, Austill and Smith attempted to fire upon the Indians. Only one weapon fired, however, as the priming of the other two had been dampened by the water from the river. When the canoes were about to meet prow to prow, the chief recognized Dale and shouted in English, "Now for it, Big Sam." The opposing canoes met side-to-side, and the chief knocked Austill down with his rifle. Dale then ordered Caesar to hold the canoes together, and after a few minutes of hand-to-hand fighting using rifles and oars as clubs, the white soldiers, although outnumbered three to one, killed all of the Indians remaining in the canoe. According to witnesses, Dale's men cheered as the bodies of the dead warriors were cast into the river. [89]

Colonel Woodward also commented upon the skirmish:

> "Colonel Austill is yet living, and of course knows more of the fight than I can possibly know. But I have no doubt that he will say that the fight has been detailed by Colonel Pickett to the best advantage for those engaged in it; and will also say that an Indian fight, either in a canoe or the bushes, alters its appearance very much by getting into a book or newspaper. I have heard the accounts given, from General Dale down to Caesar; it's a pity the eight big Indians killed in the canoe had not been taken to the shore for the landsmen to have looked at." [90]

But Woodward's account did not prevail, and another legend was born and perpetrated as history.

Soon after that, Jackson's supplies arrived and Ft. Strother was built. Friendly Creeks were besieged just south of the fort at Talladega and they asked Jackson for help. He marched with two thousand men, and on November 9 attacked the hostile Creeks. It was another success for the Tennesseans with three hundred killed, while Jackson's force lost fifteen dead and eighty-five wounded. Seven hundred Creeks escaped, and Jackson later complained that if he had been adequately supplied he could have ended the war then, "in ten days." [91]

It is always interesting to hear the story of a battle told by one of the privates. The celebrated David Crockett took part in these two actions of Tallushatchee and Talladega. He had volunteered at the first summons and was serving as a common soldier. One of the bravest men who ever lived, and one of nature's noblemen besides, his simple story of these two battles is in curious contrast to the vainglorious accounts given by the hero-worshipers.

> "We had also a Cherokee colonel, Dick Brown, and some of his men with us. When we got near the town, we divided; one of our pilots going with each division. And so we passed on each side of the town, keeping near to it until our lines met on the far side. We then closed up at both ends, so as to surround it completely; and then we sent Captain Hammond's company of rangers to bring on the affray. He had advanced near the town, when the Indians saw him, and they raised a yell, and came running at them like so many red devils. The main army was now formed in a hollow square around the town, and they pursued

---

[89] http://www.encyclopediaofalabama.org/face/Article.jsp?id=h-1815
[90] Woodward, Thomas S., *Woodward's Reminiscences*, p. 68
[91] Evans, G. G., *Life of Colonel Davy Crockett*, 1859, p. 100

Hammond till they came in reach of us. We then gave them a fire and they returned it, and then they ran back into their town. We began to close on the town by making our files closer and closer, and the Indians soon saw they were our property. So most of them wanted us to take them prisoners; and their squaws and all would run and take hold of any of they could, and give themselves up. I saw seven squaws take hold of one man which made me think of the Scriptures. So I hollered out the Scriptures were fulfilling; that there were seven women hanging to one man's coattail. But I believe it was a hunting shirt all the time. We took them all prisoners that came out to us in this way; but I saw some warriors run into a house until I counted forty-six of them.

"We pursued them until we got near the house, when we saw a squaw sitting in the door, and she placed her feet against the bow she had in her hand, and then took an arrow, and raising to her feet, she drew with all her might and let fly at us, and she killed a man, whose name I believed was Moore. He was a Lieutenant and his death so enraged us all that she was fired on, and had at least twenty balls blown through her. This is the first man I ever saw killed with a bow and arrow. We now shot them like dogs; and then set the house on fire, and burned it up with the forty-six warriors in it.

"I recollect seeing a boy who was shot down near the house. His arm and thigh were broken, and he was so near the burning house that the grease was stewing out of him. In this situation he was still trying to crawl along; but not a murmur escaped him, though he was only about twelve years old. So sullen is the Indian, when his dander is up, that he would sooner die than make a noise and ask for quarters."

That is Colonel Crockett's story of the battle of Tallushatchee, which General Carroll glorified as the most important victory of the Creek War. Col. Crockett further relates:

"The number that we took prisoners, being added to the number we killed, amounted to one hundred and eighty-six; though I don't remember the exact number of either. We had five of our men killed. We then returned to our camp at which our fort was erected, and known by the name of Fort Strother. No provisions had yet reached us, and we had now been for several days on half rations. However, we went back to our Indian town on the next day, when many of the carcasses of the Indians were still to be seen. They looked very awful, for the burning had not entirely consumed them, but had given them a terrible appearance, at least what remained of them.

"It was some how or the other found out that the house had a potato cellar under it, and immediate examination was made, for we were all as hungry as wolves. We found a fine chance of potatoes in it, and hunger compelled us to eat them though I had a little rather not, if I could have helped it, for the oil of the Indians we had burned up the day before, had run down on them and they looked like they had been stewed with fat meat."

This picture of Tennessee Christians eating potatoes cooked in the flames of the red man's house, and stewed in the grease that had oozed from the red man's body, is one of the most ghastly incidents furnished by the records of "glorious war." [92]

- - - ! ! !

Next comes Colonel Crockett's account of the Battle of Talladega:

"...in an hour we were all ready, and took up the line of march. We crossed the Coosa river, and went on in the direction of Fort Talladega. When we arrived near the place, we met eleven hundred painted warriors, the very choice of the Creek Nation. They encamped near the fort, and had informed the friendly Indians who were in it, that if they didn't come out, and fight with them against the whites, they would take their fort and all their ammunition and provision. The friendly party asked three days to consider it, and agreed that, if on the third day they did not come out ready to fight with them, they might take their fort. Thus they put them off. Then they immediately started their runner to General Jackson, and he and the army pushed over, as I have just before stated.

"The camp of warriors had their spies out and discovered us coming some time before we got to the fort. They then went to the friendly Indians, and told them Captain Jackson was coming, and had a great many fine horses, and blankets, and guns, and everything else, and if they would come out and help to whip him and to take his plunder, it should all be divided with those in the fort. They promised that when Jackson came they would come out and help to whip him.

---

[92] Watson, Thomas, , pp. 165-168

"It was about an hour by the sun in the morning when we got near the fort. We were piloted by friendly Indians and divided as we had done on a former occasion, so as to go to the right and left of the fort, and, consequently of the warriors that were camped near it. Our lines marched on as before, till they met in front, and then closed in the rear, forming again into a hollow square. We then sent on old major Russell with his spy company to bring on the battle; Capt. Evans' company went also.

"When they got near the fort, the top of it was lined with the friendly Indians, crying as loud as they could roar, How-de-do, brother, how-de-do! They kept this up until Major Russell had passed by the fort, and was moving on towards the warriors. They were all painted as red as scarlet, and were just as naked as they were born. They had concealed themselves under a bank of a branch that ran partly around the fort, in the manner of a half-moon. Russell was going right into their circle, for he couldn't see them, while the Indians on the top of the fort were trying every plan to show him his danger. But he couldn't understand them.

"At last two of them jumped from it and ran, and took his horse by the bridle, and pointing to where they were, told them there were thousands of them lying under the bank. This brought them to a halt, and about this moment the Indians fired on them and came rushing forth like a cloud of Egyptian locusts, and screaming like all the young devils had been turned loose, with the old devil of all at their head. Russell's Company quit their horses and quit into the fort, and their horses ran up to our line, which was then in full view. The warriors then came yelling on, meeting us, and then continued until they were within shot of us, when we fired and killed a considerable number of them.

"They fought with guns, and also with bows and arrows; but at length they made their escape through a part of our line that was made up of drafted militia, which broke ranks and they passed. We lost fifteen of our men, as brave fellows that ever lived or died. We buried them all in one grave, and started back to our fort; but before we got there, two more of our men died of wounds they had received, making our total loss seventeen good fellows in that battle." [93]

- - - !!!

Supplies weren't the only strategic problem: because of a lack of communication, General Cocke's East Tennessee Division was advancing toward Ft. Strother with General James White, who was Colonel Williams' father-in-law, in command of one thousand of Cocke's division. Jackson was then negotiating a peace with the Hillabee Creeks who had fought and lost at Talladega. The Hillabees knew they were outnumbered, so they sent a prisoner to Jackson asking for peace, and he agreed to terms and then sent orders to General Cocke of their capitulation. Cocke did not know this and ordered an attack. General White's troops attacked the unsuspecting Indians at dawn, and it was a massacre. The Hillabees considered it Jackson's treachery, and they fought voraciously against him for the rest of the war. Jackson wanted White and Cocke court-martialed, but cooler heads prevailed, and the East Tennessee Militia Division was sent home for supplies shortly before their terms of enlistment expired. Tennessee was not the only state supplying troops and fighting forces.

While Jackson was pinned down at Ft. Strother because of a lack of supplies, Floyd's Georgians and Claiborne's Mississippians took a hand. Striking at Autosee, on the south bank of the Tallapoosa near the mouth of Calabee Creek, November 29, 1813, Floyd, with 950 Georgia militia and 400 friendly Indians, drove the Creeks out of the town and set it on fire. Four hundred houses were burned and about 200 Creeks killed. About the same time Tallassee, too, was destroyed by Georgia troops who then returned to Ft. Mitchell.

Claiborne celebrated the holiday season in 1813 by attacking the Holy Ground (called by the Indians "Ecunchate") the day before Christmas Eve. This was a "camp meeting" site that the prophets, after the massacre at Ft. Mims, had set up as a place where they could "hold high revel, perform their magical rites, and send out objurgatory defiance to their enemies." The warriors and prophets fought until the women and children had been ferried to safety across the Alabama, then scattered into the nearby swamps. 40 to 50 warriors were killed and some 200 houses were destroyed and a large quantity of provisions taken. [94]

After a brutal winter holed up with troops deserting his cause, Jackson saw his army virtually disintegrate. The Middle Tennessee Volunteers went home in December, and were quickly followed by the West Tennessee

---

[93] Evans, G. G., *The Life and Times of Colonel Davy Crockett*, pp. 101-102
[94] Holland, James W., "Andrew Jackson and the Creek War: Victory at the Horseshoe Bend," *Alabama Review*, 1968, p. 18
[95] Williams, *The Political Mirror*

Infantry and East Tennessee troops. Col. Williams complained many years later that, had Jackson merely supplied his troops with abundant game in the fall, there would have been no shortage of supplies. [95]

> "Had the General more experience or more foresight, he would, in a country abounding in provisions and the means of transportation, have secured a seasonable and competent supply for his army, and thereby have more speedily terminated the campaign. The neglect of this essential duty, and, it is said, the haughty and passionate deportment of the commander offended his officers, and disgusted the troops, to such a degree as to greatly injure the service. The campaign, though successful, was unnecessarily prolonged, and inordinately expensive." [96]

This is entirely possible. The Creeks weren't starving. Famed woodsman Davy Crockett participated in the fall campaign before he returned to his home in southern Tennessee near Lawrenceburg. But a few years later, he bragged in his Autobiography of David Crockett that in 1825 he personally killed 45 bears in Obion County, Tennessee. It wasn't the same territory, but game could be had, as witnessed by Weatherford bringing in a deer when he surrendered.

In the Red Sticks' camp, "it was not long before it was understood that Jacks Chula Harjo (as the Indians used to call General Jackson) wanted land to pay for the trouble he had been at, and that the Big Warrior and others were in favor of giving Old Mad Jackson, as they called him, as much land as he wanted." [97]

Due to the severity of the winter and the inability of militia officers to extend their troops' enlistments, entire units were deserting the Creek campaign and were returning to their homes and families. One of the great legends about Jackson was that he personally pointed his rifle at a group preparing to leave and commanded them to stay. One such commander who could not get his men to stay was Colonel Lillard of the East Tennessee Volunteers. He wrote, "I stated that if we head not bin Decived by hour General Someney times that we wold bin willing to stay and to Serve good officers." Very few listened to Jackson's entreaty to stay, and the fact "made the old Vilion Sware outrageous.. he was greaved to the heart to think we thought no more of him." [98]

The chief source of Jackson's troubles with the army was that his men were well-nigh famished; another was that he insisted on holding them in the wilderness, starving, after their terms of service, according to the letter of enlistment, had expired. One construction was placed upon the terms of enlistment by the general and another by the private soldier.

An impartial investigation of the Act of Congress and of the various conditions of enlistment will convince any intelligent reader that the soldiers were right, and that the general was wrong.

One brave man could not hold together several thousand brave men who were equally determined and who were honest in their opinion that they had the right to go home. At one time General Jackson was left in his camp almost alone. Davy Crockett, who was one of the soldiers in Jackson's army, gives the following account of what actually happened, and it seems to this writer that Davy Crockett's word is good authority for anything that he positively stated as a fact that he himself knew to be true.

- - - ! ! !

Concerning the surprise attack at Enatachopco Creek, David Crockett had this to say:

> "In truth, I believe as firmly as I do that General Jackson is President, that if it hadn't been for Carroll we should have all been genteelly licked that time, for we were in a devil of a fix; part of our men on one side of the creek, and part on the other, and the Indians all the time pouring it on us, as hot as fresh mustard to a sore shin. I will not say exactly that the old General was whipped; but I will say that if we escaped it at all, it was like old Henry Snider going to heaven mite a damn tite squeeze. I think he would confess, himself, that he was nearer whipped this time than he was at any other, for I know that all the world couldn't make him acknowledge that he was pointedly whipped. I know I was mighty glad when it was all over, and the savages quit us, for I begun to think there was one behind every tree in the woods." [99]

Andrew Jackson needed John Williams' 39th Infantry to continue his campaign. He wrote Governor Blount from Ft. Deposit in November, "Please signify to Colonel Williams my wishes to be joined by him before I make the movement (against the Creeks)." [100] However, neither had the authority to order Colonel Williams' unit to Jackson's rescue.

---

96 Williams, *The Political Mirror*, p. 50
97 Woodward, Thomas Sp. 43
98 Horseshoe Bend pamphlet
99 *Jackson Papers*, Jackson to Blount, Nov. 29, 1813 Knoxville, TN: University of Tennessee
100 Jackson to Blount, Fort Deposit, Nov. 29, 1813, J. S. Bassett (ed.) *Correspondence of Andrew Jackson*, 6 vols, Washington, 1926-1935, I, 362
101 Jackson to Williams, December 16, 1813

Williams had raised, trained, and armed six hundred-plus Regular Army soldiers in Knoxville—soldiers who knew that if they defied an order or deserted, they would be shot. There was much difference in Regular Army troops versus state militia in efficiency, military discipline, and rank—it was uncertain if a state militia general could give orders to a US Army colonel.

On December 16, 1813, Jackson wrote Williams, pleading with him to "save the character of the state." [101]

Meanwhile, General Flournoy in New Orleans wished to be replaced, and he suggested to Secretary of War Armstrong that Colonel Williams be promoted to brigadier general and be sent there post-haste as his replacement in the Seventh Military District. On January 1, 1814, General Flournoy ordered Williams to New Orleans. The very next day, General Jackson wrote General Pinckney, specifically asking for the 39th. On January 7, 1814, Jackson wrote Colonel Williams: "Never were your services more needed than at the present moment. I am almost destitute of an army." Even General Pinckney in the Sixth District concurred with General Flournoy's decision by informing Jackson on January 9 that he needed to recruit additional militia.

The timing of these written messages is confusing, because so many persons were writing to each other at the same time requesting the same thing: Colonel Williams' 39th Infantry. Differences in the time and method of delivery make it almost impossible to determine who ordered what and when, and at which point Williams received such entreaties and orders.

The issue was put to rest by a mission that involved two members of Williams' family. John's brother, Thomas Lanier Williams, and his brother-in-law, Judge Hugh Lawson White, joined Luke Lea in a dangerous venture into the wilderness to discern Jackson's true state. Reports of his dire circumstances were reaching Knoxville, and the three men were determined to find the truth. Judge White stepped down from his bench to undertake this dangerous journey.

What they found was that Jackson's command had been reduced to little more than a personal guard. White wrote that they "were eating roots and acorns." [102] All three returned to Knoxville and begged John Williams to go to Jackson's aid; there was much indecision on Williams' part because it took them *all night* to convince him to go. Williams would later complain that he had "risked my command & my fortune" by not obeying the orders he had received to proceed to New Orleans. On January 12, the 39th Infantry left Knoxville, intent upon resupplying Jackson and preventing his demise.

Another account of Gen. Jackson's rescue:

> "Judge Hugh L. White of East Tennessee rendered to General Jackson a service, which, perhaps, more than anything else led to the brilliant termination of the Creek War. Having heard of General Jackson's danger, Judge White left the bench and hurried into the wilderness to learn for himself the actual condition of things at Ft. Strother. He found Jackson almost alone, and he returned to East Tennessee impressed with the urgent necessity of doing something at once for his support. At this time the 39th Regiment of the regular army was in East Tennessee under the command of Col. John Williams, a brother-in-law of Judge White. To Col. Williams Judge White made the most earnest appeal in behalf of General Jackson. Jackson himself had sent to Colonel Williams, through Judge White, an urgent almost despairing request for assistance. It is stated that Judge White remained with Colonel Williams nearly all night, laboring to impress upon his mind the necessity of moving to Ft. Strother, instead of marching to New Orleans, as he was under orders to do. Colonel Williams finally yielded, and the arrival at Ft. Strother of his regiment of regulars was of inestimable benefit to General Jackson during the remainder of the campaign."

This episode is related graphically in a letter which a relative of Colonel John Williams wrote for my use, when the biography of Jackson was begun several years ago. The letter is addressed to Colonel John B. Brownlow, to whom I am so much indebted for the large amount of the new data contained in this "Life."

*June 7, 1907 Col. Jno B. Brownlow*

"My Dear Sir:

"As to what literature my family may have preserved relating to Andrew Jackson, I am sure it is very limited, and any I might find would certainly be to his discredit, as I was raised to detest his name; yet all admitted that he was a very remarkable character."

"I have spent many pleasant hours looking through old historic papers, at home, in Greeneville, and all that I now remember finding, relating to Jackson, are some cartoons,

---

101 Jackson to Williams, December 16, 1813
102 Williams Family History

which I now have here, but would not care to let them get out of sight, as they are, possibly, the only ones in existence today. They could, however, be photographed and would be very interesting to the political public.

"I think it a great pity historians never came to interview my father during his later life. I believe that you will agree with me, that his was a wonderful memory of past events and prominent political characters. I believe that he knew more unwritten history than any man living, and I have often heard him tell why our family were so unfriendly to Andrew Jackson, and I will try and repeat it, for I know it is true, and should be considered generally history.

"Senator John Williams was my father's uncle, and before being Senator he was Colonel of the 39th Infantry. He married Malinda White, sister of Judge Hugh Lawson White. When, during the second war with Great Britain, New Orleans was threatened, the War Department at Washington ordered Colonel John Williams to proceed to that city, with all dispatch, to meet the British, under Packenham, and he was on the march, but before proceeding very far he was overtaken by Judge White, and several distinguished gentlemen, and informed that news had come from Jackson, who was in the wilderness in Alabama, that he and his army were in bad condition, out of provisions, half of the army down with fever, and surrounded by Creek Indians, and that squads of men were dropping out and straggling home, and the army on the eve of mutiny. Judge White and party came to explain the situation, which by now might be a great deal worse, and to beg Colonel Williams to hasten to Jackson, and that the whole State and country would stand to vindicate him with the War Department as it would take weeks to get the news to Washington, and too late to succor Jackson. Colonel Williams told my father that he positively refused to disobey his orders, that he appreciated the terrible situation of affairs; but that his orders left him no alternative but to proceed and defend New Orleans, as much as he would like to relieve Jackson and the Tennessee boys who were in such distress. My father said that they pleaded with Colonel Williams until long into the night without success, and even told him that to go was his duty, and that they knew, and he knew, that the War Department, could it know the real situation there, would change his orders, and send him to Jackson in all haste. Col. Williams told my father that Judge White pleaded with him all night, and left his tent as the sun rose, and that he had finally but reluctantly agreed to go to Jackson.

"When the 39th proceeded, they met many soldiers returning home from Jackson's army. Some had thrown away their arms, some were sick and being carried by comrades or allowed to ride the miserable horses. All were ragged and half starved, and only a few turned back to rejoin the army.

"When Colonel Williams met Jackson, he (Jackson) was overjoyed, and said: "To hell with the British, the red devils first; We will do all we can to secure you reward from Washington instead of reprimand. By the Eternal, we were about to go up bitter creek."

"While awaiting resupply, Jackson fought to keep what few men he had left to stay with him. He regarded those who had returned to Tennessee as mutineers. It was one of the thrilling moments of this mutiny when General Jackson announced, in the presence of his troops, "If only two men will stay with me, I will stay here and die in the wilderness," that Captain John Gordon, Gordon of the Spies, promptly responded, "General, I will stay with you and die in the wilderness," and then turned among the men looking for volunteers also to remain, and one hundred and nine pledged themselves to stand for Jackson." [103]

Thus the year 1813 ended without closing the Creek War. More than seven thousand men had entered the Indian country from four directions; and with a loss of thirty or forty lives had killed, according to their reports, about eight hundred Indians, or one fifth of the hostile Creek warriors; but this carnage had fallen chiefly on towns and villages not responsible for the revolt. The true fanatics were little harmed and could offer nearly as much resistance as ever. The failure and excessive expense of the campaign were the more annoying, because they seemed beyond proportion to the military strength of the fanatics.

> Major-General Pinckney wrote to the War Department at the close of the year: "The force of the hostile Creeks was estimated by the best judges to have consisted of three thousand five hundred warriors; of these it is apprehended that about one thousand have been put *hors de comba*t." [104]

"Jackson's success was in overcoming the obstacles in his path was due to his obstinacy at maintaining himself at Ft. Strother, which obliged Governor Blount to order out four thousand more militia for six months. Perhaps this force alone would have been no more effectual in 1814 than in 1813, but another reinforcement was decisive. The Thirty-ninth Regiment of the regular army had been

---

[103] Heiskell, p. 484
[104] Adams, Henry, *History of the United States During the Administrations of James Madison*, p. 790
[105] Adams, p. 794

officered and recruited in Tennessee and was still in the state." [105]

Again, the War Department failed to act decisively. Scribbled in handwriting up the side of Governor Blount's latest entreaty for the 39th was a note: "Is not this unit to be sent to Flournoy at New Orleans?" Instead, they compounded the confusion by appointing Gen. Pinckney in Milledgeville to command the Creek War on March 2nd, 1814.

En route to Jackson with orders to go to New Orleans, Williams received orders from General Pinckney to proceed to Jackson's defense before he, Flournoy, Pinckney, Jackson, or Blount knew he had such authority. Colonel Williams was therefore presented with a lose-lose situation: should he follow orders and proceed to New Orleans he would be liable for court-martial for disobeying Pinckney; should he obey General Pinckney, he might be at the mercy of the man he *knew* to command the area, General Flournoy. General Flournoy had been kind and amicable to Williams when in Georgia with the Tennessee Volunteers; General Pinckney had not. He chose the latter.

Upon his arrival, Williams notified Jackson of his predicament; clearly, he did not want to go there nor stay there. Jackson passed the matter by courier to General Pinckney, who directed Williams to stay. "The arrival of the Thirty-ninth Regiment February 6, 1814, gave Jackson the means of coping with his militia. On February 21 he wrote to his Quartermaster, Major Lewis 'I am happy in having the Colonel (Williams) with me. His Regiment will give strength to my arm and quell mutiny.' " [106] Jackson thereafter began to use Williams' law expertise and his unit's military discipline to enforce his will as commander upon the men assembled.

Jackson was still suffering from his wound in the Benton duel; thankfully, Lieutenant Colonel Benton was not present. It is fortunate for Benton that he was absent, for Jackson's mood was not good. Several court-martials were held. The seriousness of Jackson's obsession at that time with authority and ill-temper can be best shown from a pamphlet produced a few years later, *A Review of the Battle of the Horse Shoe, and The Facts related to The Killing of Sixteen Indians, on the morning after the Battle, by the Orders of Gen. Andrew Jackson.*

This pamphlet, produced as campaign literature in 1828, is written in a style altogether similar to that of Colonel Williams. Several stories are contained in the brochure, but most significant is the story of the death of eighteen-year-old John Woods, a militia volunteer from middle Tennessee, as told by a fellow militiaman, George A. Brock:

*"State of Tennessee, Franklin County*
*February 11, 1828*

"Being requested to state what I know of the circumstances, attending the trial and execution of John Woods at Fort Strother, during the late war in the Creek Nation, hereby certify that John Woods joined the army at Fayetteville, about the 22nd of January, 1814, as a substitute in place of Will Roger, who was a volunteer: and continued from that time until he was arrested, to mess with me in the same tent. Woods was about eighteen years old at this time, and was the youngest child of his aged parents, who were then, and had been for some time, living near neighbors to me. I have seen and examined the certificate of Thomas Couch and Robert Ferguson relative to this same matter. I was not present at the dispute which took place between Major Camp and Woods, but immediately afterwards heard the circumstances detailed by various persons in the same manner as stated by Mr. Couch and Mr. Ferguson. At the time of the quarrel I was in the Fort near the tent of General Jackson, and was present when a runner came from Major Camp to inform the General that a man had mutinied; the General immediately rushed out of the fort and I followed him; when out, he commenced cursing and swearing, and asked which was the man and Woods was pointed to him, who was then walking in a straight direction to his guard fire; Jackson still continued cursing and repeatedly and in great rage, reiterated shoot the damned rascal!!! Woods by this time was approaching near to his guard fire, when Jackson commanded the guard, still in a great rage, to blow ten balls through the damned rascal! As soon as Woods approached the guard he gave up his gun and surrendered himself prisoner. Woods was immediately put in irons, and conveyed to, and kept under guard in the 39th Regiment, but was not kept long ironed as I understood.

"After some days the friends of Woods, among whom was his brother, became uneasy at his detention in confinement, but without any apprehension of the sad catastrophe which was to follow. I was requested to speak to General Jackson, and accordingly I did so, and requested that his trial should be brought on soon, as we were all desirous, as he was a mere youth, that he might be placed among his friends again, and if there was a punishment, let him receive it and return to his duty. The General said that the case was a serious one, but he could have the opportunity of enlisting. I returned and consulted with his friends about it; and they opposed the

106 Adams, p. 795

idea very strongly. After some further delay I heard part of a conversation between General Jackson and an officer, who I believe was Captain of the Rangers, (Captain Hannard,) in which conversation the General told him that he must be in order on a certain day to set on the Court Martial of a fellow who had mutinied, and who he expected would have to be shot. The officer appeared very reluctant to act; neither did he sit on the trial. From hearing this conversation I became very uneasy, and got leave of the officers of his guard to carry Woods his victuals which was generally cooked in our mess; while with Woods I persuaded him to enlist, as I was fearful of the event from what I had heard; the prisoner appeared to acquiesce, and I left him, but when I told his other friends what I had done, they opposed it violently, stating that Jackson knew that he could not be hurting him for what he had done, and only wanted to scare him to enlist, and gratify their spite in that way. From this time until his trial took place nothing particular transpired, and our greatest uneasiness was at his long confinement. I think it was on the 12th day of March, that I heard his trial was progressing; I went to the spot but was not permitted to enter within the lines of the guard; the court martial was then in session between two tents, and Woods was seated eight or ten paces off on some logs, without any friend or adviser or counsel to defend him. Colonel John Williams, of East Tennessee, was acting as I understood, as Judge Advocate against him, as he was making a speech, and reading passages from books, and I think Lieutenants Parrish, Davis, and Ensign Hall, were the court martial; if there were any witnesses called to testify in his behalf, I do not know it, neither do I believe it; after looking a while my heart then yearned for what I then considered the perilous situation of the boy, and I turned away and left the place and heard nothing more of his fate, until the next day from ten to twelve o'clock, it was read in the general orders that Woods was to be shot at twelve o'clock next day (14th). Soon after this I received intelligence that Woods wished me to go and stay with him, until he left the world, but before I went, in conjunction with Dr. Fore and others, I handed about a petition for a pardon, which was signed as I thought and believed by most of the officers of the army, and I understood also by the Court Martial; I was present when these petitions were handed to the General, but whether they were handed by myself or some other person I do not recollect.

"After some general conversation on the subject, I approached the General, and told him that the prisoner had requested me to go and stay with him until his death; this the General did not refuse, but before I started I made another effort to obtain his pardon. I begged the General to take into consideration his extreme youth and inexperience, that he had left behind him aged parents, who depended upon him for their support and comfort in their declining years, that such a death would cause them great sorrow and distress. The General replied that he was sorry for his parents, and that there had been several cases before approaching to mutiny in the camps, that there was need of an example, and, said he, by the Eternal God he must be the example, he must die. I left him and went to the prisoner, where I staid until the guard came to take him to his death.

"I will remark further that at the request of the prisoner I wrote down a statement of his feelings, and his last farewell to his father and mother, and sent them in a letter to my wife, and the public are at liberty to see it.

"On the news of the death of her son, old Mrs. Woods (as I have been informed by my wife) fainted, and appeared like dying all night—of this I feel certain she never recovered from the shock, and in a few years laid her grey hairs with sorrow in the grave.

## GEORGE A. BROCK" [107]

Not a man in the army, least of all Woods himself, seems to have thought that anything very serious would result from this offense. Similar affairs had occurred, and the offender had been forgiven after a short arrest, or dismissed without pay, or, at worst, drummed with disgrace from the camp. Jackson, however, took a totally different view of the occurrence. He remembered the previous flight of Woods' company, and was not aware, *and never learned*, that Woods had not then been attached to the company. [108]

Fourteen years after it happened, and during the campaign for the presidency, which Andrew Jackson won, the execution of Private John Woods became a subject of intense discussion. It was not a deciding factor in the result of the election, but it remains a point of contention 196 years later. As in the infamous Dickinson duel, most of the accusations between rival camps depended upon eyewitness accounts of other individuals, with charges and counter-charges hurled at each other. This time it simply didn't get to the point where anyone issued another a challenge to duel. It was a case of political negative campaigning, which remains all too common in the present; it merely lacked the availability of mass distribution compared to our modern means of communication.

---

107 Williams, John, "A Review of the Battle of the Horseshoe," pamphlet, 1828, written by John Williams and published at Richmond by Chapman Johnson
108 Parton, *Life of Jackson*, vol. I, p. 508

The desperate winter of 1813 that Jackson and some seventy remaining soldiers endured greatly affected Woods' trial. He was formally accused of having been previously guilty of desertion from the militia unit under command of General Roberts.

> "The undersigned certify that we belonged to the company commanded by Captain James Harris, of a detachment commanded by General Roberts, and were out when the detachment first went and progressed near to the Ten Islands (Ft. Strother), from which place we returned. William Rager with us—and afterwards reassembled at Fayetteville, at which place John Woods joined the company, as a substitute in the place of William Rager, and went on and joined the army at Ft. Strother, during which time we were all in the habit of seeing Woods every day, and during that time know of no act of disobedience on the part of Woods, or insubordination, until the affair for which he was executed. Woods had deported himself, so far as we know & positively certify, that he never before that time either deserted or had been guilty of mutiny. And I, William Stewart, further certify, that I had known Woods from a small boy and *know* he had never served any other tour of duty than the one in which he was engaged at the time he was shot. We have also heard the statement of Captain Harris, a great part of which we know to be correct, and have entire confidence in the truth of the whole.
>
> WILLIAM STEWART
> JOSEPH ALEXANDER
> ISAAC ANDERSON"

General Roberts stated: "I had drawn up on the handwriting of Wm Burnett of this county a roll or list of the names of every man present with the following conditions upon which my company entered the service to wit.—'We the undersigned Volunteers of the Light Infantry of the 28th Regiment do agree to serve a tour of duty of three months against the Creek Indians, if not sooner discharged' upon which John Woods' name is not to be found."

Woods' commanding officer, Captain Harris wrote:

> "Woods was not quite eighteen years old, and not yet subject to militia duty according the information I then received, but having a brother Wm. Woods, going out in the Company he spoke of volunteering, but while at Fayetteville during the second rendezvous of this Company, substituted, as I have before said, and went on in that character; and until the 20th February 1814 when I left Ft. Strother for Huntsville. Woods conducted himself as orderly as any other soldier belonging to the company, so far as came to my knowledge, and was not during that period guilty or tried of any offense, so far as I knew.
>
> JAS. HARRIS" [109]

*Here follow accounts of the actual happenings that resulted in the private's arrest, trial, and execution:*

> "Being requested to state what I remember of the crime and circumstances which led to the execution of John Woods at Fort Strother, a soldier under the command of Genl. Jackson—do hereby certify and declare, that I belonged to the same company with Woods, and was leaning on a pole (having been sick for one or two weeks previous) within eight or ten steps of Woods, who was seated on the ground eating his breakfast. Having just come from his guard fire, when a man by the name of Camp, who was said to hold some commission in the Staff Department, was passing alone, and began to curse and abuse the company for permitting filth and bones to lay scattered about. Some one or two of the men were directed to carry off the bones, and proceeded to do it. Woods still continued to eat, when Camp called to him, and cursed him to get up and assist in taking off the filth. Woods observed that he was on guard, and had obtained leave of his officer for his absence. Camp cursed him for leaving his guard, and ordered an Ensign to take a file of men and to take him to his guard. Woods stated he was going himself and rose and started and threw the priming out of his gun, and primed it afresh, and then went straight to his guard fire. While he was going, Camp hallowed to the Fort to General Jackson and told him there was a damned deserter who would not be taken. Woods went up to the guard and surrendered himself prisoner. A guard from the Regulars soon came and took him into custody. Woods was ironed in the blacksmith shop (and I saw the irons put on) and then taken into the camp of the Regulars and kept there until he was shot.
>
> "I was also a witness before the Court Martial, and

---

[109] Armstrong, Dr. Joseph, *An Account of the Trial and Execution of the Poor and Unfortunate JOHN WOODS,* Charles Rhea, printer, Russellville, KY, 1828, pp. 13-14

was within the lines of the guard while the trial was progressing. General Jackson walked backwards and forwards with his hands behind his back, and remarked to the Court Martial, "To be cautious and mind what they were about for he had said, by the Eternal God, the next man that was condemned, he would *not* pardon him, and this was a hearty, hale young fellow." I think Maj. William R. Hess was Judge Advocate. No person appeared as Woods' friend or counsel to defend him.

WILLIAM STEWART"

About the same time, a person who calls himself Samuel H. Miller, a resident of Green County Ohio, made a publication also in contradiction of the account published in the Expositor, which is here inserted.

## "TO A CANDID PUBLIC

"Perceiving a false statement from the Kentucky Reporter, (which has been extracted into the columns of the Truth's Advocate) in relation to the execution of John Woods, a militia man, I deem it a duty I owe to the public to give a true statement of the facts connected with that transaction.

"The truth is as follows: John Woods deserted from his post, and started home. On his way he was met by a company of men on their march to join the army.— Woods, on seeing them, hurried from the path, and sought concealment in a cane break. He was taken, however, and brought back to camp where he was tried for desertion, found guilty and condemned to be shot. For this offense he was PARDONED by General Jackson and on promise of future subordination, he was returned to his duty—In about two or three weeks afterwards Woods was again placed on guard. On a certain morning, he stuck his bayonet in the ground—hung his cartouche box on the butt of his gun, and deserted his post—on pretense of going to his tent for breakfast. In passing the lines, he arrived at Major _____'s tent. (I forget the Major's name.) The Major asked Woods where he was going—Woods replied to get his breakfast. The Major advised Woods very strongly to return to his post—observing that he would soon be relieved—and offering him some corn bread and meat, told him that if he did not return to duty, he would certainly be taken; but Woods persisted in his determination and would not return.

"About this time the officer of the day came up and having heard a portion of the conversation, turned to the lines and inquired who commanded that company? The Captain answered, "I do." The officer of the day then told him to send a guard, and take John Woods to the Provost Guard; where he was tried by a Court Martial a second time found guilty and condemned to be shot. When the day arrived for the execution of the sentence of the Court Martial, Gen Jackson came to the place of execution and delivered a discourse which affected every heart, but that of the unfortunate Woods. By this time disaffection prevailed among several of the militia men. Woods in particular was very turbulent. General Jackson offered Woods his pardon a second time, on condition that he would serve his country like a true and faithful soldier; but Woods defied the General and Court Martial too; and swore with an oath that they dare not execute the sentence of the Court Martial. After many unavailing efforts to persuade Woods to conform to subordination, pointing out to him the consequences resulting to the army from such consequences; and Woods still remaining stubborn and irreconcilable—and swearing the Court Martial dare not execute their sentence—the General turned his horse and rode off; and Woods was shot before my own and the eyes of the whole army.

SAMUEL H, MILLER<br>Green Co. Ohio, Feb. 21, 1828"

It's important to note that there is no record of Samuel H. Miller in Green County, Ohio in 1828.

The subjoined extract of a letter from Col. John Williams of Knoxville, Tennessee, to his friend in Cincinnati exposes the profligate falsehood of the statement of S. H. Miller about the feelings and temper of Woods on the day of his execution. That a mere boy should have acted on such a solemn occasion in the manner represented by Miller is in itself unnatural and incredible. It is strange that men can be found base enough to perjure themselves in order to sustain the cause of one who has so wantonly shed the blood of his fellow men and fellow soldiers.

"Knoxville, April 17, 1828

"I was neither President, Judge Advocate, nor member of the Court Martial that condemned Woods to die; nor did I ever refuse to recommend him to mercy. No application was made to me on the subject. I neither saw nor heard the evidence upon which he was found guilty. After the execution of Woods, much was said in camp, in relation to the offense which he had committed. It was said by some, that he had been shot for an affront to a certain Thomas Camp, who had neither rank nor commission in the army. I never knew whether Mr. Camp was a commissioned officer or not. If he was, there must be a record of his commission. If he was not, it was illegal to shoot Woods for insulting him. The true state of this affair will appear, by publishing the proceedings of the Court Martial, and Mr. Camp's commission if he has one. *It is not true that Woods, on the ground of execution, with oaths and defiance, refused to promise obedience.* ON THE CONTRARY, he wept loud and bitterly." [110]

At noon on March 14, 1814 with more than three thousand army members assembled, John Woods was led to the foot of his freshly dug grave. General Jackson rode forward on his horse and read the following:

"GENERAL ORDER

"*John Woods*: you have been tried by a court martial, on the charges of disobedience of orders, disrespect to your commanding officer, and mutiny; and have been found guilty of all of them. The court which has found you guilty of these charges, has sentenced you to suffer death by shooting; and this sentence the Commanding General has thought proper, and even found himself bound to approve, and to order it to be executed.

"The offenses of which you have been found guilty are such as cannot be permitted to pass unpunished in an army, but at the hazard of its ruin. This is the second time you have violated the duties of a soldier; the second time you have been guilty of offenses, the punishment of which is death.

"When you had been regularly mustered into the service of your country, and were marched to headquarters, under the immediate Command of Brigadier General Roberts, you were one of those, who, in violation of your engagement—of all the principles of honor, and of the order of your commanding General rose in mutiny and deserted. You were arrested and brought back; and not withstanding the little claim you had to mercy, your General, unwilling to inflict the severity of the law, and influenced by the hope that you would atone, by your future good conduct, for your past error thought proper to grant you all a pardon. This ought to have produced a salutary impression on a mind not totally dead, to every honorable sentiment, and not perversely and obstinately bent on spreading disorder, and confusion in the army. It unfortunately, produced no such impression on yours. But a few weeks after you had been brought back, you have been found guilty of offenses no less criminal than those for which you had so recently been pardoned, and which, if the law had been rightfully enforced, would have subjected you to death.—This evinces but too manifestly, an incorrigible disposition of heart—a rebellious and obstinate temper of mind, which as it cannot be rectified, ought not to be permitted to diffuse its influence amongst others.

"An army cannot exist where order and insubordination are wholly disregarded—It cannot exist with much credit to itself, or service to the country which employs it; but where they are observed with the most punctilious exactness. The disobedience of order and the contempt of officers speedily lead to a state of disorganization and ruin; and mutiny which includes the other still more immediately at the dissolution of an army—of all these offenses you have been twice guilty, and have once been pardoned. Your general must forget what he owes to the service which employs him, if by pardoning you again he should furnish an example to sanction measures which would bring ruin to the army he commands. His is an important crisis in which if we all act as becomes us, everything is hoped for us toward the objects of our government—if otherwise, if everything is to be feared. How it becomes us to act, we all know, and what our punishment shall be if we act otherwise must be known also. The law which points out the one prescribes the other. Between that law and its offender the commanding General ought not to be expected to interpose, and will not where there are no circumstances of alleviation. There appear to be none such in your case; and however as a man he should deplore your unhappy situation, he cannot, as an officer without infringing his duty arrest the sentence of the court martial.

ANDREW JACKSON
Major General
*Fort Strother*, 14 March, 1814
(signed) JOEL PARISH, jr, scj" [111]

**- - - ! ! !**

John Woods' brother and father, Obediah, were still members of the state militia. They dressed their brother and son for his execution, then openly went AWOL and deserted the proceedings.

A net was placed over Woods, and seven members of the 39th Infantry on command aimed and fired. Woods fell backward into the hole and was quickly covered with dirt. Obediah Woods and his older son heard the volley of the 39th. They never returned to the militia, nor to Tennessee, and it was reported that the old man cried every time John's name was mentioned. The army left Ft.

---

110 Armstrong, pp. 8-14
111 Armstrong, pp. 7-8

Strother with a new sense of purpose about the severity of what they were leaving to do. There were no more mutinies.

"He was shot by the order of General Jackson, it is true, but I say nevertheless it was murder, being contrary to all law and to all usage either civil or military." [112]

From this point forward, everything involved in the Creek War changed.

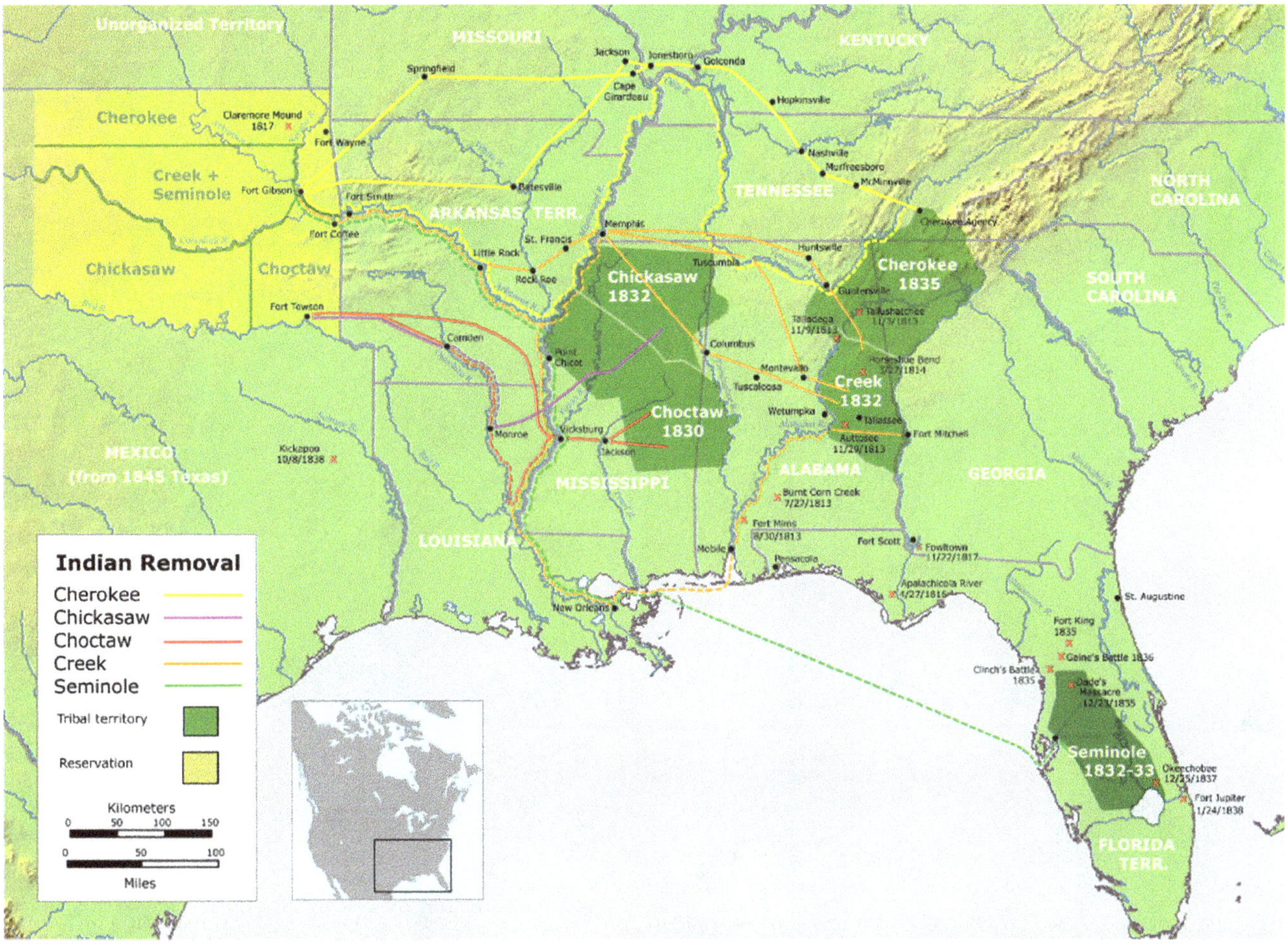

*"Trails of Tears"*

*John Woods' grave in Alabama*
Alex Brandau III

112 Watson, from a publication made in Knoxville, 1828, by John R. Nelson, p. 106

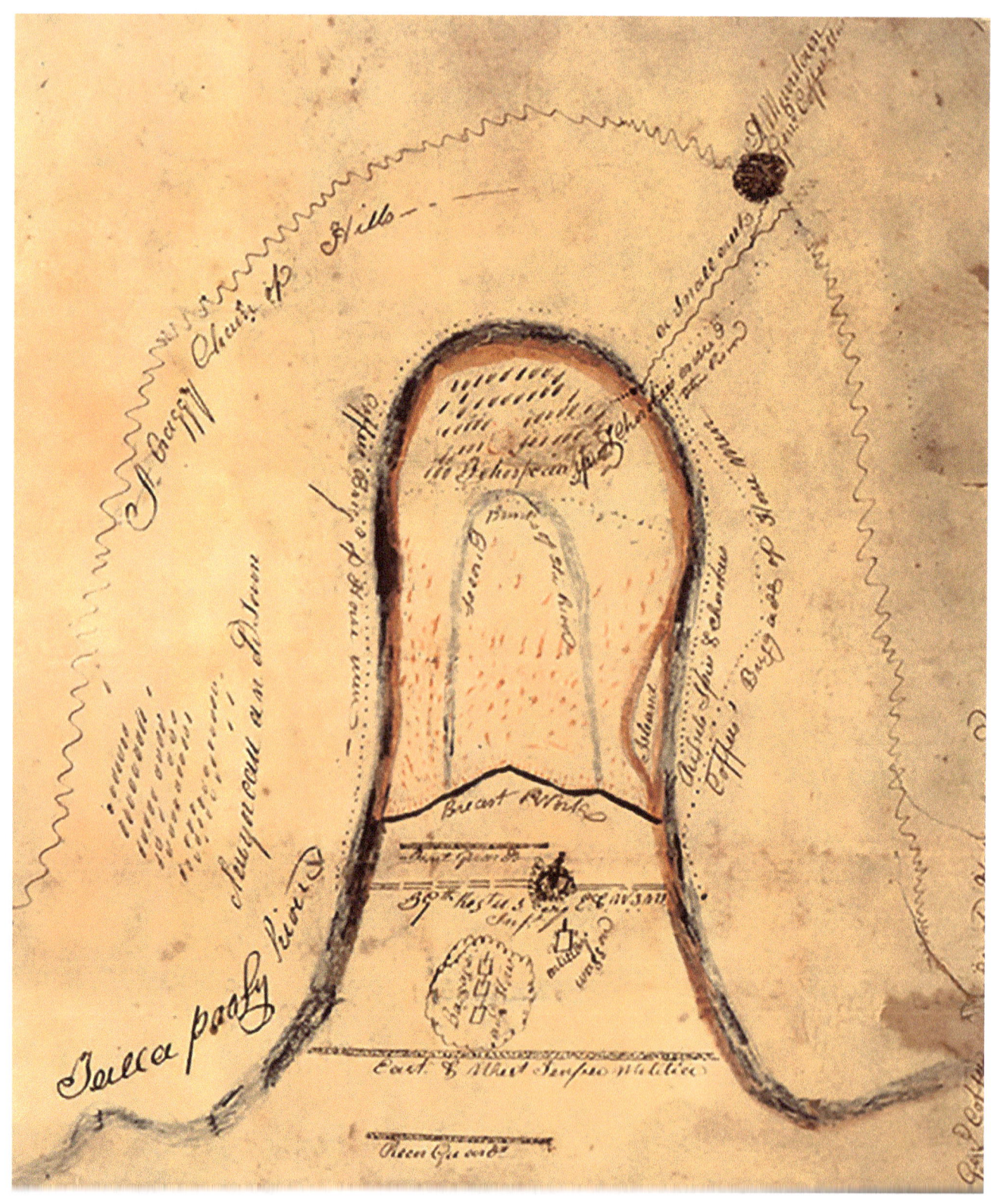

*Map of Battle of Horseshoe Bend as drawn by Col. John Williams*
Tennessee State Library and Archives

# Chapter 6
# The Battle of Horseshoe Bend

John Williams and the 39th Infantry were completely disgusted with Andrew Jackson after being made to execute John Woods, who had lived in their camp for over a month, committed no crime, and was an agreeable young man. There also was the fact that noncommissioned officers resented commissioned officers. Every noncommissioned soldier would have HATED Jackson for executing Woods.

The 39th Infantry had been stuck at Fort Strother by General Pickney and they resented that, too. They were well-trained soldiers and were ready to fight, but the conflicting passions over Woods drove a wedge between Williams and Jackson. Williams' troops wanted to get away from Jackson, who knew he had stepped on their toes by burning their petition and making them kill an innocent man. Williams never considered himself or his men as being under Jackson's command. He had been promised to NOT be under a militia officer by Secretary of War John Armstrong. Williams wrote, "You told me I was only under a militia officer in times of service."

After the junction of the 39th Infantry with Jackson's remaining militia, several other units joined the force, and by early March they were ready to attack the Creeks.

The entire Creek Nation had wintered at a bend in the Tallapoosa River that the whites called Horseshoe Bend and the Indians called Tohopeka. They had barricaded huge logs across the entire peninsula, making a protective barrier that had portholes through which to fire and fight. There were bluffs to the immediate front and left, and approximately three hundred yards of level, open field in front. The river lined both sides and the rear of their camp. It was a formidable defensive position, as long as they were not outmanned: there were about eight hundred Creek braves, and Jackson had amassed over five thousand troops.

While supplied by the British, the Indians had also been aroused by visits from other tribes. Ogillis Ineha, or Menawa, was the principal leader at Horseshoe. [113] They were excited by their spiritual leader, known as the Prophet. The Prophet had told the tribe prior to the battle that, in a vision, he had seen a cloud come upon the scene, and from it came a huge victory.

Colonel Williams moved most of the supplies from northern Alabama downriver to near the Creek campground, and, seeking to pacify Colonel Williams, General Jackson named it Fort Williams. From that staging area, the command under Andrew Jackson prepared to attack the strong Creek barricade.

On the morning of March 27, General Jackson's "spies informed him of the position of the Indians, and he at once comprehended the folly which had permitted them to assemble in a pen, as if offering facilities for him to carry out his threat of extermination." [114] Williams, though, was a student of military history and it might have been he who noticed the Creek folly.

---

113 Woodward, Thomas S., p. 43
114 Lossing, Benson J., *The Pictorial Field-Book of the War of 1812*, Harper & Brothers, Publishers, Franklin Square, 1869, p. 779 (Property of Center of Military History, Dept. of the U.S. Army, Washington, DC) ?

One of the friendly units that had joined the combined effort was a group of Cherokee mounted men. The Cherokee were led by Gideon Morgan II. Jackson sent this band, under command of his friend General John Coffee, two miles downriver to cross the river, where they would then turn north to position themselves across the river from the Creeks. This was risky at best, since no one knew how many and what kind of allies the Creeks had to the east behind Coffee's forces. No method of communication existed between Jackson and his commanders, other than visual confirmation and couriers.

"Opposing Jackson's forces were about one thousand warriors, the last sizable battle force of the Creek War Party. Prior to the beginning of the actual fighting the greatest prophet of the Upper Creeks—Monahell—was in command of the warriors. He was aided and supported by two other prophets of slightly less influence. Thus as the Creeks moved into this decisive battle the fate of the Creek Nation was in the hands of medicine men or prophets, the religious leaders of the Creeks, and not military men. The prophets claimed supernatural powers. They relied upon emotional appeal and charms and claimed personal instructions from the Great Spirit. They had selected the field of battle. The right to command was theirs—a tragic fate for the warriors, and for the Creek Nation.

"In the chill early morning of this March 27, 1814, when the first sun drove away the mists that rose from the Tallapoosa, there was Monahell surrounded by his thousand almost naked warriors who, unmindful of the sharp cold, watched their leader intently. The mighty prophet dressed in full regalia, bent his body double, then slowly straightened upward, quivering all over as he raised himself erect. Dry gourds of varying sizes were attached to a leather belt which tightly encircled his body just above the hips. Some of the gourds contained herbs, and others charms highly prized by the prophet. Some larger gourds were partially filled with small smooth pebbles and hard dried beans which rattled in a rhythm with the prophet's quivering body.

"The warriors watched Monahell, fascinated by the continuous movements of his body, and occasionally, when his jerks and twists reached the pitch of fury, they would yell and chant in a sort of cadence accompanying the hypnotic hissing sound that poured unceasingly from the gourds. The second and third prophets served as a sort of support and echo to Monahell. Their efforts blended to lend unbroken sequence to the sounds and movements created by their leader, Monahell. But though the warriors yelled, shouted, and occasionally jumped up and down, they did not dance. Unlike his northern kin, the Creek danced the war dance after the battle, not before. A Creek warrior must earn the honor of dancing the war dance in battle—so tomorrow they would dance after fighting Old Mad Jackson or never.

"Close by the whirling swaying Monahell stood Menawa (named by his warriors, The Great Warrior), the second chief, and a war chief. He looked coldly on, not believing, yet reluctant to declare his lack of faith that Monahell's magic had the power to repel the bullets of the enemy and that it would protect them and give them success in the terrible battle they were about to fight. When great danger threatened, when courage, coolness, and fighting skill were needed, Menawa was always foremost. He had fought the white man many times and in many places and knew much of the white man's ways. He distrusted the fervid words of Monahell for he knew that the white man could not be harmed or defeated by the medicine of the gourds. He preferred to fight today, as he had always fought, by stealth, with cunning and when necessary, valor. But the tyranny of pagan belief and the traditional practice of veneration of the chief held him in check. Menawa, the second chief, must not create dissent among his people upon the eve of a great battle. So Menawa remained silent.

"Monahell's fury and excitement steadily increased as he realized the opposing forces were about to join in battle. Jackson's army was now in view of the Creeks on the high ground above the barricade. About the same time, John Coffee's detachment, which had crossed to the easterly side of the Tallapoosa, was nearing the high bank across the river from the battleground. Here Coffee could attack the Creeks from the rear, control the river and prevent retreat or escape by that route." [115]

At a little past ten o'clock, two cannons opened fire on the barricade from a bluff about eighty yards away. They were completely ineffective. The green wood of the barricade merely repelled the balls and the "Indians set up a shout of derision, and the general was fairly defied." [116] This

---

[115] Brantley, W. H., *Battle of Horseshoe Bend*, Southern University Press, 1965, p. 10-11
[116] Lossing, Benson J., *The Pictorial Field-Book of the War of 1812*, Harper & Brothers, Publishers, Franklin Square, 1869, (Property of Center of Military History, Dept. of the U.S. Army, Washington, DC), p. 779

drew the attention of most of the Creeks to the front of their position and left their rear unguarded. It continued for about two hours and had little effect.

During this period of cannonading, within the barricade Monahell had constantly watched the actions and movements of the enemy while at the same time urging on his warriors and inspiring them with his magic. Monahell suddenly ordered his warriors to abandon the breastworks and prepare to meet the attack of the enemy at the river. They shouted with fanatical zeal at the thought of meeting "Old Mad Jackson" face to face, forgetting at the time that he was a seasoned general with many men, good rifles and cannon. They were certain that the magic of the prophet was leading them to a great victory.

This sudden and unexpected change in the plan of battle alarmed and enraged the realistic Menawa. Tradition yielded long enough for him to warn Monahell that he would be held to strict account if his magic proved false. [117]

When Coffee, Morgan, and the Cherokee had arrived undetected across the river, the Cherokee braves had swum across the river and captured the Creeks' canoes. Amazed they had not been caught, they went back and set fire to the Creeks' teepees. Once Monahell saw the smoke in their rear, many of his braves rushed there to see what had happened. When General Jackson saw the smoke, he considered it a sign from Coffee to commence the battle, so he ordered the 39th Infantry to charge. They responded with a spirited roar and the rolling of drums. Jackson's aide later said that the tension was unbearable.

This was the moment for which the 39th Infantry had trained. Many months of anticipation were coming to fruition… the rolling of the drums would have created an unbearable tension amongst the awaiting soldiers, and some fear amongst their opponents. Over open ground, six hundred professional soldiers under Colonel Williams formed the vanguard of the storming party. They were supported by General James Dougherty's East Tennessee brigade under Colonel Bunch. Major William Carroll's map shows that the 39th, who had been out of range from the Creeks at three hundred yards, marched forward, where, as the trained and seasoned troops they were, they redeployed into formation, similar to tactics used in ancient times by Romans. They pressed steadily forward in the face of a deadly storm of bullets and arrows; they ran across open ground, yelling and screaming all of the way. Colonel Williams later complained that his unit had been "cut to ribbons" during the charge.

The technique of charging infantry in those times was to lean forward into the opposing fire as if into a driving rain. This made a smaller target of their body and would more likely than not result in fatal head wounds rather than gruesome, debilitating limb and body injuries that could linger and be excruciatingly painful. Leading that charge on foot was Colonel Williams. Carrying the flag that was used to signal the troops was Ensign Houston. (The duty of the ensign was "to carry the flag"). [118] Williams chose Houston, though Houston had been promoted to lieutenant, because he was easily seen by all because of his size.

Menawa, observing the formation of Jackson's troops and evidently aware of the terrible consequences if the impending charge was successful, rallied all of the warriors he could in a desperate effort to set back the assault. Many of the warriors had left the breastworks, and of those who remained some hesitated at Menawa's call, wavered, and looked toward Monahell, whereupon the towering Menawa, overcome by rage at the fanatical leader whose folly had deceived the Creeks into this terrible situation, sprang upon the prophet and before the eyes of hundreds of embattled warriors Menawa slew Monahell with his own hand. [119]

Once the 39th reached the breastworks, fierce fighting began through the portholes with rifles, pistols, swords, and any other implements of destruction that were available. At one point, the fighting was so intense that rifles shoved through the portholes were withdrawn with enemy balls stuck between the barrel and bayonets. With no cover and meeting fierce resistance, the 39th was in a predicament. They had to scale the barricade to get a foothold inside the Creek fortress.

"Major Montgomery had been shot dead by a ball to the head ostensibly aimed from one of the portholes. Colonel Williams was one of the first to top the log fortifications behind which the Indians fought. He was followed by Sam Houston who was shot with an arrow" [120] in the groin. The remainder of the 39th followed and jumped into the midst of the Creeks, swinging swords and flashing bayonets after discharging their rifles.

---

117 Holland, p. 12
118 Lossing, Benson J., *The Pictorial Field-Book of the War of 1812*
119 Holland, p. 12
120 Heiskell, Heiskell, S. G., 1920, p. 496

Houston instructed another soldier to remove the arrow in his groin, but the attempt failed. Houston then threatened the soldier that, if he failed in his second attempt, he would "cut his hand off with his sword." [121] The soldier succeeded in removing the arrow, but left an abhorrent, gaping wound from which Houston never fully recovered. He was later attended to by medical officers, who treated it by pouring hot pitch upon it. (The fact that said wound never completely healed might have been the reason why he was dismissed by his new, young wife while governor many years later, at which time he resigned and left the state amid much public furor.)

As soon as a foothold was established, the rout began. The men of the 39th "fought like tigers." [122] The Creeks were no match in firepower or the use of the bayonet by the trained soldiers of Colonel Williams, and the Indians broke ranks and fled. This made them easy targets for the advancing soldiers. They retreated into the woods and thickets.

Once inside the Creek perimeter, the other units of militia and spies joined the 39th in engaging the enemy hand to hand. The fighting was fierce and continued for several hours.

General Coffee and Colonel Morgan had stationed the Cherokee across the river and would not allow them to escape. When the Creeks would dive into the water, the Cherokee simply waited for them to surface and shot them like turtles. Without canoes or means with which to dislodge the Cherokee, there was no escape.

At one point, a spent ball hit the Cherokee commander, Colonel Morgan, in the forehead, knocking him from his horse. Believing himself mortally wounded and experiencing the heat of a fire-hot bullet, the Cherokee said he "danced like a prairie chicken." [123]

One Creek made it to the other bank of the river by swimming the entire width underwater. When the Cherokee captured him, they made menacing motions with their tomahawks. He stuck out his head, exposing his neck and inviting a mortal wound. The Cherokee so respected this show of bravery that they let him live.

The advancing American units were wreaking a heavy toll on the Creeks. They were sought out and shot in whatever hiding places they could find. Near midday, a large group of Creeks were backed into a defensive position. Since the battle had been decided, an effort was made to end the battle by sending a rider forward bearing a white flag. Jackson used this lull to bring his cannons full-force upon the enemy, bringing them inside the barricade.

About that time, a small thundercloud came over the peninsula. Remembering their prophet's tale of success under a prophetically seen cloud, the Creeks shot the flag-bearer, and the Americans resolved to show them no mercy. Jackson fired grapeshot from his cannons and tore huge holes in their defensive line. Ironically, the prophet was found with "grapeshot to the mouth." [124]

Tales of personal heroism abounded from the actions of that day, but some humor was later told as well. One man recalled he had been a mere youth and, needing to cool his rifle barrel, had gone to the river to soak it in the water. While doing so he heard a crying sob and saw an officer crying behind a tree.

Trying to console the soldier who was wiping his eyes, the youth assured him everything would be all right. The soldier said, "Will you then do me a favor?"

"Certainly," the youth replied.

"There's an Indian behind that oak tree who shot the bark off a tree into my eye; would you kill him for me?" [125]

After a short, small chuckle, the deed was done.

Toward the end of the day, soldiers had trapped a band of Creeks inside a cave just over the side of a cliff. Before setting fire to the brush, they decided to give them an opportunity to surrender. A volunteer was needed to expose himself and wave a white flag. Sam Houston had returned to the battle and volunteered for this duty. For his effort, he received two balls to the shoulder. The soldiers then lit the brush afire and shot the burning, escaping Creeks off one by one. Houston was considered mortally wounded and was left upon the field to die.

Once darkness came, a few Creeks were able to escape into the night, but their nation lay in ruin. Most of their braves were dead, and 350 women and children had been captured in total defeat.

Nighttime brought rest to the weary, agony to those suffering, and a chance to evaluate the victory that had been gained. Late in the day, General Jackson had ridden upon the field of battle and, seeing Major Montgomery's

---

121 Williams Family History
122 Opcit, Loessing, p. 779
123 Used by permission of Paul Ghiotto, Jacksonville, FL, September 5, 2018
124 Heiskell, S. G., p. 500
125 Ghiotto

body, cried, "The flower of my army is gone!" and was said to have wept. [126]

This reference is made in almost every retelling of the story and it was stressed in the publicity and history books that followed. It should be remembered that Major Montgomery was loyal to his commander and was apparently at odds with the general, and it conveniently let a dead man who could not speak become the hero of the battle instead of Colonel Williams.

Major Montgomery was buried near where he fell, and many years later, the citizens of Tallapoosa County honored his memory by "exhuming his remains and burying them with military ceremonies at the capital of the county." [127]

To Colonel Williams Jackson stated: "You, sir, have put me on the road to military fame and glory." Of all the men present, Jackson and Williams knew more than others how much had been won that day. Parts of what would become several states were taken from Indian control, and millions of acres would be opened up for settlement and expansion. The British had been dealt a severe blow in their efforts to punish the Americans, and a true pathway to defend the Gulf Coast had been opened up. All of this left New Orleans less vulnerable and easier to defend than ever before.

- - - ! ! !

"Menaway who had five wounds was badly wounded and discovering the whites and friendly Indians paid but little attention to dead women, he got some women's clothes, put them on, dragged two or three dead women together, and lay between them until night, and then escaped." [128]

The next day, Jackson ordered a body count be made, and to keep from counting dead Creeks twice, nose ends were clipped off to show they had been counted. Many of the Creek bodies were weighted with rocks and sunk into the river. Sixteen more Creeks were discovered that next morning and were quickly killed. The scene was one of carnage, with 800 dead Creeks; 350 women and children were taken as prisoners. The Americans had lost twenty-six, with 107 wounded; the Cherokees eighteen killed, thirty-six wounded. The 39th Regiment, which spearheaded the charge against the breastwork, suffered the most casualties, with seventeen killed and fifty-five wounded. Among these casualties were Major Montgomery and Lieutenants Somerville and Moulton;

three cities of northern Alabama still bear their names, and several members of the 39th eventually returned and settled there.

Wounded soldiers were brought back to Fort Williams for treatment and recuperation, but in truth many succumbed to dysentery and infection. Those who had died were buried and their graves marked. The commanders went about justifying in reports what had happened.

"Mr. Warren Wilbanks of Noxabee County, Mississippi, who died in 1882, ninety years of age, is authority for the statement that many of the Tennessee soldiers cut long strips of skin from the bodies of the dead Indians and with these made bridle reins. Also that when the Horse Shoe village was set on fire some of the soldiers noticed a very old Indian, a non-combatant, sitting on the ground, pounding corn in a mortar, as though unaware of the tumult and danger around him, and that a Tennessee barbarian, though called a soldier, deliberately shot him dead, assigning as his reason for so doing that he might be able to report when he went home that he had killed an Indian.

"Mr. Archibald McArthur, an aged man of Winston County, Mississippi, is authority for this statement, that in the heat of the fight a lost, bewildered, little Indian boy, five or six years of age, came among the soldiers, when one of them struck him on the head and killed him with the butt of his musket. When reproached by an officer for barbarity in killing so young a child he replied that the boy would have become an Indian some day.

"An aged man, Mr. Evans, of Neshoba County, Mississippi, is authority for the statement that the party detailed to count the dead warriors found on the battle field of Tohopeka, so as to make no mistake in the count, cut off the tip of each dead Indian's nose so soon as the count was made. "They counted up," says Pickett, "five hundred and fifty-seven warrior bodies found on the field. The Indians take off the scalps. These soldiers took off the nose." [129]

Jackson said in his report to Governor Blount, "The loss of Colonel Williams' reg't of Regulars is seventeen killed and fifty-five wounded; three of whom have since died."

About Colonel Williams, he stated, "The regular troops,

---

126 Heiskell, p. 497
127 Loessing, p.772
128 Woodward, Thomas S. p. 117
129 Halbert, H. S. and Ball, T. H. *The Creek War of 1813 and 1814*, Tuscaloosa: University of Alabama Press, 1895, p.277

led on by their intrepid and skillful commander Colonel Williams, and by the gallant Major Montgomery were presently in possession of the nearer side of the breastwork; and the militia accompanied them in the charge with a vivacity and firmness which could not have been exceeded and has seldom been equaled by troops of any description." [130]

Colonel Williams reported to Secretary of War John Armstrong that "One half of the officers and about one sixth of the troops of the 39th engaged in the battle of Tohopeka on the 27th are among the killed and wounded. The officers remaining with the regiment fit for duty, are insufficient for ordinary camp duties." Colonel Williams' reports on the battle were listed in the directory of war records, but have never been found; those items before and immediately thereafter remain.

Colonel Williams was also writing General Flournoy, wanting to return to east Tennessee to be allowed to recruit and fill his ranks, thus getting him directly out from under Jackson's control.

General Flournoy knew of Williams' previous Volunteer efforts, having vilified him and the Tennessee Volunteers previously at Savannah. He stated, "Should it become necessary to draw men from Tennessee, Colonel Williams' personal influence would enable him to effect that object with facility." [131]

Colonel Williams was returned to Knoxville for recruiting service and Colonel Thomas Benton, Jackson's old ally/adversary, was recalled to lead the 39th into lower Alabama, where they were used as an important rear guard at Mobile while the Battle of New Orleans raged later that year.

Militia General Andrew Jackson returned to Nashville, where he was promoted to commander of the 7th Military District at New Orleans and was made a major general in the United States Army. He instructed his aide, Major Reid, to begin an autobiography almost immediately. Thus began the public relations campaign seeking military fame and glory.

William Weatherford, the Creek "chief," surrendered and supposedly gave a stirring speech to Jackson:

> "Here I am; kill me if you like; I fought you as long as I could; I would fight you still longer if I could. My warriors are dead or scattered; their bones are at the bottom of the river, or whitening on the battlefield; our homes are burned; our fields have been laid waste; our women and children are huddled in the wilderness, with no shelter over their heads, with no food to stay their hunger. I cannot fight you longer, I surrender. Your men want me killed, kill me; but send food to the helpless women and children." [132]

Version two of this speech is that Jackson had tried to offer a reward for the capture of Red Eagle to the other Indians, but they all refused to accept it. For several months Jackson's army and allies tried to capture Chief Red Eagle, but were never successful. When Weatherford had heard that Jackson was pressuring his fellow Indians and chiefs into capturing him, he decided to ride to Fort Jackson and turn himself in, thus sparing his friends and other chiefs the humiliation of turning their head chief over to the one white man they hated the most, Andrew Jackson.

Version three is that Red Eagle rode up to Fort Jackson. He inquired where the general's tent was and went right to it. Jackson had just come out of his tent when the Indian came up to him. The chief said: "Are you General Jackson?" When the man replied yes, the Indian said, "I am Bill Weatherford." Jackson was furious and he told Weatherford (also known as Red Eagle) to go into his tent. "How dare you show yourself to my tent after murdering the women and children at Fort Mims?" Jackson continued, "I had directed that you be brought to me confined; had you appeared to me in that way I should have known how to treat you."

Chief Red Eagle replied: "I am in your power—do with me as you please. I am a soldier. I have done the white people all of the harm that I could: I have fought them and fought them bravely. If I had an army I would yet fight, and I contend to the last: but I have none: my people are all gone. I can do no more than weep over the misfortunes of my nation…. General Jackson I am not afraid of you. I fear no man for I am a Creek warrior. I have nothing to request of myself; you can kill me if you desire. But I beg you to send for the women and children of the war party, who are now starving in the woods. Their cribs have been destroyed by your people, who have driven them to the woods without an ear of corn. I hope that you will send out parties, who will safely conduct them here, in order that they may be fed. I exerted myself in vain to prevent the massacre of the women and children at Fort Mims. I am now done fighting. The Red Sticks are nearly all killed. If I could fight any longer I would most heartedly do so. Send for the women and

---

[130] Jackson to Blount, March 31, 1814
[131] Flournoy to Jackson, *Jackson Papers*, University of TN, March 1814
[132] Watson, p. 190

*Menawa*
Wikipedia

children they never did you any harm. But kill me, if the white man wants it done."

General Jackson replied: "I will not ask that you lay down your arms and become peaceable. The terms of which your nation can be saved, and peace restored, has already been disclosed; in this way and none other, can you obtain safety. If you want to continue to fight you are at liberty to leave and rejoin your war party. If later you are captured under those circumstances you will pay for your crimes with your life."

Chief Red Eagle replied: "I want peace, and relief for the suffering and deprivation of my people. But I may well be addressed in such language now. There was a time when I had a choice and could have answered you. I have none now, even hope has ended. Once I could animate my warriors to battle, but I cannot animate the dead. My warriors can no longer hear my voice. Their bones are at Talledega, Tallushatchee, Emuchfaw, and Tohepeka. I have not surrendered myself thoughtlessly. Whilst there were chances of success I never left my post, nor supplicated peace. But my people are gone and I now ask it for my nation and myself. On the miseries and misfortunes brought upon my country, I look back with the deepest sorrow, and wish to avert even greater calamities. If I would have been left to contend with the Georgia army I would have raised corn on one bank of the river and fought them on the other; but your people have destroyed my nation. You are a brave man; I rely on your generosity.

"You will exact no terms from a conquered people, but such as they should accede to: whatever it may be it would now be madness and folly to oppose. If they oppose you will find me among the sternest enforcers of obedience. Those who would still hold out can be influenced only by a mean spirit of revenge; and to this they must not and shall not sacrifice the remnant of their country. You have told us were we must go and be safe. This is a good talk and my nation ought to listen to it. They shall listen to it."

A crowd had gathered outside the general's tent. When Red Eagle was finished talking, the soldiers started yelling, "Kill him, Kill him, Kill him." This made the general mad and he ordered them to silence.

Then Jackson stated: "Any man who would kill such a man as this would rob the dead." [133]

*Is this not a bit overstated?*

Colonel Thomas Woodward, *who was there*, later stated: "I read what purported to be Weatherford's speech when he surrendered to Gen. Jackson; but if I recollect right,

133 http://www.weatherfordenterprises.com/surrenderpage1.htm
134 Ibid. Woodward, Thomas S., *Woodward's Reminiscences*, p. 37
135 Dunlap to Jackson, July 2, 1823

he was made to say that he would whip the Georgians on one side of the river and make his corn on the other. That was all a lie and for effect."

Woodward also stated Weatherford had "never been a chief, though exercising as much or more influence over a part of the nation than many that were chiefs." [134]

The 39th camped in south-central Alabama to regroup, and called their stopover Camp Montgomery. The county of Montgomery and the political capital of the State of Alabama were named in honor of this brave soldier.

Sam Houston refused to die. After several days it was decided he would be taken home to Maryville in a litter dragged behind a horse. By the time he arrived at his mother's home, he was so emaciated that the only way his mother knew it was her son was by the ring she had given him inscribed with the single word, "HONOR." It is highly unlikely that these events occurred because the ring has never been found and there is no quote from his mother.

With over eight hundred dead, the ability of the Creeks to resist was gone. Jackson's troops found the scalps of those murdered at Ft. Mims in another Creek village and gave them a proper burial. In one town they found a Creek mother hiding among the tent poles of a teepee; they shot her and then discovered she had a child with her. This child was returned to Tennessee, was named Lincoya, and was reared by Jackson in an attempt to provide future leadership for the decimated tribe. That same action *could* have been considered an attempt to cover up the massacre and Jackson's extermination plans by ascribing to him an act of benevolence.

General Jackson's report to Governor Blount was widely circulated and reprinted in the *Nashville Whig*. It was painstakingly written to include, but not glorify, Colonel Williams. However, by word of mouth, his bravery that day became widely known. Behind his back, Jackson and General Dunlap wrote of him later and deridingly referred to him as "the Horse Shoe Colonel." [135] Earlier histories have stated that Colonel Williams resented Jackson not giving him more credit for the victory than he did. That is perhaps true because, apparently, he did not give him his due that day or any day thereafter. The damage to the friendship of the two men had already been effected.

Indeed Jackson had been charged by the legislators of Tennessee, who had resolved to *exterminate* the Creeks. To some gentle spirits it seemed unnecessary to kill so many Indians, but to the people of Tennessee, who remembered fifty years of border warfare, it seemed just and appropriate. When someone asked Governor Blount how it was that Jackson killed so many Indians he replied, "Because he knows how to do it." [136]

On April 19, Militia General Jackson was a brigadier general of the United States Army; the next day, General Pinckney arrived and took command. He immediately ordered Jackson to Fort Williams to erect forts and plant garrisons in the conquered territory. Near the Hickory Ground, a strong fort was built and called Fort Jackson.

On May 1, Major General William Henry Harrison, in a quarrel with the federal government, resigned his command from the northern quarter of the war. John Williams wrote to his mentor General Flournoy at New Orleans, "the Creek war is over;" and on May 4 the Nashville Whig printed the same thing. By May 12, with less than a month in grade, General Jackson was promoted by Pinckney to major general, and because of Harrison's resignation, on the 28th he assumed command on the Seventh Military District, which included Louisiana and the Mississippi territory. In five months, Colonel Williams' prospects for command evaporated, and General Jackson's entire future was assured. "Thus did the frontier soldier, who eighteen months earlier had not commanded an expedition or a detachment, come to occupy the highest rank in the army of his country. No other man in that country's service since the revolution has risen to the top quite so quickly." [137] That day at Horseshoe Bend, Colonel Williams put Andrew Jackson on a higher road to more military fame than either of them could imagine.

> The work of the Army was over; Jackson turned his face toward Nashville, where honors were prepared for him. To his soldiers he sent a triumphant peal by way of parting. "Your vengeance, has been glutted. Wherever these infuriated allies of the arch enemy assembled on the field of battle, you have seen them overthrown.... The bravery you have displayed on the field of battle, and the uniform good conduct you have manifested in your encampment, and on your line of march, will long be cherished in the memory of your general, and will not be forgotten by the country which you have some materially benefited."

> In Tennessee the rejoicings were tumultuous, for it was the state's first important historic achievement.

---

136 Blount to Jackson, January 15, 1814, Jackson, MS.; Bassett, p. 118
137 Bassett, p. 123
138 Bassett, p. 120

When the campaign began seven months earlier, Jackson had many enemies. Two months later, when mutiny existed at Fort Strother and when some of the sanest heads began to shake at what people said of his obstinacy, these enemies were exultant. Now all opponents were silenced and shamed, and from that time he was the state's military hero. [138]

John Williams stayed neither silent nor ashamed very long.

Andrew Jackson returned to his wife, Rachel. What follows is an example of her affection, which he had received during the previous winter:

*Hermitage, Feb. 10, 1814*

"My dearest Life;

*I received your letter by Express. Never shall I forgit it. I have not slept one night since. What a dreadful scene it was—how did I feel. I never can describe it. I Cryed aloud and praised my god For your safety how thankful I was—Oh my unfortunate Nephew he is gon how I deplore his Loss his untimely End—My dear praqylet me conuur youby every Tie of Love of friendship you to let me see you before you go againe I have borne it until now it has thrown me into feavours I am very unwell—my thoughts is never diverted from that dreadful scene oh how dreadful to me & and the mercy and goodness of Heaven to me You are spared perils and Dangers so maney troubles—my prayer is unceasing how long O Lord will I remain so unhappy no rest no Ease. I cannot sleepe all can come home but you I never wanted to see you so mutch in my life had it not have been for Stokel Hayes I should have started oute to Huntsville let me know and I will fly on the wings of the purest affection I must see you pray my Darling never make me so unhappy for aney Country I hope the Campain will soon end the troops that is now on their way will be sufficient to end the ware in the Creek Country You have now don more than any other man ever did before you have served your country long enough You have gained many Laurels You have bind them and more gloriously than had your situation have been differently and instid of your enemyes injuring of you as theay intended it has been an advantage to you You hae been gon a long time six months in all that time what has been your trialls daingers and Difyiculties hardships oh Lorde of heaven how can I beare it—Colo Hayes waites once more I commend you to god his providential eye is on you his paternal Care is guarding you—my prayers my tears is for your safety Day and night farewell I fell too mutch at this moment our Dear Little Son is well he sayes maney things to sweet papa and happy Dayes until we meete—Let it not be Long from your "Dearest friend and faithfull wife until Death"* [139]

Mrs. Jackson was an illiterate woman; probably most of her education came through a deeply religious life. Many of her phrases are conventional expressions in the fervid pulpit language of the day, but she had an extremely benevolent nature, and through her emotions she ruled her husband's affection until the day of her death. It was no slight achievement, and whatever her education, it indicates that naturally she was a woman of distinction.

Most of the defeated Creek Indians had resettled in Florida. It was expected that General Pinckney, commander of the Sixth Military District, and Indian Agent Benjamin Hawkins would negotiate a treaty with the Creeks, but nine of Jackson's officers signed a protest and Jackson was assigned the duty.

When the council met on August 1, Jackson surprised all by making incredible demands: besides existing military forts and roads, liberty to use the rivers, and an end to their relationships with Spain; additionally he demanded a concession of twenty million acres of what had been described as "the best unsettled country in America." The friendly Creeks sought the advice and consent of their brothers in Florida, but Jackson insisted on immediate acceptance, so they signed the treaty on August 9.

Colonel Williams returned to a waiting wife and three young children in Knoxville. His newest daughter, Margaret McClung Williams, had been born while he was away on February 5. He was thirty-six years old; Melinda was twenty-five. "Colonel Williams and Benton are almost the only Tennesseans of prominence who went through the war without achieving distinction." [140]

Total casualties in the Creek War were 1,902 Creeks and 133 white and Cherokee; virtually a ten-to-one loss for the Creek Indians.

139 Bassett, p. 122
140 Bassett, p. 87

*Artist depiction of barricade at Horseshoe Bend in 1814*

# Chapter 7
# Politics and Lafayette Returns

In the aftermath of the War of 1812, many changes took place. The Creek War ended with incredible concessions by the Indians that opened huge parts of Georgia and Alabama for white settlements.

The full-fledged feud between Andrew Jackson and John Williams through two elections changed politics in the United States. To celebrate the fiftieth anniversary of the American Revolution, President Monroe invited the Marquis de Lafayette to tour the country. There was great emotion throughout the land. There were winners and losers; some were with honor and some were without.

General Andrew Jackson returned to Nashville and received a hero's welcome. He had recovered enough from his wounds that he was feted at parties around the town. His friend, John Overton, realized he now had a path to political fame; the country was ripe for a new generation of heroes and was growing rapidly in population from new immigrants, and they were going to let them vote! Even before New Orleans, there had begun a groundswell of publicity among the common people; it was partially orchestrated by Overton and others of Jackson's friends. Timing was everything as his rapid rise became a grassroots sociological movement from the old aristocratic system (to which the country had been born) into one that was more "for the people."

John Williams returned to Knoxville, licked his wounds, and crossed the mountains to see his father. He was probably devastated that he had lost his opportunity for promotion and the glory of battle. Plus, a dangerous suicidal charge across open ground will change you. He had been put into a position where he was duty-bound to risk his and his men's lives in the better good of the Battle of Horseshoe Bend. He obviously objected to the execution of John Woods, but could do nothing since he had to obey orders. That issue would return.

He was asked for bravery, command, leadership, toughness, and brutality. He saw images that would never go away. Like a file that never closes, he would have remembered that campaign and would have been forever changed by it.

His father was a consummate politician, and he knew Andrew Jackson as a young man all too well. With several family members in Congress, the Williamses had more than their share of political power. What plans the Williamses had were never divulged, but Jackson and Williams would exchange only several more notes in the remainder of their entire lives.

One note was Williams' excuse for not returning to his unit, due to failing to attract many new recruits, and he advised Jackson he had gone "across the mountains to see my aged and infirm father." His aged and infirm father, sixty-six at that time, would live another thirteen years.

Jackson virtually begged Williams to return to service under him. Williams would not. Jackson severely rebuked Williams for not giving up arms to the Kentucky Militia passing near Knoxville. Williams and Kentucky Militia General Taylor had exchanged bitter letters regarding the arms, and on whose authority they might be delivered; Williams prevailed, and his last communication stated, "You have been informed that it is not in my power to part from the arms in my possession. I am under the necessity of refusing positively a Compliance with your order. I deem it unnecessary at this time to investigate your authority to give me an order." [141]

On October 17, Jackson reprimanded Williams, stating:

> "I regret that you could not furnish him all the arms that could be spared from the Deposit in your hands. I have deemed it necessary to make this communication to you as well to prepare you for an event which must happen, if insisted upon by Gen. Taylor, as to guard you against the repetition of an act which might prove so injurious to the safety of the country. This is not a time to investigate nice military questions of rank." [142]

Colonel Williams had ordered his executive officer, Lieutenant Colonel Thomas Benton, to reorganize the remaining troops of the 39th, and advised him that another company would be marched from Knoxville soon. Williams planned to return to command them.

> Then arrived the General's letter of censure and rebuke. Secure in the conviction that he had acted according to military regulations, Williams immediately wrote a long and complete defense of his refusal to surrender the supplies. He expressed regret and astonishment at the reprimand. The old question of rank had arisen again, and he assumed that Taylor had no more right as a militia general to take the arms than the clothing of the regulars. [143]

He stated to Jackson in another letter:

> "In either case I should have been accountable to the Government, and bound to have paid the amount, out of my private funds.... I am assured that General Taylor's correspondence with me, was not commenced, with an expectation of promoting the public service.... And it would afford me infinite satisfaction to deliver over all the public stores in my possession to promote the service, if I had a legal order to that effect. But I never will envolve myself in ruin by squandering the public stores confided to my care. And I will resist every attempt to make me responsible for others faults. I am always ready and willing to have every act, both of my civil and military life, investigated. In the exercise of your discretion you seem to think these are sufficient grounds for my arrest. I shall therefore hold myself in readiness to receive your order of arrest, and to repair without delay to such place as may be appointed for my trial." [144]

Jackson did not order Williams' arrest; Colonel Williams' loyalty and honor had been assailed, and it kindled the fires of resentment that had been borne between the two lawyers prior to Horseshoe Bend. Jackson used every means at his disposal, but he could not persuade Williams to return. General Taylor did not press charges, and remained poorly regarded in military circles/.

General Jackson concluded the treaty with the Creeks in August, commenced an expedition into Florida in September, and concluded 1814 by arriving at New Orleans and declaring martial law, which incensed the citizens of that city and the public officials alike.

On December 23, the first battle against General Packenham's British troops occurred at New Orleans, followed by a second on January 1. The final and concluding battle occurred on January 8.

Late in his life, Williams wrote anonymously: "If the victory at New Orleans gained for the commanding General a high military character, his conduct at that post did not less firmly establish the evil dispositions which render it dangerous to civil institutions." [145]

It proved to be a final step in the "military glory and honor" path General Jackson had proclaimed after Horseshoe Bend. He soon became a national hero at New Orleans, even though he had been reviled and hated by the citizenry there. Even after the battle in February, Louisiana Governor Claiborne regretted "the violence of his character." [146]

The country of new, free men needed a spiritual boost, and another victory over the British was just what it deserved. There was evidence that the Treaty of Ghent, which ended the War of 1812, had been greatly influenced by the news of the American victory at Horseshoe Bend. Said treaty did not arrive until *after* the battle at New Orleans. Knowing that national prominence awaited him, Jackson did all of the politically expedient things. He visited American and British wounded. He attended numerous banquets in his honor, and he formed many alliances within the circles of military and political leaders. He had seen how the leaders of the Revolution had profited from their fame, and it would only logically follow that he desired to receive some of the same.

---

141 Williams to Taylor, Sept. 20, 1814
142 Jackson to Williams, Mobile, Oct. 17, 1814, Jackson Letter Book, H, pp. 96-97
143 Driver, Leota Maiden, *The East Tennessee Historical Society's Publications*, Nov. 30, 1958, p. 27
144 Williams to Jackson, Knoxville, Nov. 1, 1814, Bassett (ed.), *Correspondence*, II, pp. 88-89
145 Anonymous, Col. John Williams, The Political Mirror, Or Review Of Jacksonism, J. P. Peaslee, New York, 1835, p. 52
146 Official Letter Books of W CC Claiborne, Mississippi Hissorical Society, Volume VI, Feb. 24, 1815

Williams responded in February to General Jackson: "you have knocked off John Bull's horns." In May, the 39th Infantry was consolidated into the 3rd Infantry Regiment; on June 15, Williams was discharged from active military service and the Flag of the 39th was returned to Colonel Williams. Jackson remained in the military, and John Williams turned to law and politics as a civilian. There was great enmity between them, and though many mutual friends tried to reconcile the two warriors, neither would do so.

John Williams received some accolades for leading the charge at the Battle of Horseshoe Bend. He remained popular, especially in East Tennessee, where he had led those Volunteers only two years earlier. He was proposed for public offices, including Governor of Tennessee. However, on October 15, 1815, John Williams was appointed to fill the unexpired term of Joseph Campbell in the United States Senate. He was reelected by the state legislature in 1817, and was a quiet, behind-the-scenes senator who formed alliances with powerful men from the traditionally strong original states. He was a Whig and sided with the Adams' view of politics rather than Jefferson's.

As handsome as they came, he was admired by Dolly Madison, who called him "the Chesterfield of the Senate" after the gentleman's gentleman, Lord Chesterfield of the British Parliament. He was an advocate of states' rights, was considered a constitutional expert, and generally did his job without major conflict. He loved the pomp and circumstance of the nation's capital. He admitted he was fond of martial music and enjoyed watching the ladies of society in their finery.

He served as head of the Senate Committee for Military Affairs. That committee considered military courts' martial witnesses, reorganization of the military medical staff, and organization of the military academy at West Point. As head of the Military Affairs Committee, Williams was in the uncomfortable position of being out of the chain of command, but in charge senatorially of his many friends and few enemies in the military. Now that the War of 1812 was over, the mood of the country was one of war avoidance. The legislative body had been whittling down the military expenditures since the war's end, and theirs was the continual question of why there were so many generals and so few wars. Naturally, the continuing on-duty officers of the military had their very existence at stake. They sometimes conspired among themselves, both officially and otherwise. As head of that military committee, Williams probably received much of the blame for the reductions he was obliged to suggest. His record indicated he voted for the United States Bank, the Missouri Compromise, and states' rights.

While John Williams courted the powers that were in the Senate, Jackson continued to pursue his military career. His fame continued rising by word of mouth among the populace—particularly in the frontier West that the then-Southwestern United States had become. The end of the War of 1812 so quickly followed Jackson's victory at New Orleans that the idea was popularly planted that *he* had won the war. [147] By his forty-eighth birthday on March 15, 1815, when the average life expectancy was mid-forties, General Jackson was elderly. He had reason to be concerned about his health.

As a youth he suffered from drooling, spitting and dribbling when under duress. He had survived smallpox during the Revolutionary War—the disease that killed his mother and brother. He suffered from dysentery most of his life and he had chronic urticaria (hives) that caused him to itch all over. By the time he was an adult, his teeth had decayed to the point that he could not eat solid food. When later president, he was nearly six feet tall, but only weighed 129 pounds. [148]

Jackson had been shot twice—once by Jesse Benton in the shoulder, and once in the duel with Dr. Dickinson. The latter wound pierced his side and the ball lodged in his chest. By the end of his life he suffered from severe headaches, indigestion, shortness of breath, hemorrhaging, blindness in one eye, blurring of vision in the other, reduced hearing, and occasional deep chest pains. [149]

Jackson's treaties with the Creeks and Choctaws opened huge tracts of acreage for white settlement. Only the Seminoles in Spanish-owned Florida remained hostile. Former territories Indiana and Mississippi became the 19th and 20th states in 1817 and 1818. John and Melinda Williams suffered the birth and death of yet another child, James White Williams, named for Melinda's father, who lived only one year. Their son, John Williams II, married Rhoda Campbell Morgan in March 1818, and yet another generation of Williamses came of age.

In 1817, Jackson and his United States forces entered Florida under questionable authority for the purpose of punishing the troublesome Seminoles. Their march into the swampy lowlands was both arduous and slow. They

---

147 History Channel documentary
148 Google
149 Google

met little resistance, because the Seminoles would know of their approach and would retreat by abandoning villages and food stores, just like they had done on Williams' earlier excursion.

One incident that occurred on this campaign became an issue of national discussion. Jackson knowingly executed two English subjects, Ambrister and Arbuthnot, and accused them of being spies. This knowledge was received with much consternation in Washington, for the fledgling country did not want to provoke another war with either England or Spain. Cries for an official inquiry prompted an investigation by the Military Committee of the Senate that was headed by Senator Williams.

Many thought Jackson should be reprimanded for illegal entry into Florida and for the excessive punishments used against the British subjects. In 1821, Jackson traveled to Washington to answer criticisms of his actions. One of his defenses was that Williams himself had illegally entered Florida in 1813. Senator Williams pointed out the success of his campaign as well as the Spanish Governor's acceptance of it.

However, the two Tennesseans continued to bitterly contest each other.

In 1819 Jackson accused Williams of spreading false information damaging to his reputation on two matters: the report, which apparently was widespread, that Jackson had invested in real estate in Pensacola and then, as he put it, "in order to enhance the value of my property...had marched my army there and seized the place"; and the story that Jackson had "made the reservation of the salt lick in the Chickasaw treaty for myself, and that the ink had not dried on the treaty before I had obtained a lease for it." [150]

Williams maintained, late in his life, again writing anonymously:

"On the 26th of December 1817, the War Department issued orders to him, then at Nashville, to repair to Fort Scott, and assume the command of the forces in that quarter of the Southern division; to call upon the Executives of the adjacent States, if, in his opinion, the troops of the United States were too few to beat the enemy; and to adopt necessary measures to terminate the conflict. On the receipt of this order, General Jackson, instead of calling for the militia, summoned to his aid 1200 volunteers from Tennessee and Kentucky. This corps was organized, and officered, under his directions, and mustered into the service of the United States. About the same period, General Gaines, also, raised 1600 men, among the friendly Creeks. General Jackson entered upon the campaign with a force of about 3000: that of the enemy, at the utmost did not exceed one thousand; and at no time did half that number present themselves to oppose his march. Of course little resistance was made. The Indian towns were destroyed and their inhabitants dispersed. (Note as footnote: In this campaign the troops of the United States suffered no loss, save in the death of *six militia men* executed with the approbation of the General, for desertion.)

- In his progress, he captured, caused to be tried by court martial, and executed Arbuthnot and Armbrister, two Englishmen, residents among, and averred to be instigators of the hostility of, the Seminoles; and he hung without trial, two Indian chiefs, who, by wiles, had been drawn into his power. He invaded the Spanish territory of Florida, reduced the forts of St. Mark and Barrancas, and the city of Pensacola, and commanded the reduction of St. Augustine; transported the Spanish officers, civil and military, to the Havana; abolished the revenue laws of Spain, instituted those of the United States; and; on his own authority, established civil and military officers.

- The preceding sentence records, almost as many offences as facts; and if it were separated from the context, the reader might readily suppose that he was perusing an account of the progress of an independent sovereign, or of a Roman Consul bearing the eagles of the "gowned nation" over new conquests. Whilst the events were fresh before the nation, the following charges were alleged, by our most eminent statesmen, against the General.

**1.** That in substituting volunteers, raised upon his own authority, for the militia, he assumed a power which did not legally belong, either to him, or to the administration of the Government; for, that, whilst the general law, provided for the use of the militia, no statute warranted the evocation of volunteers; and that, whatever the law provided, whether in form or substance, was obligatory on its agents;

**2.** That, by the organization of the volunteer corps, the officers and privates were independent of the Government and dependent upon the General;

**3.** That, the invasion of Florida was unwarranted, that if warranted, it was only in pursuit or reduction

---

150 Opcit, Driver, p. 31

of an enemy, who overpowered the neutral or was sustained by him; that, if such cause justified the capture of St. Marks it did not extend to the seizure of Fort Barrancas nor the city of Pensacola; that, if it even extended to them, it did not give a right to conquer the country, expel the governor, abolish the laws, and convert the territory into a colony of the United States; that, by these acts, the General had made war upon Spain, had changed the regulations between us and that Government, and had, thus, assumed powers which could be exercised only by Congress;

**4.** That, although, it might be true, that, the cruelties practiced in war by one belligerent, might, lawfully, be retaliated by the other, and that, white men associating themselves with savages were associated with their fate; yet, that, in the present case, the retaliation was unnecessary, the war being over, and was forbidden by the rule of mercy which a practice of three hundred years had established in North America; that, if the law of nations, in this respect, had not been thus abrogated, it has been executed without the knowledge or the sanction of the Government; and that, if the General had a right, without specific authority, to enforce this law, it was exercised with indecorous and cruel precipitation.

**5.** That, in the cases of Arbuthnot and Armbrister, he had alike, grossly, mistaken, the law, under which their offences were cognizable, the mode in which they should be prosecuted, and the evidence necessary to their conviction, that, the principle assumed by him, 'that they by uniting in war with the savages against the united States, whilst we were at peace with Great Britain, became outlaws and pirates, is not recognized in any code of national law; that, if it were, LaFayette, De Kalb, Pulaski, and a host of foreigners, who had aided in our Revolution, were outlaws and pirates, liable, if captured by the British, to suffer death; That, though these unfortunate men might, be subjected to the extremity of pain under the *lex talionis*, they were not the proper subjects of a court martial, being at the disposal of the commanding General, or more properly of the Government of the United States; that, as the court martial was resorted to, for the protection of the General, he had delegated his authority and should have been concluded, thereby; that his rejection of the sentence of the court, decrying stripes and imprisonment for Armbrister, and substituting the punishment of death, was arrogant, despotic and cruel; and that, the testimony upon which the sentence was founded would have been rejected in every Court governed by established rules of evidence.

• We do not purpose to investigate, at this day, all or either, of these charges. But we will state the manner in which they were disposed of. The irregularity in raising the troops was unobserved by the Government, or if observed, was, disregarded, nay, commended, in the hope that a more speedy termination of the campaign would be thereby attained. The seizure of Florida was condemned; the colony, with all its towns and fortifications, were delivered up to the Spanish authorities. The homicide of the Indian and white agitators was deemed an event too good for banning and too bad for blessing. Those who suffered were held to have merited their fate; but every man of sensibility deplored, that, the reputation of the country, for civilization and humanity, had been stained by the execution; all responded to the following sentiment, of an eloquent gentleman, who, ably, discussed the subject before Congress: "When," said he, "the General the exultation of conquest has passed away, and he shall look back upon the transaction with the feeling of man stripped of the pride of the conqueror, this deed of bloody justice, will weigh heavily upon his heart, and embitter his days. I would not endure the remorse that is in store for him, for all his laurels, and all his eulogiums."

The justice and humanity of this sentiment will not be disputed, but its prophetic character may be questioned. Your true hero is always so constituted, that he "looks with composure upon blood and carnage (note a footnote: Letter of General Jackson to Mr. Monroe commenting on the character of Mr. Madison.)" Your ambitious men, your Alexanders, your Caesars, your Cromwells, your Bonapartes, your Attillas, your bandits of every species, who will, intensely, march resolutely to their goal, though every step extinguish a life. The love of glory eradicates the love of man. Remorse comes only, when fortune deserts them.

• But we have in the events of this campaign, the most satisfactory evidence of the General's disregard of the Constitution and laws, as of his ignorance of the principles upon which the powers of his office, should have been applied. In the levy of his troops he looked only to the end, disregarding the illegality of the means; in the invasion of Florida, he violated the rights of a friendly nation, and the Constitution of his own country; in the unnecessary execution of the wretched savages and their more criminal seducers he stained the reputation of his nation; and in all, he trod beneath his feet every principle save his own will. Here, as at all times, his motto was legible upon his sword, *'sic volo, sic jubeo; stet pro ratique voluntes.'* Which may be freely rendered, 'not *thine*; Oh Lord, but let *my* will be done.'" [151]

### - - - ! ! !

An interesting anecdote from Jackson's Seminole campaign was written many years later by Thomas Woodward, a young man of mixed blood who fought on the American side and stated:

> "This was in March, 1818. We occasionally fired a few guns at straggling Indians, and they in turn would fire upon us; now and then one was killed, and a prisoner or two taken. There was nothing that could be called a fight upon our route to the spot on the Appalichicola, where Gen. Clinch had blown up Ft. Woodbine, a year or two before. The Army at that time consisted of the 4th and 7th Regiments of United States Infantry, two Regiments of Georgia Militia, under Gen. Glasscock, a Company of Kentuckians, under Capt. Robert Crittenden, and a Company of Tennesseans, under Capt. Dunlap, this last Company composed General Jackson's Life Guard, and some five hundred Indians, under the two half-breed Chiefs, Kinard and Lovet, and myself.

> "We set about building Fort Gadsden, on the site of old Fort Woodbine. And at that place Gen. Jackson and myself took our first split, and as the matter has been often talked of, and misrepresented by some, I will here give you the particulars of that affair, as there are as yet those living who witnessed it. General Twiggs of the Army, witnessed the whole of it, and Colonel John Banks of Columbus, Ga., Major Samuel Robinson, of Washington County, Georgia and Captain Isaac Brown, of this state, are all familiar with the circumstances.

> "Captain Dunlap was a gentleman and a good officer, and his company was composed mostly of the sons of the first families about Nashville, and some of them were very young, as well as very mischievous. They performed no duty more than to ride along the trail on our march, and when in camp strolled when and where they pleased. I had noticed them, or some of them, several times on our march from Fort Scott to where we then were, making fun and cutting their capers with the Georgia Militia. I tried to put a stop to it as often as I could; told them that we were all engaged in the same service, and should be one people. It did no good. One day, while at work on Fort Gadsden, I had a parcel of Indians taking the bark from the pines to cover the huts in the Fort; many of the officers were present, noticing how neatly the Indians arranged the bark. Among those present that I recollect, were Gens. Jackson, Gaines, and Glasscock; Colonels Breasley and King; Major Floyd and Captain Bee. While we were there, a Georgian by the name of Jabez Gilbert came up. I knew Gilbert, he was pretty well smoked—soap and water would have helped the looks both of himself and clothes. Some eight or ten of these Nashville youngsters seized him, and said they would throw him into the river, which was but a few yards off. One of the young men, I think, was named Ayres, and perhaps a Lieutenant. He stepped up to General Jackson and said: "General, we have a notion to wash that fellow." The General said nothing, but hung his head and smiled. That made me mad. They dragged Gilbert nearly to the water's edge. I remarked to General Glasscock, that was one of his men; I repeated it several times, but Glasscock said nothing. I then spoke out loud, and remarked that he was a Georgian, and had claims on me. I then walked to where Gilbert was, pulled him away from them, and ordered him to go to his quarters. They then attempted to seize me. I tapped, or pushed one of them over; and another I pushed into the water where it was about knee deep.

> "Colonel Breasley, who had been, or was looking to be arrested, had made me a present of his side arms, which I had under my hunting shirt, and showed to the boys, and that ended the row at the water.

> "I walked back, and took my seat not far from where Gen. Jackson and the others were sitting. This man Ayres came up and commenced a sort of quarrel with me, and said that General Jackson saw it, and had not interfered, and that it was none of my business; besides, he said, I had no command among the whites, and that I had better attend to my Indians. I told him it mattered not where my command was, that when I saw such chaps as him out of their place, I would put them in it. I discovered that the General was mad, for I had not been very choice about words or insinuations. He rose to his feet and said he had seen as big men as I was thrown into the water. I remarked to him that he might, but that he had not men enough in his Life Guard to put me in, and if he

---

151 Williams, John, *The Political Mirror or Review of Jacksonism*, J. P. Peasley, New York, 1835, pp 58-61

liked, he could try it.

"Major Twiggs at this time stepped near, and gave me to understand that I had better say no more, and to go to my quarters, and remarked to Ayres at the same time, "Young man, you put out from here." Twiggs and Capt. Bee were the only men that said a word. Capt. Bee turned off and spoke to be heard by those who were listening, and said: "Woodward is right, and the Georgians ought to love him."

"As I walked off, General Jackson cursed me for a damned long, Indian looking son-of-a-bitch. I recollect his language well. As he made that speech, I turned and said to him, that I had some of the blood, but neither boasted of, nor was ashamed of it. I went to my quarters, and either sent a note, or got Captain Brown to go to the General, (I now forget which,) and say to him that I regretted having incurred his displeasure, and that if he had no further use for my services, I would quit his camp.

"That evening or the next morning he sent for me to go to his quarters. He said to me that I had done right in preventing the volunteers from throwing the militiaman in the water, but said I was too self-willed, and did not observe a proper respect towards my superiors, and that he wished the matter to drop there, and wished me to remain. There the matter ended.

"I could not help laughing to myself at the idea of the difference the old General then made (and which is often made yet) between volunteers and militia, for I had always looked upon volunteers and drafted men both, as being militia, until they had been well trained. Though I believe the word militia signifies a national force or trained band—and all new troops, both volunteers and drafted men, are alike until they are made regulars by training." [152]

- - - ! ! !

In truth, Spain realized by those two incursions by the United States into their territory that, while at war with France, they could no longer defend Florida. They sold it to the United States in 1819; it would not become a state until 1845. Jackson effectively squelched the political uprising in the Senate about Florida and left Washington a bigger hero than he'd entered it.

Other notable events were happening while the colonel was a senator too. In 1819, Beethoven was confirmed deaf. John Williams filed a subdivision plan of what is currently a part of downtown Knoxville, and Simóne Bolivar liberated Colombia, Venezuela, and Ecuador.

Rising Jackson protégé, Sam Houston, became a lieutenant and remained in the United States Army. He had become a Jackson protégé after surviving his wounds from Horseshoe Bend. Being six-foot-six, blond, handsome, and rugged, he had a way with words, and sought favor from Jackson, who gave it. Having attended what became Maryville College in his pre-military days, the president of that school, Dr. Isaac Anderson, said that often "[he] had determined to whip Sam Houston, but he would come up with such a pretty dish of excuses that [he] could not do it." [153]

His knowledge of the Indians served him well, for he was appointed as sub-agent of the Cherokee under Return J. Meigs. While accompanying some tribe members to Washington, Houston invoked the wrath of Secretary of War John C. Calhoun, who objected to his wearing of tribal garments. Due to an internal investigation, Houston resigned his commission in 1818. Houston then returned to Nashville, where he studied law, and moved to Lebanon, Tennessee, to practice his trade. In 1819, he was named prosecuting attorney for Davidson County (Nashville) and adjutant general of the Tennessee Militia. Only two years later he was elected major general of the same organization, and he served two consecutive terms in the House of Representatives.

Somewhat a calm before the storm intervened in 1820. John and Melinda had another daughter, Cynthia; the loss of infants was all too common in those days, but Melinda, who was the primary caregiver, took the deaths especially hard. John had been appointed a charter member of the East Tennessee College Board of Trustees, and wrote a merger of that institution with Hampton Sidney Academy. Daniel Boone died. The US population in 1820 was 9,618,453. John's younger brother, Dr. Alexander Williams, moved to nearby Greeneville, Tennessee, where he gave up his medical practice to run the estate of his future father-in-law, John Dickson. Dr. Williams married Katherine Douglas Dickson, John Dickson's only daughter. He became a noted fox hunter.

About that time, another of John's brothers, Lewis Williams, came to Knoxville to visit. Lewis was in the House of Representatives for so long that when he died

---

152 Woodward, Thomas S., pp. 159-161
153 Haley, James L., Sam Houston, University of Oklahoma Press, 2002

he was proclaimed Father of the House. While there, he became ill and apparently died. As the family was preparing him for burial, someone noticed a bit of color yet in his cheeks, and they began to massage him and he was revived. The incident scared Alexander's wife, Katherine, so badly that she made the family swear that they would wait for three days after her death just to make sure. Unfortunately, when her time came, it began to rain on the third day and did so for a week. When they finally could inter her in the cemetery in Knoxville the service was notoriously brief.

In 1821, James Madison was elected to a second term, and Guatemala, Santo Domingo, and Panama became independent of Spain. John Williams bought Melinda a carriage with which "to take the children to church." John's older brother, Robert, died unexpectedly at forty-eight while visiting in Knoxville, and John settled his estate and assisted his heirs. Robert's daughter, Malinda Robert Williams, married John's son, Joseph Lanier Williams, who was named after their grandfather, in 1842; they were first cousins. Melinda White Williams' father, General James White, the founder of Knoxville, died on August 14; and on May 27, General Andrew Jackson resigned from the Army, as Missouri became the twenty-fourth state.

Senator Williams continued to remember the folks back home and to keep their welfare constantly in mind. In 1819 he had generously given a parcel of land as the site for a meeting house. When, by mistake, those settlers were ordered off of the public land near Hiwassee, he immediately laid the matter before the Secretary of War. [154] Then early in 1823 he introduced into the Senate a resolution authorizing Tennessee to sell her vacant lands north and east of the reservation line for such price as the legislature might deem expedient. A bill with such provisions passed the Senate on February 5, 1823. By the Compact of 1806, which had remained in force, the state was prohibited from selling land at less than the minimum price set for that sold by the United States government. By this revision, however, many small pieces which otherwise would have remained vacant would have been disposed of for 50, 25, or even 12 ½ cents per acre, the amount which eventually became the sales price. Such sales would add to the revenues of the state. One editor estimated that this law would produce no less than $210,000 from the Hiwassee District alone. [155]

Thus, one of his last official acts in Congress was a bill that consummated a plan held in mind from the date of the ratification of the Indian Treaty in 1819. Also, during that last year of service, a bill was reported from the Senate Military Affairs Committee providing for the establishment of a national armory on the western waters, the location to be determined by a skilled engineer. Williams wrote in a letter to Governor William Carroll, expressing the hope that the citizens of Tennessee would call to the executive's attention the suitable sites in their state: "Perhaps no state in the union contains more situations for water power than Tennessee. In East Tennessee they are to be found in every county."

He named Bell's works on the Big Harpeth, Stone Fort on Duck River, and the iron works near Sparta all as "admirable situations for a national armory.". [156] Here he was the prophet, foreseeing the value of national locations which were to be capitalized upon a hundred years later. [157]

John Williams was known to utter disparaging words about Jackson in Washington. Privately, Jackson and his allies mockingly referred to him as "the Horseshoe Colonel," but they did not do so to his face. Those opponents were determined to defeat him for election in 1823, because if Jackson were to run for president in 1824, they could not have John Williams openly opposing and denigrating him in Washington.

After one comment he happened to make on the floor of the Senate, the general's supporters cautioned him he had best not rile the general or he might face his challenge to a duel. Williams stated on the floor of the Senate that, should the general challenge him, he would "choose rifles from twenty paces and that "I shall shoot him between the eyes where he cannot pad with paper." [158] Williams was an expert rifle shot and Jackson knew this as a fact.

Senator Williams heard of these plots to unseat him at the next meeting of the Tennessee state legislature in Murfreesboro. He left Washington early, visited all of the legislators in their home districts, and secured many to promise to vote for him. He wrote John Overton, who had married Melinda's sister, that he heard he was to be "turned out in the Senate" but that he "fears not." [159]

---

154 *Knoxville Register*, April 28, 1818, Nashville Clarion and Tennessee Gazette, Feb. 1, 1820
155 *National Constitutional Advocate*, Jan. 14, 1823; Williams to the Editors, Feb. 5, 1823, *Knoxville Register*, April 18,1823
156 John Williams to Carroll, Washington, Feb 1., 1823, *Knoxville Register*
157 Driver, Leota Maiden, *The East Tennessee Historical Society's Publications*, No. 30, 1959, p. 35
158 *Williams Family History*
159 Williams to Overton, Jan., 14, 1823

The coming senatorial election of 1823 in Tennessee would change forever the way elections were conducted in the United States.

Judge John Overton was a friend to Andrew Jackson, Robert Overton Williams, and John Williams. All four were originally from North Carolina, and were involved in the small world that was the legal system in early Tennessee.

Robert Overton Williams and Judge John Overton had corresponded for years with John Williams, often securing hard-to-get books and other intellectual items for Judge Overton. Visits to each other's homes were common, and with Overton long remaining a bachelor, some raucous behavior probably had occurred too.

Of all the many things he was, Overton was a good politician. In modern society he would have owned his own public relations firm and would have run successful election campaigns. In those days, however, such a profession and expertise did not exist.

Since the days of Washington, elections were held with candidates mostly from the aristocratic families, with much free alcohol poured on election day. Buying of votes for alcohol or money was common. The general rule of thumb was that candidates would not campaign for their election; rather, they would stay at home and await the decision so that they could accept the position when it was *offered*.

Overton also knew Washington. He had influential contacts there, knew how it worked politically, and had been the federal government contact in the early years of Tennessee's statehood.

In Nashville, he lived in an impressive home and estate known as Travelers Rest. Both Jackson and Williams were guests there. He posssibly was one of those gentlemen who sought to reconcile the two feuding veterans. Williams and Overton never corresponded again; the friendship between the Overtons and Williams' was broken.

When Horseshoe Bend was over, Overton immediately saw the potential gain from Jackson's newfound fame. He and other gentlemen helped push Jackson toward national prominence. That ended the friendship between Overton and Williams. Correspondence between Williams and Overton and Jackson all but ended about the same time. Overton probably was pleased with General Jackson's rising fame, but it cost him a long-term friend and brother-in-law in Williams. John Overton later married Melinda White Williams' older sister, Mary McConnell White Overton.

With the Battle of New Orleans eclipsing Horseshoe Bend in public knowledge and importance, the latter slipped out of consciousness and the former was on the tip of everyone's tongue. Of all of Jackson's advisors, Overton knew best what was at stake. With the legislature meeting early in 1823, a few miles to the southwest of Nashville at Murfreesboro, he stationed spies at the site, who reported the happenings back to him. Even President Monroe had associates strategically placed, monitoring the political activity; the governor of Illinois was lurking in the area, and was suspected of being in league with him.

Jackson's supporters felt it obligatory that Williams be replaced if the general was indeed to mount a campaign for the presidency. Williams was fond of telling his Washington associates that Jackson was not nearly as popular in Tennessee as he was in DC, and in East Tennessee that yet was possibly true.

When the legislature convened in September 1823, the plan of Jackson's men was to have Williams replaced by Pleasant M. Miller or John Rhea. Several polling ballots were held and it was found that Williams would prevail handily.

> Senator Eaton and Major Lewis had Jackson's name placed before the legislature as the only hope of furthering their own ambitions. Overton and Grundy, by this time, somewhat appalled by the upsurge of Jackson's presidential stock outside of Tennessee and dismayed at his emerging social philosophy, actually sought to kill his presidential candidacy by the reelection of Williams. However, the boom they had helped to generate now was beyond their control; unintentionally they had aided Andrew Jackson on his way to the Senate and eventually to the White House. [160]

The night before the scheduled election, straw polls indicated Williams would defeat Jackson's "in name only" candidacy. Overton's spies informed him of this, and the little judge mounted his horse and rode the significant distance to the Hermitage and spent considerable time convincing Jackson what he must do.

Overton and Jackson rode through the night to the Murfreesboro conclave. There was much joy at Jackson's appearance the next morning and he indicated he did indeed wish to become Tennessee's senator. This tipped the balance in the election. When the votes were counted, Jackson prevailed thirty-five to twenty-five. Of those twenty-five who voted for Williams, only three were reelected in the next election. "For the first time, the tradition of choosing the senators from the two divisions of the state had been disregarded." [160]

One of those who pledged their vote to Williams was former Congressman David Crockett. He wrote in his autobiography, published shortly after his death:

> "The term of Colonel John Williams had expired, who was a senator in Congress from the state of Tennessee. He was a candidate for another election, and was opposed by Pleasant M. Miller, Esquire, who, it was believed, would not be able to beat the colonel. Some two or three other were spoke of but it was at last concluded that the only man who could beat him was the present "government", General Jackson. So, a few days before the election was to come on, he was sent for to come and run for the senate. He [Jackson] was then in nomination for the presidency; but sure enough he came, and did run as the opponent of Colonel Williams, and beat him too, but not by my vote. The vote was, for Jackson thirty-five; for Williams, twenty-five. I thought the Colonel had honestly discharged his duty, and even the mighty name of Jackson couldn't make me vote against him.
>
> "But voting against the old chief was found a mighty uphill business to all of them except myself. I never would, nor never did, acknowledge I had voted wrong; and I am more certain now that I was right than ever.
>
> "I told the people that it was the best vote I ever gave; that I had supported the public interest, and cleared my conscience in giving it, instead of gratifying the public ambition of a man. I let the people know as early as then, that I wouldn't take a collar around my neck with the letters engraved on it. MY DOG. Andrew Jackson." [161]

Afterward Jackson wrote to his friend, John Coffee:

> "It will, I have no doubt, astonish to you to hear that I have been elected senator, but I can assure you it has astonished me as much and a circumstance which I regret more than any other in my life, on several accounts, not having anticipated such an event I am unprepared to leave home, and my feelings and wishes all conspired to remain at home, but it was thought expedient by my friends that my name should be brought out. The vote stood 35 for, 25 against me. Every intrigue that could exist, and indeed corruption was resorted to." [162]

It was often said that the general had *never sought* political office. By actively *campaigning* for the Senate seat, American electioneering was changed forever.

Williams, also on the scene at Murfreesboro, made the long journey home to Knoxville a defeated man for the first time in his life. He reported a few days later to his colleague, Senator Rufus King of New York:

## TRANSCRIPT OF A LETTER FROM COL. JOHN WILLIAMS, KNOXVILLE, TENNESSEE, TO SEN. RUFUS KING OF NEW YORK, DATED Nov. 19th, 1823

*"D. Sir,*

*"Your letter of the 4th inst(ant) was this day rec'd. It is dear to my feelings to express the satisfaction derived from the receipt of a letter from one, whom it has become the habit of my life to cherish adoration and respect. To the inquiry of your letter I answer yes. I will not hazard the declaration that this was done by & with the advice and consent of Mr. Monroe.*

*"But the effect as regards me was the same. And there is little doubt he was aided by two of his Secretaries. Gov. Edwards was harboured about Nashville for some time this summer. Some think he was charged with a mission which was unsafe to be committed to paper. He is a fit agency for such an embassy. Mr. Monroe is a great man upon a small sea. I have never entertained unfriendly feelings toward him. He wants magnanimity when passing judgment on the conduct of others. The direct influence of the Palace corps was totally disregarded. But they could & I believe did operate thro' others. From the time of return home in March last I have been buffeting the political tempest which raged with unexampled fury in Tennessee. Candidates for the legislature were set up in every County of the state in opposition to my reelection. Four or five Gentlemen were spoken of as my opponents & each declared to be the opposing candidate in those parts of the state where he was supposed to be most popular. In the mean time county meetings were got up thro' the state nominating Gen'l Jackson for President. On all of these occasions State pride was excited & the public mind inflamed against me as much as possible. I was denounced as a Radical of the worst order, as hostile to Mr. Monroe & his administration &c &c. when the Legislature met it was soon ascertained that out of 60 members 40 were for me against all the declared candidates & about 50 against any one of them. Gen'l Jackson was then brought forward as my opponent. At first it was supposed he could beat me without his appearing on the ground. Finding however that I would out poll him he was sent for & brought on the turf. At sun set the evening before the election I should have beaten him*

---

160 Driver, p. 36
161 Crockett, David, *The Autobiography of David Crockett*, Charles Scribner's Sons, New York, 1923, p. 111
162 Smith, Sam B., *The Papers of Andrew Jackson: 1821-1824*, Jackson to Coffee p. 302

4 or 5 votes. But that night & the next morning I was out maneuvered & defeated by the superior <u>discipline</u> of the enemy. I do not plead as an excuse that I was surprised in any part of the campaign. I knew for weeks in advance & took my position accordingly. But they <u>broke</u> my column & <u>dispersed</u> my troops in despite of every effort to rally them. Nor do I complain of the means used to insure my defeat, they were such as are to be expected in the progress of human affairs. If the fate of the World had been at stake more could not have been done on either side. Being a solitary individual without patronage or power & having nothing to rest on except the partiality of personal friends; the odds were ag't me when I had to contend with the present & next Prest., their cabinets & adherents. I ardently desired success. But I preferred living beaten by the old War horse to any of the cider nags that first run ag't me. Perhaps its all for the best. From the want of <u>facility</u> in my temper I never could get along with those in power. I commenced my career in 1803 & never before was disappointed. I have been treated perhaps better than I desired. It is true I delight in the Society of most of the Senators & many others whom I met in Washington, but I can give up all this without a pang & live at home with my little family. My resources are small but competent for those who have but few wants. I can say without vanity there is a disposition in the state to give me employment. But there is nothing in their gift which is desirable to me. In a review of what has passed I am satisfied with myself. And I retire from the bustle with an approving conscience. The humble part which it has been my lot to take in public affairs had enabled me to form personal friendships which I shall cherish for life. Permit me to number yourself among those for whom I shall ever entertain a sincere esteem.

"Your friend,
John Williams" [163]

Much can be read between the lines of the emotion Williams felt at his first defeat. Seldom can presidential interest be so easily identified in a state election prior to this time. A second letter complained more bitterly of Jackson:

## TRANSCRIPT OF A LETTER FROM Col. John Williams to J.B. Thomas dated November 2, 1823. Knoxville, Tennessee, in the Illinois State Historical Library, Springfield, Illinois

"Dear Thomas;

"During my absence from home of six weeks attending our Legislature your acceptable letter of the 26 Aust. Reached this place. I made my retreat good from Murfreesbo: two weeks after remaining 8 or 10 days on the Politic ground. We have had terrible storms during the summer & fall. I am beaten, but not vanquished. <u>The hearts of the people are with me</u>. If you have ever seen a race where three horses ran in concert against one you may have some idea of the late contest in Murfreesbo: If the fate of the World had been at stake greater efforts could not have been made on either side. Miller & Rhea were the candidates against me until the legislature met. Our Legislature is composed of 60 members. At least 40 of them were for me agt Miller & Rhea both. When this fact was ascertained beyond doubt, Genl. Jackson was started & his friends Miller & Rhea withdrew. My enemies expected to beat me with Jackson & let him stay at home. But in this they were deceived & they dispatched a messenger for him & brought him in great haste on the ground. On the day before the election I should have out polled him. But the night preceding the election they out maneuvered me & I was beaten by the superior <u>disciple of the enemy</u>. I was not surprised in any part of the campaign, My credits informed me of all that was passing. But I was finally overpowered by their superior disciple. Many people in this state are silly enough to believe that Jackson is to be our next Prest. Being an humble individual & possessing neither patronage nor power & having nothing to rest on except the _____ of personal friends the odds were agt me when I had to contend against the <u>President & next Presidents</u>, their cabinets, etc. etc. I have no proof that the weight of Monroe, Adams & Calhoun was exerted against me but I believe the fact to be so. Even the State of Illinois was medling agt. Me. Gov: Edwards made his head quarters at Nashville & visited Genl. Jackson some time before the Legislature met. Whether he was charged with a mission that could not be entrusted to the mail I cannot say. Judge Phillips of the same state was at Murfreesbo: and violently agt. me. This is the first time I was ever defeated in any thing I set about seriously. I am not mortified. And would not at this moment exchange conditions with some of those who think they have gained a victory over me. The avowed object of the General's friends of sending him to Congress was to place him on a footing with the other candidates for the Presidency. And to afford him an opportunity of testing his civil qualifications for that office. As he is going there to make a figure in the political world it would be proper to make him Chairman of the military committee of the Senate. And I hope my friends will unite with the generals & place him at the head of that comtee: No doubt resolutions will be offered directing the comtee: to report a bill to reduce the staff of the army. To abolish the office of Adj. Genl & dispence with the office of Colo. Of the 2nd Regt. Of Artillery. This will bring him into discussion. If the wheel of fortune should not make a turn in my favour I am content to live at home. I shall expect to hear from my old friends at Washington this winter. Present my respects to Mrs. Thomas & Miss Rebekah.

"Yours sincerely
John Williams" "Honb J.B. Thomas" [164]

---

[163] Williams to King, Nov. 19, 1823
[164] Williams to Thomas, Nov. 7, 1823

Colonel Williams was beaten by the man he had rescued from starvation in northern Alabama. He must have felt very badly, but his knowledge of the political prospects was still current. He had many friends in both houses of Congress, and he projected forward to the presidential election only months away by stating in another letter about Jackson, "He is with all his *fury* decidedly the most cunning man I have ever encountered. I speak from experience as you all will before the contest is over in the H. of Repr." [165]

Jackson's political star had been rising since New Orleans, but still some opposed him and considered his rise to contending for national office surprising. Thomas Jefferson was said to have stated in 1824:

"I feel much alarmed at the prospect of seeing General Jackson President. He is one of the most unfit men I know of for such a place. He has very little respect for law or constitutions, and is, in fact an able military chief. His passions are terrible. When I was president of the senate, he was a senator, and he could never speak on account of the rashness of his feelings. I have seen him attempt it repeatedly, and as often choke with rage. His passions are, no doubt, cooler now; he has been much tried since I knew him, but he is a dangerous man." [165]

Williams was but one of many superlative men who fell victim to Andrew Jackson's rise to fame. The temperament of the country was simply ripe for such change.

Jackson's victory at New Orleans led to previously unprecedented adulation that was manipulated by his political handlers. The biography that had been completed immediately after Horseshoe Bend was proof that these friends of Jackson knew both what they were doing and where they were headed. It was perhaps the first public relations campaign ever waged for the presidency.

Given the public's lack of education, its immaturity as a nation, and the euphoria of defeating their former masters for a second time, the effect on the minds of the people was narcotic in nature. J. T. Mangrum of Oxford, North Carolina, wrote to his kinsman, W. P. Mangrum, a US representative in Washington, the following assessment of the political feelings from his home on April 19, 1824:

"I think I may safely inform you of a fact, which you will dislike to hear & be inclined to disbelieve, that exhibits the character of our people in a very unfavorable point of view. The fact is, that Genl. Jackson will in my opinion get the vote of this State.

"I think so, because the people are fascinated and influenced by the splendor of his military fame alone! It is not that they think of or care about his being an able statesman that they will vote for him— consideration of this sort never enters into their minds. They claim he has done much for his country, he has slain the Judiciary & flogged the British & spilled his blood in defense of his country's rights. Therefore, he is the bravest, wisest, & greatest man in the nation —even the memory of Washington is lost in the blaze of the Genl's glory & in the glare of his bloody laurels."

In spite of his expressed magnanimity, Williams did not give up. His family still held much political power and there is some evidence they tried to participate in Jackson's defeat in the House of Representatives in 1824. John Williams' older brother, Lewis, was a long-time member of the House. In a letter to North Carolina Congressman W. P. Mangrum, Lewis wrote:

"On the road and since my arrival here (N.C.) I have had much talk about the Presidential election. From all I can hear there can be no doubt that Crawford will get the vote of this State. But in politics as in war the enemy should not be despised—on the contrary the action should be planned as if the most formidable opposition was to be expected, and I trust all of us will do our duty." [168]

On November 25, 1824, John Williams wrote to Martin Van Buren, "he [Jackson] is with all his fury decidedly the most cunning man I have ever encountered. I speak from experience as you will before the contest is over in the House of Representatives! Altho I fell early in the action, I feel a deep solicitude as to the result."

Williams concludes the letter with a request to Van Buren that he write him through his brother, Lewis Williams, a senior member of the House. This suggests that his mail was being watched and concludes with the accolade, "The devoted Jews never groaned under a more merciless despot than is practiced toward me." [169]

- - - ! ! !

---

165 *Knoxville Register,* Oct. 19, 1823; Williams to Van Buren (then a Congressman); Nov. 25, 1824, Van Buren Papers, IV
166 Bassett, p. 329
167 Rep. Lewis Williams to Rep. Mangrum
168 Williams to Mangrum
169 Williams to Van Buren, November 25, 1824

In 1824, President James Monroe invited Marie-Joseph Paul Yves Roche Gilbert du Motier, Marquis de Lafayette, to the United States as the "nation's guest"; during the trip, he would visit all of the then twenty-four states. For his contributions to the American Revolution, many cities and monuments throughout the United States bear his name (Fayetteville was the only one of those he actually visited in person), and he was the first person granted honorary United States citizenship. [170]

An interesting description of Lafayette's visit in Alabama to the Indians follows:

*"Wheeling, Winn Parish, La.*
*July 8, 1858*

*"J.J. Hooper, Esq.:*

*Dear Sir: The entry of Gen. LaFayette into Alabama, was the most imposing show I witnessed while I lived in the State. In 1824, I think it was, LaFayette was looked for in Alabama. I was the first and oldest Brigadier General in Alabama, (after it became a State.) Gen. Wm Taylor, I think, was the oldest major General; and Israel Pickens was Governor. There may have been his equal, but there never has been his superior in that office since Alabama became a State. At the time LaFayette was expected, Gen. Taylor was absent, I think, in Mobile. The Indians were a little soured, from a treaty that had been, or was about being made with the Georgians. Gov. Pickens requested me to take an escort and conduct LaFayette through the nation. The Hon. James Abercrombie then commanded the Montgomery Troop, and Gen. Moore of Claiborne, commanded the Monroe Troop, both of whom volunteered their services. Before the escort left Alabama, (which then extended only to Line Creek,) Gen. Taylor arrived and took the command.*

*"That was before the day of platforms and conventions—men lived on their own money. You must guess then there was some patriotic feeling along, for there were between two and three hundred persons, all bearing their own expenses. Some in going and coming had to travel four hundred miles, and none less than two hundred miles. Besides the military, there were a number of the most respectable citizens of Alabama—among whom were Boling Hall, ex-member of Congress, ex-Governor Murphy, John D. Bibb, John W. Freeman and Col. James Johnston, one of the best men that ever lived or died. If there are any such men these days, I have not had the pleasure of their acquaintance. Our trip to the Chattahoochee was pleasant indeed. We made our head-quarters three miles from Fort Mitchell, on big Uchee Creek, at Haynes Crabtree's. Had that been a war, and if it had continued till the present day, all of that crowd that's now living would be soldiers. After some three or four days stay at Crabtrees, we learned that Gen. LaFayette had passed White Water, and we knew at what time he would reach the river. The Indians seemed to take as much interest in the matter as the whites. All hands mustered on the west or Alabama side, where we could see the Georgia escort approach the east bank of the Chattahoochee, with their charge. On the east bank, Gen. LaFayette was met by Chilly MacIntosh, with fifty Indian warriors, who were stripped naked and finely painted. They had a sulky prepared with drag-ropes, such as are commonly used in drawing cannon. The General was turned over by the Georgians to the Indians. That was the greatest show I ever saw at the crossing of any river. It beat all of Gen. Jessup's wind bridges across the Tallapoosa, and other places where there was never much more water than would swim a dog, only at a high rise. As the ferry-boat reached the Alabama side, the Indians, in two lines, seized the ropes, and the General seated in the sulky, was drawn to the top of the bank, some eighty yards, where stood the Alabama Delegation. At the proper distance from the Alabama Delegation, the Indians opened their lines, and the sulky halted.*

*"Everything, from the time the General entered the ferry, till this time, had been conducted in the most profound silence. As the Sulky halted, the Indians gave three loud whoops. The General then alighted, took off his hat, and was conducted by Chilly MacIntosh, a few steps, to where Mr. Hall, with head uncovered, white with the frosts of age. I knew Mr. Hall from my boyhood. He always showed well in company; but never did I see him so finely as on that occasion—he looked like himself—what he really was—an American gentleman. As McIntosh approached Mr. Hall, he said, "Gen. LaFayette, the American friend"—"Mr. Hall, of Alabama," pointing to each as he called his name. Mr. Hall, in a very impressive manner, welcomed LaFayette to the shores of Alabama, and introduced him to the other gentlemen. Dandridge Bibb then addressed the General at some length. I heard a number of persons address LaFayette on his route through Alabama—none surpassed Dandridge Bibb, and none equalled him, unless it was Hitchcock and Dr. Hustis at Cahaba. I have always been looked upon as rather dry-faced; but gazing on the face of the most distinguished patriot that it had ever fallen to my lot to look upon, and the feeling remarks of Mr. Bibb on that occasion, caused me, as it did most others that were present, to shed tears like so many children.*

*"After the address at the river, all marched to Fort Mitchell hill, where there was an immense crowd of Indians, the Little Prince at their head. He addressed the "French Captain," through Hamley, in true Indian style. I could understand much of his speech, but cannot begin to give it as Hamley could. The Prince said that he had often heard of the French Captain, "but now I see him, I take him by the hand, I know from what I*

---

170 https://en.wikipedia.org/wiki/Gilbert_du_Motier,_Marquis_de_Lafayette

see, he is the true one I have heard spoken of; I am not deceived—too many men have come a long way to meet him. He is bound to be the very man the Americans were looking for." The Prince, after satisfying the General that he (the Prince) was satisfied that the General was the true man spoken of and looked for, then went on to say, that he had once warred against the Americans, and that the French Captain had warred for them, and of course they had once been enemies; that he (the Prince) was getting old, which his withered limbs would show—making bare his arms at the same time—that he could not live long; but he was glad to say, that his people and the whites were at peace and he hoped they would continue so.

"But he had raised a set of young warriors, that he thought would prove worthy of their sires, if there should ever be a call to show themselves men; and that as a ball play was, outside of war, the most manly exercise that the Red Man could perform, he would, for the gratification of the General and his friends, make his young men play a game. The old man then turned to his people, and said to them—they were in the presence of a great man and warrior; he had commanded armies on both sides of the Big Water; that he had seen many nations of people; that he had visited the Six Nations, in Red Jacket's time, (the General told the Indians he had visited the Six Nations,) that every man must do his best—show himself a man, and should one get hurt he must retire without complaining, and by no means show anything like ill humor. The speech ended, about two hundred stripped to the buff, paired themselves off and went at it. It was a ball play sure enough, and I would travel farther to see such a show than I would to see any other performed by man, and willingly pay high for it, at that. The play ended and all hands went out to head quarters at Big Uchee, where we were kindly treated by our old friend Haynes Crabtree.

"There was a man, then living among the Indians, Capt. Tom Anthony, who long since found a last resting place in the wilds of Arkansas. He was a man of fine sense and great humor. There was also an Indian known as whiskey John. John was the greatest drunkard I ever saw; he would drink a quart of strong whiskey without taking the vessel that contained it from his lips, (this is Alabama history, and there are plenty now living that have seen him do it.) To see John drink was enough to have made the fabled Bacchus look out for a vacancy that frequently occurs among the Sons of Temperance. Capt. Anthony told John that all hands had addressed the French Chief, and that it was his duty to say something on behalf of those that loved whiskey. John could speak considerable English in a broken manner. It so happened that the General and others were walking across the Uchee Bridge when John met them. John made a low bow, as he had seen others do. The General immediately pulled off his hat, thinking he had met with another Chief. John straightened himself up to his full height, (and he was not very low,) and commenced his speech in the manner that I will try to give it to you. "My friend, you French Chief! Me Whiskey John," (calling over the names of several white persons and Indians;) "Col. Hawkins, Col. Crowell, Tom Crowell, Henry Crowell, Billy McIntosh, Big Warrior Indian, heap my friends, give me whiskey, drink, am good. White man and my very good friend me, white man make whiskey, drink him heap, very good, I drink whiskey. You French Chief. Tom Anthony say me big Whiskey Chief. You give me one bottle full. I drink him good." The General informed John that he did not drink whiskey, but would have his bottle filled. John remarked, "Tom Anthony you very good man, me you give bottle full. You no drink, me drink him all, chaw tobacco little bit, give me some you." Now the above is an Indian speech, and no doubt will appear silly to some who have not been accustomed to those people. Should it, however, fall under the eye of those who were along at the time, they will recognize John's speech, and call to mind our old friends, Capt. Anthony and Col. James Johnson, who was the life of our crowd.

"We remained that night at Crabtree's and the next day reached Fort Bainbridge, where an Indian country-man lived, by the name of Kendall Lewis, as perfect a gentleman, in principle, as ever lived in or out of the nation, and had plenty, and it in fine style. The next day we started for Line Creek.

"It fell to my lot to point out many Indians, as well as places, for we were stopped at almost every settlement to shake hands, and hear Indian speeches. Among many things and places that were pointed out to the General was the place where Lot was killed, the old "lettered Beech." At Persimmon swamp, the old Council Oak, Floyd's battle ground, the grave of James McGirth, the place where McGirth made peach brandy, many years before, and many other things. That night we reached Walter B. Lucas'. Everything was "done up" better than it ever will be again; one thing only was lacking—time—we could not stay long enough. The next morning we started for Montgomery. Such a cavalcade never traveled that road before or since.

"On Goat Hill [171] near where Capt. John Carr fell in the well, stood Gov. Pickens, and the largest crowd I ever saw in Montgomery. Some hundred yards east of the Hill, was sand flat, where Gen. LaFayette and his attendants quit carriages and horses, formed a line and marched to the top of the hill. As we started, the band struck up the old Scottish air, "Hail to the Chief." As we approached the Governor, Mr. Hill introduced the General to him. The governor tried to welcome him, but,

---

[171] Woodward, T. S., p. 71

*like the best man the books give account of, when it was announced that he was the commander of the whole American forces, he was scarcely able to utter a word. So it was with Gov. Pickens. As I remarked before, Gov. P had no superior in the State, but on that occasion he could not even make a speech. But that did not prevent Gen. Lafayette from discovering that he was a great man; it only goes to prove what is often said, that many who feel most can say least, and many who have no feeling say too much.*

*"The people of Montgomery did their duty. Col. Arthur Hayne, who was a distinguished officer in the army in the war of 1813, and who was the politest gentleman I ever saw, was the principal manager. If the Earl of Chesterfield had happened there he would have felt as I did the first time I saw a fine carpet on a floor and was asked to walk in; I declined saying, "I reckon I have got in the wrong place." Several steamboats were in waiting at the wharf, and the next morning all hands went aboard and started for Cahaba, at the time the seat of government.*

*"At Cahaba, as in Montgomery, everything was "done up" as it should be. There the General met with Major Porter, whom he had known in the Revolution. There I shed more tears. The General examined the old ditch that had been cut by his countrymen many years before. An old cannon was shown him also, which was left by the French Army, when they quit the country. He remarked that those relics caused sad feelings, that there was still a pleasure, a kind of melancholy pleasure, which he could not describe.*

*"About this time a gentleman was wounded from the firing a canon on a trading boat. The General visited the wounded man, and took much interest in his welfare; he was told that the gentleman had many friends who would care for him; I told him that he was an old camp mate of mine; he replied, "one good soldier will always take care of another." I remained in Cahaba until the General embarked on board a steamboat for Mobile; I accompanied him on board, and on bidding him farewell, said, "I have done what little I could to make your journey to this place as pleasant as possible, and I now have to leave you." He took me by the hand and said, "I thank you kindly; may God bless and prosper the young State you live it; I shall always cherish the kindest feelings for you and the other gentlemen that escorted me through the nation, as well as all others who have taken so much trouble to make me welcome among you." The last words I heard him utter were, "Farewell, my friend! Take care of that wounded man."*

*Yours,
T. S. W."* [172]

General Lafayette was said to have calmed the situation resulting from the election of 1824, and he returned to France in September 1825. Lafayette died on May 20, 1834, and is buried in Picpus Cemetery in Paris, under soil from Revolutionary War battlefield Bunker Hill. [173]

*Williams Family Crest owned by Alex F. Brandau III*

172 Woodward, T. S., pp. 66-73
173 http://en.wikipedia.org/wiki/Gilbert_du_Motier,_marquis_de_Lafayette

*Williams House*
Photo by Bill Ferguson, 2018

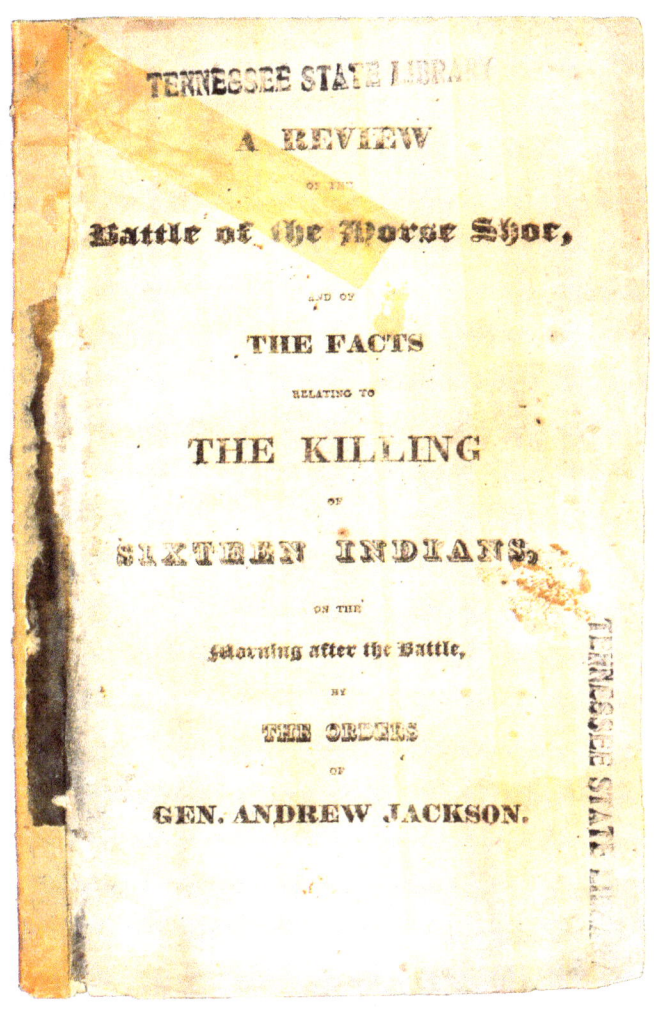

*Horseshoe Bend Pamphlet written mostly by Col. John Williams*
Tennessee State Library and Archives

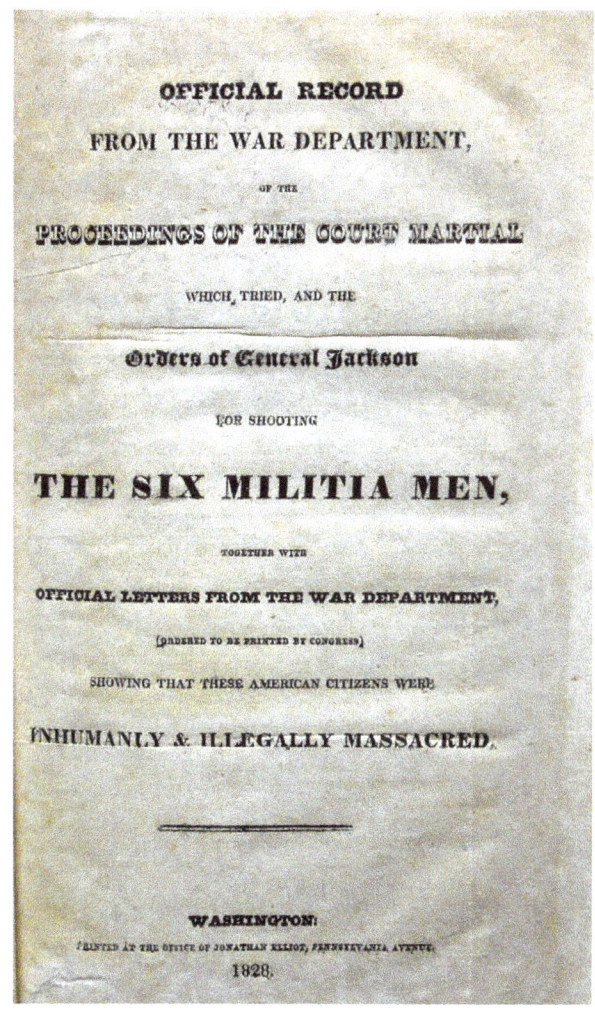

*Election campaign literature partially written by Col. John Williams 1824*
Tennessee State Library and Archives

*Artist Depiction of Weatherfold Surrender*
Public Domain

*Artist Depiction of Major General Jackson*
Sold at Fort Jackson, AL

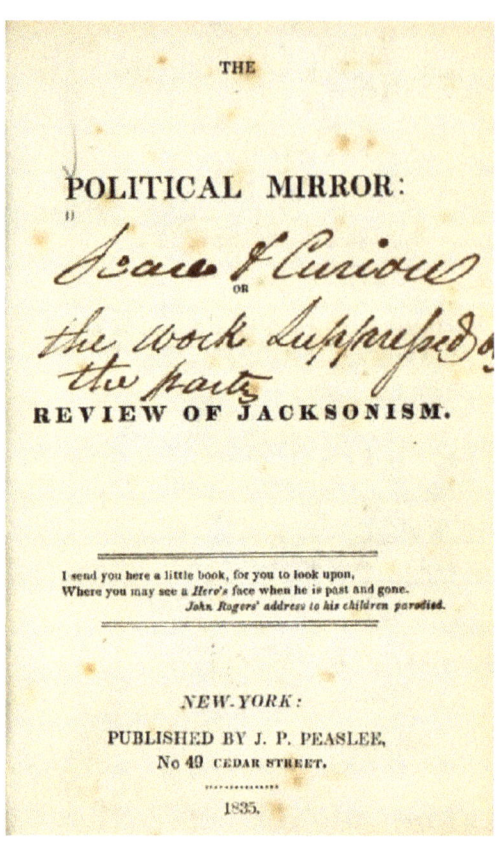

*Title page of Political Mirror with Library of Congress attendant handwritten: Curious & Suppressed By The Party proving Col Williams was written out of history*

*Chief John Ross of the Cherokee*
Public Domain

*(litho), American School, (19th century) / Private Collection / Peter Newark American Pictures / Bridgeman*

*https://www.bridgemanimages.com/fr/asset/256368/american-school-19th-century/jackson-is-to-be-president-and-you-will-be-hanged-litho*

*Brandau Family during WWII: Dorothy, Buddy, Alex Jr. and Dottie*
personal property, Alex F Brandau III

*Azaleas at Sneed Vault*
personal property Alex F Brandau III

*John Williams House 1920s*
Personal property Alex Brandau III

*TSD black school history 2013*
Personal property Alex Brandau III

# Chapter 8
# The Election of 1824, Guatemala Mission, and a New House

Having lost his Senate seat to Jackson, John Williams resorted to what he did best—he wrote. Many campaign documents against Jackson were his words. It appears he, his kin, and his friends had anticipated what had happened in the election of 1824. How did they know it would end there?

Given some intrigue, it is possible that Williams was dispatched to Central America, thus preventing him from being questioned about the perceived "corrupt bargain." Williams would return home in 1826 with disparaging prospects—no job, a new son, and a new house. Said house would later be purchased by the State of Tennessee; it was bought in disrepair and was restored in 2008 by John and Melinda Williams' descendants.

John Williams retired from public life to his law office and continued to use his unique talents to write politically oriented material. He chose anonymity so as not to provoke Jackson, but Jackson knew his style.

There is no evidence that John Williams was active in the presidential election of 1824, but, being only a year removed from the Senate, and with family members still in Congress, it is possible that he was. The candidates were John Quincy Adams, Andrew Jackson, Henry Clay, and William H. Crawford. Ex-Senator John Williams had known the cabinet members of both Monroe and Madison; he was a known Crawford man.

Beginning his career in 1803, the same as John Williams had, William H. Crawford was elected to the Georgia House of Representatives, and by 1807 he was in the 10th United States Congress midterm as a US senator from Georgia. He rose to power quickly and was elected president pro tempore of the Senate in 1811. When Vice President George Clinton died in April 1812, Crawford became "acting vice president" until March 4, 1813. President James Madison then appointed Crawford as the US minister to France; Crawford held that ministerial post until shortly after the end of the War of 1812. Upon Crawford's return, President Madison appointed him to his cabinet as Secretary of War. A year later, Crawford moved jobs to become Secretary of the Treasury. He remained in that position through the rest of Madison's term and Monroe's administration for a total of nine years. He was an acknowledged leader inside Washington and aspired to become president. By fulfilling cabinet posts in previous administrations, he had followed the "proper" career path toward accomplishing that goal. Crawford was a leading candidate, but a massive stroke in 1823 ended his chances. That stroke was kept from the public knowledge for a long time. [174]

Henry Clay Sr. was a leading American politician who represented Kentucky in both the House and Senate. He served as secretary of state from 1825 to 1829, and was influential in the federal government. He was known as "The Great Compromiser" for his ability to bring others to agreement; he was the founder and leader of the Whig Party and advocated programs for expanding the economy, tariffs to protect fledgling American industry, a national bank, and internal improvements to promote canals, ports, and railroads. He was a war hawk and,

[174] http://en.wikipedia.org/wiki/William_H_Crawford

according to historian Clement Eaton, was "more than any other individual" responsible for the War of 1812.

Though his multiple attempts to become president were unsuccessful, he was a major supporter of the American System, and had success in brokering compromises on the slavery issue, especially in 1820 and 1850. He was part of the "Great Triumvirate" or "Immortal Trio," along with his colleagues Daniel Webster and John C. Calhoun. In 1957, a Senate committee chaired by John F. Kennedy named Clay as one of the five greatest senators in US history. In his early involvement in Illinois politics, and as a fellow Kentucky native, Abraham Lincoln was a great admirer of Clay. [175]

Ex-Senator John Williams knew Senator Henry Clay as a colleague in the Senate; he also was a known relative of John's wife, Melinda White Williams.

John Quincy Adams (1767-1848) served in both the Senate and House of Representatives. He was a member of the Federalist, Democratic-Republican, National Republican, and later Anti-Masonic and Whig parties. Adams was the son of the second president, John Adams, and his wife, Abigail Adams; the name "Quincy" came from Abigail's maternal grandfather, Colonel John Quincy, after whom Quincy, Massachusetts, is also named. He was a diplomat and served as secretary of state for James Monroe, helping to formulate the Monroe Doctrine.

Late in his life, Adams was elected a US representative from Massachusetts after leaving office, the only former president ever to do so, and served for the last seventeen years of his life. In the House, he became a leading opponent of the Slave Power and argued that, if a civil war ever broke out, the president could abolish slavery by using his war powers, which Abraham Lincoln partially did during the American Civil War in the 1863 Emancipation Proclamation. [176]

Ex-Senator John Williams would have known the founding father and former president, John Adams' son, John Quincy Adams, as a learned colleague. Their great-grandchildren married. Gideon Hazen Williams, son of James Chamberlain "JCJ" Jones and Ann Strong Hazen, married Marguerite Johnstone Adams on April 3, 1914. She was the great-granddaughter of John Quincy Adams. [177]

Andrew Jackson (March 15, 1767-June 8, 1845) rose to command and public fame after the Battle of Horseshoe Bend. His victory over the British at the Battle of New Orleans (1815) put the United States upon a new path of democracy and political agenda. He is the only American president for whom an age is named.

A polarizing figure who dominated American politics in the 1820s and 1830s, his political ambition combined with widening political participation, shaping the modern Democratic Party. His legacy is now seen as mixed, as a protector of popular democracy and individual liberty, checkered by his support for Indian removal and slavery.

As he based his career in the developing state of Tennessee, Jackson was the first president from the American frontier.

- - - ! ! !

In the midst of the campaign of 1824, John and Melinda Williams birthed another daughter in November: Susan, who married John Leese Moses and lived to the ripe old age of fifty-two (dying in 1877). Her descendants inherited the portrait of Colonel John Williams, and they were famous for being early proponents of and officials at the Tennessee School for the Deaf.

Ex-Senator John Williams allowed his name to be put forth for the state legislature in 1825, but he did not campaign for the office and lost to Colonel James Anderson, 982 to 931. [178] Colonel Anderson, while serving the previous term, did not cast a vote in the crucial decision about where to place the state capitol. He stated he had kin in both Nashville and Murfreesboro, and, living in Knoxville, did not wish to choose between them. Knoxville lost to Nashville, and Colonel Williams claimed that Anderson's abstaining cost Knoxville the vote.

In February 1825, John Quincy Adams was elected president by the Electoral College and was sworn in as the sixth president of the United States on March 4. Lack of modern telecommunications prevented voters from actually seeing and judging candidates. The familiar moniker, "Old Hickory," and the legend he became, flourished as a grassroots movement. Indeed, Jackson won the popular vote, but was defeated in the House of Representatives.

In a distributed circular dated July 20, 1826, in the Mangrum papers, Chandler Price, a Jackson supporter, offered the Jackson camp's view of what happened:

---

175 http://en.wikipedia.org/wiki/Henry_Clay
176 http://en.wikipedia.org/wiki/John_Quincy_Adams
177 Williams, Lewis James, Joseph Lanier, Rebecca Turner, and Lewis Lanier, Williams: *300 Years of Leadership in America*, Panther Creek Publishing, Lewisville, N.C., 1997, p. 68
178 Knoxville Register, Aug. 5, 1825

"It will be remembered that in the House of Representatives, the Presidential election is conducted by states—that General Jackson though far ahead of his competitors on the returns of the electoral ballots, there received but eight votes: that the Representatives of Kentucky gave their state vote to Mr. Adams, in favor of whom not a single man of their constituents had, by suffrage, declared himself: that the Representatives of Illinois, unmindful of a public pledge, acted in the same manner; that the Representative from Missouri followed in this wake, even after the repeated and protracted struggles of a conscious sense of duty: and that Louisiana, whose soil had been redeemed, and whose matrons had been shielded by the translucent heroism of Jackson from the barbarous pursuit of "beauty and booty," abused by two of her representatives, turned upon her server, and against the will of her citizens, pierced him with the fang of unparalleled ingratitude." [179]

Given the bold language voiced by the Monroe Doctrine protecting the Western Hemisphere, it was important that the emerging countries and former colonies now being founded by Simón Bolivar be addressed and evaluated. Williams became our first diplomat to serve in Central America. President Adams wanted John Williams as Secretary of War, but was persuaded to select someone from New York as a political favor. [180] New President Adams then appointed Colonel Williams chargé d'affairs to Guatemala; he became our first diplomat to reach the emerging countries of Central America.

A trip of that distance was perilous in those times. On March 23, Colonel Williams sailed for Guatemala from Hampton Roads, Virginia, aboard the ship John Adams. He arrived at Amoa on April 17 and Isabal on the 21st, and he began an overland trek toward Guatemala City by mule on the 23rd.

From Guatemala, Colonel Williams wrote several letters to friends and relatives late in the year that are all quite similar:

## TRANSCRIPT OF A LETTER FROM COLONEL JOHN WILLIAMS TO JEREMIAH MASON

"May 20th, 1826, Guatemala

"Mason,

"*I sailed on the ship John Adams from Hampton roads on the 23rd of last March. And that evening met the equinoxial gale off the capes of Va which continued for five or six days. This was my first excursion to sea. Altho a storm at sea has some terrors it has been greatly overrated by mariners. We touched at Matouzas on the 3rd of April at Havana on the 7th sailed from the latter place on the 11th doubled Cape Antonio on the 12th. On the 15th touched at Trusello on the continent & for a ____ & on the 17th anchored in the harbour of Amoa my port of destination. On the 19th dispatched the ship John Adams. On the 20th sailed in a small schooner I chartered & on the 21st landed at Isabal at the bottom of the gulph of Dulce which is connected with the bay of Honduras by a natural canal very deep & in some places not 300 feet wide. With perpendicular banks more than 200 feet high. I remained at Amoa as short a time as possible. It is a perfect graveyard & for unhealthiness is only equaled by Vera Cruz, Porto Ballo, and Acapulco. From Amoa to Isabal is 150 miles. On the 23rd I left Isabal mounted on a mule & on the 2nd of May arrived in this city distance from Amoa 210 miles. You will think this was slow traveling. But I assure you we set out nearly every morning at 2 or 3 o'clock & performed the journey in about half the time usually taken. The country is an alternation of very high mountains mostly without timber & rich valleys. The journey for seven days was thro' an especially hot climate. The air was like the atmosphere of an oven. There had been no rain since last December & water was scarce. The clouds of dust want of water, and the vertical rays of a blazing Sun rendered traveling disagreeable. An English gentleman who is here informs me he has traveled much thro' the East & West Indies & in S. America & he has never seen so bad a road as that from Isabal to Guatemala. This city is situated in latitude 14 No. in a rich valley & in a most delicious climate. The elevation is 5000 feet above the ocean. The inhabitants scarcely know any change of temperature during the year. The weather reminds me of one of our sweetest May days in Tennessee. It is comfortable to wear either winter or summer clothing. When the thermometer stands at 80 the freshness & elasticity of the breese is delicious. Within 20 leagues of this place there is every climate. In view & distant about 6 leagues is the great volcano called here the Volcan de Aqua which demolished old Guatemala estimated at 14 or 15,000 feet high, from which this city is supplied with ice. In a few leagues from thence is the climate of the coast of Africa. Hence is to be seen in this market the productions of all climates. If the statements of the people can be confided in there are inexhaustible mines of the precious metals in many parts of the country. No country in the world needs industry & enterprise more than this. The population of this city is variously stated at from 40 to 60:000. The houses are all one story high (except the churches) with thick walls to resist the earthquakes, plastered inside & out with lime & covered with tile. The gardens are ornamented with orange &*

---

[179] Price to Mangrum, Jul;y 20, 1826
[180] Heiskell, p. 191

*lemon trees. And each yard has a bath & fountain of pure water. The streets are 36 feet wide, paved with lime stone, with a small _____ running in the centre of each street. The public square is rectangular 450 feet. One side of the square is filled up with the Cathedral & its appurtenances. On the other three sides are public edifices. In the center of the square there is a fountain or reservoir containing many thousand gallons of water. There are perhaps 40 churches & from 4 to 500 Priests of the different orders. Most of the churches are magnificent buildings. Some of them it's said cost more than two millions of dollars & few less than 50:000$. What a pitty that some of this money was not applied to making a road to the east. Here as everywhere the women go more to church than the men. The Priests have absolute control over the religion & cash too of the people. The operation of the new Government will in the progress of time in a great degree correct this evil. On the news of my arrival at Amoa reaching the _____ by express the Government commenced preparations for my reception which were not completed until day before yesterday when I was presented officially to the President & the other authorities of the country. In order to conform to the custom here I had to make a diplomatic speech. I presume some account of this will be published in the Gazette. Colo. Beneske has succeeded as agent of the New Company in contracting for the canal between the No. & So. Seas. He had many difficulties to encounter but has overcome them all. The ship passage will be thro' the lake Nicaragua. The excavation will be only five leagues over low ground into the Pacific from the lake. There are 3 or 4 bars in the river St. Johns to deepen. This done a frigate can pass from one ocean to the other. The lake is connected to the Atlantic by the river St. Johns. A 74 ship can now pass this river except at these few bars. The lake is 80 leagues long & 25 or 30 wide is fed by nearly two hundred streams besides lake _____ & is of great depth. The water to be used in the canal can never be missed. The English were very desirous to get the making of this canal. Their agent is still here. This matter has terminated very advantageously for the navigation of the United States. Our country is first in the affections of these people. I have only room on this sheet to request that you will remember me to Mrs. Mason & to subscribe myself as heretofore your friend.*

*John Williams"*

## TRANSCRIPT OF A LETTER FROM COLONEL JOHN WILLIAMS TO WILLIAM DICKSON AND ALEXANDER WILLIAMS

"May 20, 1826, Guatemala

"Mr. Wm Dickson

"Dr. Alex Williams

"On the 23rd of last March I sailed from Hampton roads in the ship John Adams. On the same evening we met the equinoxial gale which continued for five or six days with much violence. This was my first excursion to sea. The terrors of a storm at sea have been greatly overated by mariners. We touched at Mata Matqanzas & Havana on the island of Cuba. At Truxallo on the continent & landed at Amoa my port of destination on the 17th of April. I dispatched the ship John Adams on the 17th for Carthagenia. On the 20th sailed on a small schooner I had chartered thro' the bottom of the bay of Honduras & into the Gulph of Dulce & landed at Isabal on the 21st distant from Amoa 150miles—I remained at Amoa as short a time as possible. It is a perfect graveyard & is fatal to many strangers. On the 23rd I left Isabal mounted on a mule & a Spanish saddle the like of which neither of you has ever seen. And on the 2nd of May arrived in this City distance from Amoa 210 miles. I was detained one day for the want of transportations. You will say this was slow traveling. But I assure you I started nearly every morning at 2 or 3 o'clock & traveled industriously & performed the trip in about half the time usually taken. I never traveled less than 18 nor more than 30 miles per day. I doubt whether there is so bad a road in the world where human creatures pass. There had been but little rain since December. The clouds of dust want of water and the vertical rays of a blazing sun rendered the journey disagreeable. The country thro which I passed is an alternation of high mountains mostly without timber & rich valleys. For seven days it was excessively hot. The air was like the atmosphere of an oven & was difficult of respiration. This City is situated in Latitude 14N in a valley of rich land & in a most delightful climate. The inhabitants scarcely know a change of temperature during the year. The weather reminds me of one of our last May days. There is one continued normal season. Yet the people do not live to a great age. Within twenty leagues there is every climate. In six leagues & in view is the great volcano called the Volcan de agua which destroyed the old city of Guatemala from which this city is supplied with ice. Within a few leagues from there are the shores is the Pacific is to be found the climate of Africa under the Equator. The volcano is estimated at 14 or 15000 feet high. The population of this city is perhaps 50:000. The streets are 36 feet wide well paved with lime stone with a _____ in the center of each street. There are about 40 churches & about 4 or 500 Priests of the different orders. Most of the churches are magnificent buildings. Some of them its said cost *more than two millions of dollars & few of them less than $50:000. The houses are low with thick walls to resist the earthquakes. There is a neatness & uniformity in this city which I have never seen equaled. Rents are moderate. The house I occupy has 10 rooms stables & with two fountains of water & a piazza of 156 feet. I pay for it $25 per month. I was the first minister ever recd at this court. The government made considerable preparations and gave me a splendid reception. General Morales Minister from Columbia arrived a few days after I did. The United states stand first in the affections of their people. Colo Beneske formerly of the French army but now the agent of a New York Company has obtained the contract to make a ship communication between the No & So seas & thro' the lake Nicaragua. There is no doubt of the practicality of this enterprise. The lake is connected to the Atlantic by the river St. John which is not navigable for cargo ships except for a few places where sand bars are formed & which can easily be removed. A canal of 14 miles thro' low clay ground from the lake to the Pacific will complete the communication. The English were extremely anxious to obtain this work. There agents are yet here. Colo Beneske thinks my arrival contributed to his success. It is fortunate for the commerce & navigation of the United States that this channel has not fallen into British hands. The completion of this work will give a new direction to the commerce of the world. And whilst the contract will be highly beneficial to this government it cannot fail to be a source of great profit to the contractors. They are to get ten per cent on the amount _____ & other advantages equal to that sum. I contemplate visiting the United States next winter. If I should I will probably reach Tennessee early in February. Remember me kindly to your two better halfs. Say to Mrs. Dickson some rogue between Isabal & stole the spectacles she gave me. Present my respects also to Mr. John Dickson & his lady. I should like to know how you come on farming. I expect my wife will beat both of you. I have not heard any word from the U States since I left it. I am looking for the arrival of news with great solicitude.*

*"With great respect your Obedient Servant*

*John Williams"*

## "This version to his brother, Alexander, and Alexander's father-in-law.

*"Misters*
*"Dickson & Williams*

*Note: scribbled on the outside: "The canal contract was procrastinated from day to day & from week to week & was not finally executed until this day. Colo Beneske will start for New York in a few days & will take charge of this letter.*

*John Williams*
*June 16, 1826"*

While in Guatemala, John Williams presented himself to the Central American court with his best foot, manners, and posture forward. Simón Bolivar was said to have referred to him as "the elegant gentleman."

Late in his life in 1835, Colonel Williams described the mission thusly:

"41. The object of the Panama Convention, to which Columbia, Central America, and Mexico were originally parties was to deliberate of the great and common interests of several new and neighbouring nations. In such deliberations, the interests of the United States were deeply involved; and, were it, merely, that our government might be, speedily, and correctly, informed of the proceedings of the Congress, and the issue of their negotiations, it was advisable to have an accredited agency with them, in such confidential relation as would ensure the authenticity, and the safe and prompt transmission, of its reports.

"42. The objects of the United States in this conference were: 1. The establishment of some principles of international law, whose unsettled state had been productive of much evil; as the perpetual abolition, among the American states of private war upon the ocean, or at least such modification of the practice as would make the friendly flag protect the cargo: the curtailment of the contraband of war; and the proscription of fictitious paper blockades: 2. To consider of means for the abolition of the slave trade: 3. Of means to defer the European powers from further colonization on the American continent, and from interference in the contest between Spain and her former colonies: 4 To determine in what light the political condition of Hayti should be regarded—a case highly important to the southern portion of our own country: 5. To consider the views of Columbia and Mexico in their proposed invasions of the islands of Cuba and Puerto Rico; an event which might result, ultimately, in putting them in the hands of some European power, other than Spain—to prevent which, the United States were interested by preserving the existing tranquility of the islands, and the peace and security of the inhabitants: 6. To obtain from the nations of the South, a recognition of the principles of religious toleration: 7. To establish general principles of intercourse, applicable to all the American powers, for the mutual regulation of their commerce and navigation, founded on the basis of perfect equality and reciprocity: 8. To consider the means of making a canal through the Isthmus of Panama; a measure of great importance to the commercial world, but more especially to the United States: 9. And lastly, to conciliate the affections of our sister republics, by aiding them, at their earnest request, with such wholesome counsel as our greater experience might suggest.

"43. These views were not peculiar to the administration of Mr. Adams. The only proposition, which by *possibility*, might result in foreign alliance, the prevention of European interference in American affairs, had been profoundly considered by Mr. Monroe, and the commanding position taken by him upon the subject, was sustained by the nation.

"45. The Congress at Panama might not accomplish any of the transcendant benefits anticipated; It was, in its nature, a measure speculative and experimental. Unforseen accidents and mischances might baffle its high purposes, and disappoint its fairest speculations. But its design, the amelioration of the condition of man, was great and benevolent. "It was congenial with that spirit which prompted the Declaration of Independence; inspired the preamble of our first treaty with France; dictated our first treaty with Prussia, and the instructions under which it was negotiated, and filled the hearts and fired the souls of the immoral founders of our Revolution."

"46. Although the mission at Panama would be *diplomatic*, not *legislative*, and indeed *consultative* merely, and acting under the declaration, that the United States would engage in no discussion inconsistent with entire neutrality...." [181]

John Williams returned from Guatemala to Washington in 1826 to find his political patrons becoming increasingly unpopular. Jackson supporters claimed a conspiracy in the election of 1824, and the rising tide of Jackson's legend continued to grow. Williams returned to Knoxville and was met with a celebration and parade by the citizens. As they passed his house, much mirth was made of his quizzical pleas as to why they were not stopping. In his absence, his wife, Melinda, had taken slaves to the riverbank and had kilned the brick from the riverbank clay for a new, two-story, federal-design house two miles from Knoxville out the Dandridge Pike. "John's been gone so long he doesn't even know his own house?" the taunts arose.

- - - ! ! !

When the party arrived amidst much drinking and celebration, Williams found his wife and the results of her efforts—unbeknownst to him, she had also birthed their final son, Charles, and met him at the door of his new two-story brick home. Needing badly to be alone with his wife and to be away from the inebriated mass, he broke up the assembly by riding up to one of the windows and smashing it with his riding crop. The party disassembled quickly.

- - - ! ! !

On July 4th of that year, President Adams' father, John, and former president Thomas Jefferson both died. A grudging admiration for each other may have developed in their later years. Nonetheless, Adams always proclaimed that, though Jefferson was seven years younger than himself, "I will outlive Jefferson."

On his death bed on Independence Day, 1826, John Adams uttered his last words. They were: "Thomas Jefferson survives."

It is rumored that upon Adams' death the messenger dispatched to carry the news to Jefferson's Virginia home actually passed a messenger dispatched from that site to Adams' home, also bearing sad tidings.

Just a few hours earlier Thomas Jefferson had passed away. Both architects of the document that gave birth to this new nation died, fifty years to the day from the birth of the country they founded. [182]

- - - ! ! !

Though he lost the election of 1824, Andrew Jackson was the leading candidate to win in 1828. He resigned the Senate seat (that he had won from John Williams) in 1825, preferring to live at the Hermitage as peacefully as possible. Party managers kept his temper from becoming public knowledge, and though there was much political maneuvering between the national leaders of the day, the election of 1828 was Jackson's by a large majority.

In the remaining years before the election of '28, many friends tried to reconcile the two former military allies. Jackson still demanded an apology from Williams that he would never make and the stalemate continued. At one point shortly before her death in 1828, Williams had formed a mercantile company and, while in Nashville, sold to Rachel Jackson a pair of reading glasses. [183] Where such meeting occurred is unknown, but

---

[181] *The Political Mirror*, pp. 18-21
[182] http://www.homeofheroes.com/profiles/profiles_jeffadams.html
[183] Feller, Daniel, editor, *Papers of Andrew Jackson* at University of Tennessee; Wilmington, DE: Scholarly Resources Incorporated 1987; Williams, John & Company, 1828, p. 524
[184] Jackson to Coffee

apparently Williams thought he might prevail upon her to end Jackson's enmity. She died before the general went off to Washington, and Jackson continued to see Williams and his associates involved in every conspiracy against him, whether they were or were not.

In a letter to his friend John Coffee, Jackson wrote, "I am branded with every crime, and Dr. McNairy, Colonel Erwin, Anderson, and Williams are associated for this purpose." [184]

When Andrew Jackson was inaugurated as seventh president, there was much drunken revelry. Jackson himself did not spend the night in the White House, and it is good he did not, for the celebration there got out of hand quickly. The White House was covered with mud inside, and some inebriated individuals were seen swinging from the chandeliers.

The rule of the aristocrats who had founded the country came to an end. Jackson became the hero, the "common man" who had ascended to the most powerful position in the nation. Andrew Jackson would, in the next eight years, assume more powers for the executive branch of government than had ever been imagined to be possible.

John Williams stayed at home. It was not politically expedient to be his friend, and many of his former senatorial colleagues abandoned him. Some of his known friends lost their jobs because of it. In 1830, Williams wrote to his friend, John Floyd, "I was hurt at the removal of Major Callaway late Marshall of East Tennessee because he was my personal friend. I had withdrawn from public life & it was cruel to punish a man because he had a good opinion of me."

Attempts were made to put Williams into a job of worth, but he twice refused appointment to the Tennessee Supreme Court. To Jackson's vice president, Martin Van Buren, he wrote in 1831,

"Within the last twelve months I have been strongly urged to represent this district in Congress which I could do without a struggle. But I have determined not to go to Washington to be put under the bow of the Emperor." [185]

The political base in Knoxville had changed so drastically that it interfered in the White family itself. With John's political demise, Jackson, at first, cast favor upon Melinda's brother, Hugh Lawson White—the man who had stepped down from his judge's bench to find Jackson starving in the wilds of Creek territory and had set in motion the 39th Infantry's rescue of him. As Hugh Lawson White rose up the political ladder, John Williams opposed him. White complained of his brother-in-law to Jackson, stating "he has taken the stump against me" and "is a mean politician." [186]

John Williams built a small law office in the front side yard of his home and received occasional law clients there. He was shunned by some of the citizens of Knoxville and was ostracized socially by local fear of Jackson and his supporters' reprisals. Williams' brother-in-law, Hugh Lawson White, succeeded him in the Senate upon Jackson's resignation. There was great dissension and emotion within the White family. Bereft of friends, persecuted by Jackson and his associates, he tried to do what he said he would do after his defeat in 1823: "live" with his little family.

Once Andrew Jackson became president, the feud with John Williams was effectively over. Jackson had won! They continued to snipe and complain about each other, but not *to* each other officially. Having ridden the court circuits while young men and conducted many cases together, Jackson and Williams knew each other more closely than most. Certainly, they knew each other's writing and speaking style when they read it, so it was possible for Williams to get his words and thoughts to the president through correspondence and anonymously in the newspapers.

Williams remained in Knoxville and kept his active mind astute by doing occasional legal work for the few who would still work with him. He remained very close to his friend John Ross and gave behind-the-scenes legal advice in the Cherokee's quest to remain on their land. He remained a trustee of the East Tennessee College for a total of over thirty years and wrote several of their merger documents with other educational institutions.

One interesting fact found in the notes of the Trustee meetings was that on several successive meetings, he was asked by the headmaster to write a code of conduct for the students. Apparently, he chose not to do this, for the headmaster himself finally accomplished the task. [187]

John Williams made the transition from statesman and senator on the national stage to father of his family in small-town Knoxville. His and Melinda's children were becoming adults, and life generally slowed down for him. He was surrounded by those whom he loved.

---

184 Jackson to Coffee
185 Williams to Van Buren, March 22, 1831, *Van Buren Papers*, XIII
186 Hugh Lawson White papers 1838-1840
187 Board of Trustee Minutes, University of Tennessee, Knoxville, Hoskins Library, Dept. of Special Collections

Andrew Jackson's fame and popularity reflected the pride of the emerging new nation. Yes, there were scandals, and people attacked him relentlessly, but the old firebrand of temper was gone.

Jackson founded the Democratic Party, visited France, and accomplished many things to make the executive branch of the federal government considerably more powerful.

Jackson was not a magnificent physical specimen. He had long outlived his expected lifetime, and, being thin and tall, he gave a visage of a frail elderly man. How he survived with at least two lead balls in his body for forty years is unknown. Whomever had named him "Old Hickory" was correct. He was tough!

John Williams tried to stay out of the political arena. After some scandal in 1831 regarding the old Florida Inquisition, he wrote that he *"hoped never again to see his name in print."* [188]

But when the nullification question arose in 1833, Williams again wrote to his friend John Floyd:

> "For the last four years I have lost confidence in our political institutions. I have read in history of the downfall of the ancient Republic the ruin of our own. I sounded the (tocsin) of alarm without effect. Many of my best friends would not hearken. They ascribed my opposition to every motive but the true one. I have suffered proscription and persecution little short of the Spanish Inquisition without exciting even the sympathy of my old friends. Thus opposed and abandoned I determined for the remainder of my life to devote myself to my personal concerns. This district would at any election for years past or at the next election have sent me to Congress. But I have declined all public employment. I still, however, feel a deep interest in the welfare of my country without the means of rendering any service. I deplore the present condition of things. My heart sickens at the almost certain prospect of having our once happy land deluged with our kindred blood. My skirts are clear of censure & I thank God for it. I voted for the Tariff of 1816 with the double view of raising revenue & protection. I then & still believe it was constitutional. No one doubted at that time (that I remember) except Mr. Randolph. On most subjects he was considered under hallucination. The seeds, however, sewn by him at that time have taken deep root & now threaten to dissolve the union. I heard Mr. Calhoun's tariff speeches & remember his doctrines. He had attained the years of discretion. He cannot plead infancy & like an infant avoid his ____. He is a man of splendid genius but without judgment. He has not sufficient ballast to steer the ship of State. His vaulting ambition is his great vice. His late made physical disquisitions in relations to our government will not do. He is caught in the snare set for him. I wrote you immediately after Calhoun's association with Jackson that his fate was sealed. I told Colo. Semkens the same thing at Greenville two years ago. I entertain a personal regard for Calhoun altho he, Mr. Monroe, Gov. Edwards and others conspired against me in 1823. My offense was that I acted honestly in relation to the reduction of the army in 1822. The conduct of S. Carolina cannot be justified on any principle consistent with the theory of our Govt. The suppression of insubordination in that quarter will add to the power of Jackson already too great & is therefore to be deplored. For myself I will say that I will not shed the blood of S. Carolina for nullification & sustain a more odious nullification in Georgia. The former are under a delusion & have my sympathy whilst the latter are animated by sordid averice & a wish to assess the Helpless & unprotected Indians. The conduct of Georgia is sufficient to incite the wrath of Heaven on our country. If our land should be visited with "War, Pestilence, & Famine" it will be nothing more than a just Dispensation of Providence for our national crimes. The attitude of So. Caro: is unfortunate for the country & more so for the prominent men concerned. They will not be sustained by the American people. If it does not terminate in an explosion of the Union & despotism it will end like the Pena. Insurrection in '94 or the Hartford Convention in 1814. In the cumming storm may Heaven protect you & yours is the sensere wish of your steadfast friend.
>
> John Williams

"Gov: Floyd

"Do not publish my letter which you say is Prophetic, I wish never again to see my name in the news paper. The little Judge is married!!!!! I entertain a hope she will improve his manners & learn him to conduct more like a gentleman than he has done for some years past." [189]

---

[188] Williams to John Floyd 1833
[189] Williams to Floyd, Jan. 5, 1833

Said "judge" relates to Nashville judge, Jackson confidant, and brother-in-law John Overton through their wives. Their correspondences stopped in 1817. He was of small stature, was long unmarried, and capable of bachelor behavior with his friends. Mary McConnel White Overton exuded a profound influence in the Overton family that lasted for many generations.

John Williams continued his friendship with Martin Van Buren, ex-senatorial colleague and Jackson's vice president in 1832. Van Buren has been described as "everybody's friend," but Williams suggested their letters be sent "under cover" through Gov. Dickerson of North Carolina. It is possible that Williams wrote said letters knowing that the content would be given to President Jackson. Given that perspective, he wrote:

**Transcription of Williams to Van Buren, March 22, 1831:**

"Knoxville, March 22nd, 1831

"Dear Sir;

"Mr. Calhoun's pamphlet is all the absorbing subject of conversation in this part of the country. The pamphlet and contents of the Telegraph newspaper have made a strong impression on the public mind in favor of the _____ Prest. Great pains have been taken to give an intensive circulation to Duff's paper & his influence at once cannot be extinguished. When in the Senate I voted against Duff's nomination to a land office in Missouri on the ground of his want of principle & have never subscribed for his paper. When any publication appears in the Globe relative to this controversy, I have not permitted myself to take part in it. But I feel an interest in what is said on both sides and I still retain some of my old partialities. Perhaps no man living (except Mr. Monroe and his cabinet) knows as much as I do about the events connected with the Seminole campaign. It was at my insistence that Mr. Monroe was prevailed upon to extend the orders to the commanding General to enter Florida in pursuit of the Indians. The prospect of obtaining a formal intimation from the administration to Gen'l Jackson to take possession of Florida originated with me. My anxiety to occupy the Floridas was so great that I was willing to risque a war with Spain to effect that subject. I believe General Jackson on such an intimation would cheerfully incur the responsibility of that measure. When discussing the propriety of authorizing the commanding general to cross the boundary of the United States to pursuit of the Indians Mr. Monroe often remarked, "We must respect the Spanish authorities wherever their flag is maintained or ere become involved in a war not only with Spain, but likewise with the holy alliance." On hearing that Gen'l Jackson had occupied St. Mary's & Pensacola I supposed it probable the administration had given the information I had suggested thro' some other channel than myself. Shortly after the manifests of the administration was published in the Intelligencer the letter from Washington referred to by Mr. Crawford appeared. Many reports were industriously in Ten(nessee) calculated to prejudice Mr. Crawford. On my arrival at Washington in 1818 I sought the first opportunity to inquire of CR: (Crawford) what part he had taken in the Cabinet council. He then gave me the same account contained in his letter to Mr. Forscyth. General Jackson arrived in Washington during the discussion of the Seminole campaign in the H. of Repre: On hearing that he was profuse in his abuse of Crawford I stated to many persons with the view of this reaching the Gen'ls ears, that he was misinformed to the part Mr. CR: had taken in the deliberations, that it was Mr. Calhoun and not CR: who had proposed the court martial. On returning home in the Spring of 1819 I continued to make the same statement to prove it by the Prest & his Cabinet if desirable to Gen'l Jackson. But this all went for nothing. Public prejudice had been incited against CR: I was identified with him and a thousand slanders were circulated vs. me. Finding that the Gen'ls wrath could not be appeased, I determined on a defensive position. The Gen'l and some of his friends determined to have an investigation into my conduct before the succeeding Legislature. I prepared my defense containing all the facts within my knowledge relative to the campaign & embracing many of the circumstances disclosed in the late correspondence. No movement was made, however, in the Legislature, altho Gen'l Jackson in a letter to a gentleman in Nashville now in my possession stated that such a measure was intended. I had witnessed the obsequisness of Mr. Calhoun to Gen'l Jackson in Washington. I supposed that the latter knew that the former had moved his arrest in the Cabinet council. I could not account for what had passed in Washington except for the supposition that all the pretenders to the throne except Clay had confederated to demolish CR: This strengthened my zeal for him, as I knew he had been unjustly assailed. In December 1818 CR: stated to me that Calhoun was highly censurable for not answering Jackson's letter to Monroe in which Mr. Rhea's name was introduced & that this circumstance had great influence in determining his cause in relation to the incidents of the campaign. CR: I knew had no unkind feelings towards Jackson until after he had been much traduced. I was intimate with him & believed him to be a man of unsullied honor. The only thing that has ever transpired to his discredit is that he is now mustering in the ranks of his enemies without any atonement having been made (to my knowledge) for the outrages committed to his character. My lot in life has been singular. I have rec'd the greatest injury from those on whom I had conferred the greatest _____. On my arrival in Ten(nessee) when a young man I contracted a partiality for Gen'l Jackson. I stood by him thro' good & thro' evil reports and there were times when he needed friends. At one period when on his return from Richmond as a witness in Burr's trial persons of this place who now have his confidence shunned him as they would contagion. He cannot have forgotten this. When his militia army mutinied & abandoned him on the Creek campaign he wrote me on the 16th December 1813, by Judge White requesting me (having no power to order me) with my Regiment of regular troops in order he said, "to support the campaign & save the character of the state from disgrace." In violation of the orders of the War department of the 29th of October 1813 I did risque my com:(mission) & my fortune march to his relief, support the campaign, & save the state from disgrace. After the close of the war without the slightest provocation on my part unless it was preferring an other for Prest. He declared an interminable war against me which I presume will be prosecuted until death. Altho the General has some good points and expresses an extraordinary knowledge of human character yet he can be approached thro' his credulity & induced to make war on his best friends. I doubt whether any one whose life has been spared has ever rec'd as much injustice at the hands of another as I have from him. I expect to die in total ignorance of the causes of his unplacable & deadly hostility. The character of our former relations, & the nature of the war which he waged in 1815 precluded me from inquiring after the cause. I must beg pardon for this effusion. It is a subject in which you can feel no interest. And perhaps it is improper that I should have said so much to you. I am laboriously pursuing my profession, & expect to do so during the remainder of my life. I was provoked into a cavass for our Legislature in 1827 by persons who ought to have been my friends. On ascertaining that I should have no opposition the next election I withdrew. Within the last twelve months I have been strongly urged to represent this district in Congress. Which I could do almost without a struggle. But I have determined not to go to Washington to be put under the bow of the emperor. I shall be content to assist in putting out the late incumbent & putting in any other of a little better capacity & who has not descended from a Tory stock. This will seem strange to you, but the elections in August will probably verify it. I understood that Mr. Balch of Nashville has assumed the superintendence of your future views in this state. He is without much personal or political consideration. And the Prest. Will tell you so if you make the inquiry, I was a little surprised at Crawford's correspondence with him.

John Williams" [190]

---

[190] Williams to Van Buren, March 22, 1831

# Chapter 9
# Removal of Southern Indian Tribes

From Columbus' arrival in 1492 until John Quincy Adams took over the presidency in 1825, 333 years had passed. John Williams, in his anonymous book, *The Political Mirror*, ten years later in 1835 would say that "the fate of the North American people was that of any conquered people." Everyone knew what would eventually happen, but Williams fought it until he died in 1837.

John Williams spoke and wrote Cherokee. His writings are in the Cherokee *Phoenix* newspaper. He was friends with Cherokees since his boyhood in North Carolina. John Ross was his dear friend, and Williams used his pen to direct their legal defense in the courts.

> "After 1825 the history of the Southern Indians is limited to the epic and tragic theme of removal. The constant and unrelenting pressure by the United States warped all Indian relations; Indian resistance to removal determined practically all tribal actions. Their leaders were chosen because of their attitude toward removal, their councils deliberated only on the subject of removal. Removal was the subject of their thoughts, and the dread of it virtually paralyzed their lives."
> 
> Cotterill, R. S., *The Southern Indians*, Norman and London, University of Oklahoma Press, 1954, pp. 231-239

By the time John Quincy Adams became president, he had to deal with five tribes: Seminole, Creek, Cherokee, Choctaws, and Chickamauga... the only tribes still east of the Mississippi River. The Red Stick Creeks moved into Florida with their Creek cousins and were outnumbered there in the combined tribes.

Florida Governor Andrew Jackson wanted the Creeks returned to Alabama. Under pressure from both sides, the Seminole chiefs settled for a reservation in Central Florida, but it was doomed to failure for lack of good soil and prey animals. Starving Seminoles took white settlers' cattle. This resulted in the demise of the Red Stick Creeks and the return to prominence of the Muscogees. Three treaties later the Seminoles' fate still was not settled with settlers in Alabama and Georgia fighting their return there.

With the defeats of the Creeks, Seminoles, and Chickasaws, most of the great Southwest was Indian-free. Settlers had immigrated to these lands and had begun peaceful lives. The Cherokee, who had so valiantly helped at Horseshoe Bend, were simply trying to do the same: lead peaceful lives. They retained ownership of the mountainous lands in Tennessee, North Carolina, and Georgia.

There was a sentiment and a demand that those Indians east of the Mississippi River be removed west of it. Since negotiations had failed to accomplish this goal, legislative methods were being used to force it upon the Cherokee.

John Williams saw this crisis evolving. He had for several years opposed the methods and motives of the Georgians, but he was without power to prevent it. He chose to become involved. John Williams spent the last winter of his life at New Echota, Georgia, with John Ross, chief of the Cherokee, and his people. It is possible that he might have known Sequoia while there; Sequoia (also known as

George Guess) put the Cherokee verbal language into a written language, enabling them to provide a written history of their own for the first time. Williams wrote anonymous articles in the *Cherokee Phoenix*, which also printed about thirty percent of its content in Cherokee.

Little is known of what occurred during that winter. Enough occurred that Williams again called upon Martin Van Buren. His letter of April 2, 1837, voiced his concerns and plans:

*"Dear Sir;*

*"I have spent the greater part of the last winter at New Echota attending to professional business before the com. Under the late treaty with the Cherokees. Having an opportunity of knowing the condition of things in that Country I feel it my duty to give you correct information. The treaty of Ridge party does not constitute one twentieth of the nation. The common Indians have been told by John Ross that the treaty is no treaty; & that they will continue to occupy their Country. Ross possesses a more absolute contract over the common Indians, than the Pope does over his Papal dominions... Many of the Indians are building houses & extending their farms, as if they were to remain presently where they are. Unless some other arrangement is made, the Indians will have to be removed at the point of a bayonet. When this is done some of them will be killed; their relations will take satisfaction & an Indian War will be the consequence. It will be as difficult to drive them out of the almost inaccessible mountains of No Carolina & Tennessee as it has been to hunt the Seminoles in the hammocks of Florida. This would cost a vast expenditure of both blood & treasure. The only remedy is to make a supplemental article to the treaty, give the Indians an additional sum for their Country, vest one half of it in the Charleston & the other half in the Georgia railroad. This appropriation would be the surest means of reconciling Georgia to the measure, and would probably have the effect of sending the Cherokees West in a good humour. From the advancement of the Cherokee in civilization, they will exercise a controlling influence over the other tribes, West of the Mississippi. If disposed to do so, they could array from the different tribes a vast Indian force, & drive the White population across the Mississippi before an army could be raised & marched to that frontier. The Government has been fortunate in the selection of General Wool to command the Cherokee Country. He has conducted his operations with great prudence & confidence of both the red & white people. I beg you to consult him about our relations with the Cherokees. I feel great solicitude that a War with the Cherokees should be averted. I am sometimes almost tempted to proceed to Washington & have a personal interview with you. I wrote a letter last winter to my old friend Col. Benton on the subject, but rec'd no answer. I have determined to address you directly & call your attention to this subject.*

*"Please accept of my best wishes for Your personal & political prosperity*

*John Williams"* [191]

General Wool, whom Williams mentions, wrote the adjutant general:

*"The whole scene since I have been in this country has been nothing but a heart-rending one, and such a one as I would be glad to get rid of as soon as circumstances will permit. Because I am firm and decided, do not believe I would be unjust. If I could, and I could not do them a greater kindness, I would remove every Indian tomorrow beyond the reach of the white men, who, like vultures, are watching, ready to pounce upon their prey and strip them of everything they have or expect from the government of the United States. Yes sir; nineteen twentieths, if not ninety-nine out of every hundred, will go penniless to the West."* [192]

All the tribes except the Cherokees soon ceased to struggle. The badgered Creeks, bereft of leadership by the death of Little Prince, and seeing their lands increasingly appropriated by white intruders whom they were powerless to remove, sent to Washington a delegation that, on March 24, 1832, signed an agreement to remove. The Seminoles yielded on the following May 9th. The Choctaws, after their other chiefs had resigned in fear of the Mississippi law, were influenced by Le Flore to accept removal in the infamous treaty of Dancing Rabbit Creek on October 28. The Chickasaws agreed on October 20. The Cherokee alone continued the contest, driving the intruders off their lands, removing their capital to Tennessee, and appealing to the Supreme Court of the United States for protection. These measures postponed but did not avert the final doom. On December 29, 1835, at New Echota in the absence of John Ross and other officials, a few dissident chiefs were corrupted into signing a treaty of removal, which Jackson shamelessly utilized as an expression of tribal consent. [193]

Colonel Williams wrote in 1835 of the event:

"223. The Condition and ulterior destiny of the Indian tribes within the United States have ever been subjects of deep interest with the Government. It has sought to introduce among them the arts of civilization, and to divert them from a wandering life. But these benevolent purposes have been marred,

---

[191] Williams to Van Buren, *Van Buren Papers*, April 2, 1837
[192] Conley, Robert J., *Cherokee Nation*, University of New Mexico Press, 2005,
[193] Cotterill, R. S., *The Southern Indians*, University of Oklahoma Press, 1954, pp. 231-239

generally, by the impracticable character of the aboriginal race, which make it necessary for the preservation of peace, and the progress of the white population, that the Government should avail itself of every favourable opportunity to purchase their lands, and, consequently, to drive the tenants further into the wilderness.

"224. From this fate, it seemed as if the Cherokees, the Choctaws and the Chickasaws, having made great advances in civilization, were to be redeemed. But, the two last have been unable to withstand the instances of the present administration, and have been swept beyond the Mississippi; there, it to be feared, to dwindle and perish, as the mass of their red brethren have done. The Cherokees have firmly resisted every effort to remove them; and the transition through which they are passing, is a case of absorbing interest in the history of man. Already do they till the ground, and manufacture, extensively, for themselves; they have workshops, schools, churches, a regularly organized government, a written language, invented by another Cadmus, and printing press. So great, indeed, has been their improvement, that individuals of this nation, as admitted, on all sides in Congress, are qualified for seats in that august body.

"225. The soil upon which these tribes reside, lies within the States of Georgia, Alabama, and Mississippi; which, claiming to be the only sovereigns, within their respective territories, have extended their laws over the aborigines; and former State having seized, surveyed, and distributed, without compensation, the Indian lands, thus committed a grievous oppressions, to which the General Government has become a party. But to understand this properly, we must develop, consisely, the relations between the Cherokees and the United States.

"226. It would be vain, now, to discuss the equity of the power, assumed by the States of Europe, and their American successors, over the aborigines of our continent. We characterize it, sufficiently, by observing, that the right of discovery, upon which it is founded, is that which force and art obtain over weakness and simplicity. Selfish as it is, the moral sense has moulded it into something resembling justice—has restrained it by principles which may not be abandoned, without the reproach of broken faith, and the condemnation of the world. These principles originate in a species of national law, and in special compacts between the Indians and the General Government.

"227. The source of all right to property, is possession and continued use. That, the Indian derived from his Creator; and it has been, in a qualified manner, acknowledged by his discoverer. Under the right of discovery, the Indians are admitted to posses a present right of occupancy, subordinate to the ultimate dominion of the discoverer; and, in a certain sense, to exercise sovereignty over the soil. They might transfer these right to the sovereign of the discoverer, but to none others; until transfer, they were deemed sovereigns, de facto. In a word, the Indian nations were always considered as distinct, independent, political communities, retaining their original natural rights, as the indisputed possessors of the soil, from time immemorial; with the single restriction, imposed by irresistible power, which excluded them from intercourse with any European potentate, other than the first discoverer of the coast of the particular region claimed; and this restriction the European potentates imposed upon themselves, as well as upon the Indians. With the rights of the discoverer, the United States adopted their obligations.

"235. With a view, however, to remove, the inconvenience under which the States of Georgia, Alabama, and Mississippi certainly laboured, the President proposed, 'to set apart an ample district, west of the Mississippi, and without the limits of any State or territory, to be guaranteed to the Indian tribes, so long as they shall occupy it; each tribe having a distinct control over the portion designated for its use.' This measure is of very doubtful policy. The Cherokees deprecate it, as one of utter ruin. The congregated Indian races may soon destroy the game; and with it, many of them must perish; The tribes, which range over a much larger territory than will be given to the exiles, suffer, annually, from famine, and the emigrants, as hunters, cannot escape it. As agriculturalists, they have much to learn, for which their new state would be illy adapted; and it greatly to be feared, that, in this respect, retrogradation will attend their removal, even should they be unable to escape the horrors of war, almost inevitable, among the commingled tribes. It is a question, however, which can be determined by experiment only; and Congress have consented to make it, appropriating a half million of dollars, for the allotment of a district beyond the Arkansas, and the removal of such tribes as will consent to emigrate.

"237. But the Cherokee will not depart. They have been assailed by order of the administration, with bribes and threats, but they are immovable. They cast themselves upon the graves of their fathers, and implore the Government, by the remembrance of their former power and hospitality, not to tear them from these relics of departed greatness; they point to their farms, their dwellings, their churches, and their schools, and cry, *"These are the fruits of the white man's benevolence, let him not destroy the good work of his hands."* We fear, however, they pray in vain. The administration has sped the bolt, which, unless averted, must prostrate the nation. But, if the Indians were disposed, for the sake of present peace, to abandon their country, they cannot rely upon the promise of the United States for protection. To every assurance of this kind, they reply, we now hold your most solemn pledge for the same purpose. We have called upon you to redeem it in vain. How, then can we confide in promises which we have found utterly worthless?" [194]

---!!!

About ninety years later, Knoxville historian S. G. Heiskell sought to memorialize the Cherokee in his writings. A portion of the tribe had escaped to the mountains and still survive on a small reservation given them in North Carolina. They never totally gave up:

"The combat between the pioneers of Tennessee and the Cherokees was bold and bitter and bloody on both sides, and the white man finally conquested. It is of interest to Tennesseans, therefore, to know something of this tribe that caused their ancestors so much toil and exposure, anguish and death, and who, finally, through the persistent policy of Andrew Jackson, a Tennessean, took up their march toward the west, where they now are.

"Unlike many other tribes of American Indians, the Cherokees seemed to prefer a mountain country, and they were the mountaineers of the South, and at one time claimed ownership of more than one hundred thousand square miles which covered all of Kentucky, all of Tennessee except west Tennessee, large portions of North Alabama and North Georgia almost as far down as Atlanta, one-half or more of South Carolina, and the mountainous section of North Carolina. This territory constituted the original claim of the Cherokees.

"When their final cession was made and they transferred all of their holdings to the United States government holdings, their territory consisted of lower East Tennessee, beginning at Fort Loudon, about one-half of the northern third of Georgia, and a small triangle in north Alabama. In the days of their greatest power their principal towns were along the headwaters of the Savannah, Hiwassee, Tuckaseegee and a large part of the Little Tennessee. The latter river rises in a spring in North Carolina, breaks through the Smoky Mountains into Tennessee and empties into the Tennessee River at Lenoir City, Loudon County, on the line of the Southern Railways. Telassee was the last Indian town going up the river before getting to the mountains, and it is the site of the present town of Alcoa in Blount County, Tennessee, where is located the plant of the Knoxville Power Company.

"The crest of the Smoky Mountains is the boundary line between North Carolina and Tennessee and is five thousand feet high and above the timberline. It has peaks 6,000 feet high, and one, Clingman's Dome in North Carolina, 6,619 feet. This range is the boundary of the Cherokee nation in Tennessee, and with it the Cherokees were familiar in all their history, and in it, around it, and about it, were perfectly at home. Beginning with this range, they lived along the full length of the Little Tennessee. We are justified in thinking that the God whom the Hebrews of old said made the world in six days, must have intended that the Smoky Mountains and the Little Tennessee River should be considered twin masterpieces of His handiwork. Connected with no other mountain range in the world is the element of mystery so pronounced as with the Smoky Range— none so impress the beholder with awe and solemnity. We look upon their vast domes and majestic heights and wonder how they came about, and when, and how it was possible that the Little Tennessee cleft the range in twain, and plowed its way from its initial spring in North Carolina, through Blount, Monroe, and Loudon Counties to its junction with the Tennessee River. In the combat between the mountains and the river—in the struggle of the water to pierce the towering land—there must have been a warfare of countless ages, when the river at last came off conqueror and broke through. Yet how important the river looks compared with these vast mountains! As we stand and gaze upon them, the Smokies seem to look down in everlasting silence, as if extending a

---

[194] Col. John Williams, the Political Mirror, pp. 113-118

speechless benediction upon the beautiful river as it wanders along beneath the cold white glory of the East Tennessee stars, with the sheen and glimmer of its waves reflecting the grandeur of the mountains and landscape, and the splendors of a beautiful land. When dusk comes, the Smokies seem so vast, so mysterious, so passing understanding, so typical of infinity, so inscrutable in meaning, with their peaks, and crags, and towering heights! Who can wonder that the solemn mountains were selected as the place where the Law written upon tablets of stone was handed to Mosses! Dread and tireless sentinels telling of Omnipotence and the Infinite, mysterious as life's fathomless mystery! In pondering the Smokies, we can but recall Coleridge's *Hymn Before Sunrise in the Valley of Chamouni*.

"But thou most awful form!
Rises from forth thy silent sea of pines,
How silently! Around thee and above
Deep in the air, and dark, substantial, black,
An ebon mass; methinks thou piercest it
As with a wedge! But when I look again
It is thin own calm home, thy crystal shrine,
Thy habitation from eternity!
O dread and silent mount! I gazed upon thee,
Till thou, still present to the bodily sense.
Didst vanish from my thought: entranced in prayer
I worshipped the Invisible alone.

"Chota, which was on the south bank of the little Tennessee, a few miles above the mouth of the Tellico, and between twenty and twenty-five miles from where the Little Tennessee enters the Tennessee River, was the capital of the Cherokee Nation and also a city of refuge. It was in the present Monroe County, Tennessee. Its population is not stated by any of the historians who have written about the Cherokees, but the Ethnolgical Report says the evidence about it indicates "a somewhat extensive ancient village." Chota being a city of refuge, any person, whether white or red, who had committed a wrong against another, could take refuge in it and be safe from attack, but this exemption did not continue after leaving Chota.

"...the Little Tennessee a gem among rivers, a very queen among waters. It glides like a stream of silver towards the sea from its home beyond the Smokies, and but the magic of its moist touch has carried gladness to the land through centuries without number. It does not count the years in its travel, it cannot gauge its measureless beneficence, and is mute in its ever-varying panorama of hills and meadows, lofty crags and blooming fields, glamorous landscape and scenic splendor. In the long ago it caught the eye of the stalwart Cherokee and enamored him with its charms, folded him to its bosom, and held him as a devotee on its banks for ages; and he, like his ancestry before him, swore by the Great Spirit that as long as life was in him and he could meet a foe on the battlefield, should mortal power drive him from its sparkling waters. Along these waters the daily life of the Cherokee was exhibited at its best.

"Whence the Cherokee came, and when, no voice tells us. All we know is that sometime in the long misty past, he came to this beautiful river, claimed it as his own, and in defense of his habitation along by it, he challenged John Sevier to mortal combat on many a blood field; and never, until 1838, when he voluntarily left it, was he so crushed that he quailed to offer the gage of battle to Sevier again.

"The Indian policy of the United States was always dictated by an expressed desire to get rid of the Indian, the method of doing so not considered very important. There was at least one virtue in the land-greed of the white man, which there was absolutely no hypocrisy or cant in his openly expressed intention to get the Indian's land, and drive the Indian away, no matter where.

"In its general aspect the battle for land between the white man and the red man is the same old battle of the strong against the weak, of trained and organized prowess against the untrained and unorganized children of the forest, of civilization against savagery; and this same battle has been going on ever since two men first wanted the same thing at the same time, which, of course, the stronger man eventually got.

"As the white man has come up from savagery, he claims that he has left behind him, as the snake leaves behind its shed skin, the traits, methods, and tendencies, of his original state; and, in a measure, this is true, but in essence, human nature does not change, and cannot, and the man and woman of five thousand years hence will love and hate, will strive and yield, will be master and vanquished, will be loyal and treacherous, will be fearless and cowardly, will be generous and avaricious, will be noble and pusillanimous, and in every other intrinsic quality, will be just the same as the man and woman of today. Conditions and environment may change and thereby influence human conduct; our mental outlook may be enlarged by science and discovery year after year and thereby our view of the wisest course to take under given circumstance be aided; all the innumerable things that go to make up that vast complexity we call civilization—its vices, crimes, diseases, ideals, splendors, hypocrisies, squalors, weaknesses, aspirations, achievements, great men and great women—may sway us and move us and impress us and inspire us, but we are the same men and women in essential character, after all and everywhere.

"The treatment by our Government of the American Indian is a closed chapter in history. The tribal governments have been dissolved, and the members have been merged into the general body of the American people. Our Indian chapter being closed, we have every facility for judging of the conduct of the American people of that day toward the red man, and it must be confessed that that conduct produced the same results as in every age of the world where the stronger and the weaker nations met in combat, the weaker were crushed and demolished. While it is true the United States spent many millions of dollars on the red man, it is also true that the government's policy was not always straight, above board and honorable. In fact, in the course of the years, for a man to be an Indian Agent was, in effect, to be classified as a swindler and cheat, and the Indian his victim." [195]

Most of the Cherokee, including Chief John Ross, did not believe that they would be forced to move. In May 1838, seven thousand U.S. Army troops under the command of General Winfield Scott began arresting the Cherokee and moving them into stockades until they could be removed west. Altogether, there were thirty-one forts constructed for this purpose.

For eight years prior to the removal, the Cherokee were confronted with their future on a daily basis. Illegal stockades were built on their land, intended to house the Cherokee people long before their forced journey on the Trail of Tears actually started. As settlers moved into the area, these forts were built for the purpose of housing the Cherokee before their removal. The earliest of the forts was built in Georgia in 1830, shortly after the Congress passed the Indian Removal Act.

In spite of orders to troops to treat the tribe members kindly, the roundup was very cruel. Men, women, and children were taken away from their homes, families were separated, the elderly and ill were forced out at gunpoint, and people were given only a few moments to collect their belongings before being herded into forts with minimal facilities and food.

One member of the guard would later write: "I saw the helpless Cherokees [sic] arrested and dragged from their homes, and driven at the bayonet point into stockades. And in the chill of a drizzling rain on an October morning I saw them loaded like cattle and sheep into 645 wagons and started toward the west." [196]

It is difficult to imagine the hardships that the Cherokee who made the forced march to the Indian Territory had to face. Most of them hoped that the government would not force them to leave, and so made no plans for the long journey. When the government roundup of Cherokee began, many were forced from their homes with only the barest possessions. Sixteen thousand Cherokee were divided into sixteen detachments of about one thousand each.

Three groups left in June 1838, traveling by rail, boat, and wagon primarily on the Water Route. But the detachments found themselves making the journey in the hottest part of the year, when the river levels were too low for navigation.

Under the generally indifferent army commanders, human losses for these first groups of Cherokee removed were extremely high. Sickness and death rates caused by drought, bad water, bad diet, and physical exhaustion were especially high among children. Some of the Cherokee left almost naked and without shoes, or only in moccasins, and refused government clothing because they felt it would be taken as an acceptance of being removed from their homes. Some refused government food; others were given food that was not normally part of their diet, such as wheat flour, which they did not know how to use. One military estimate of the death in one of the parties was 17.7 percent, with half of the dead being children.

Fifteen thousand captives still awaited removal. Poor sanitation and drought made them miserable. Many of them died. Chief Ross and the National Council of Cherokee appealed to General Scott to permit the rest of the Cherokee to wait until fall to move, and to supervise their own removal. General Scott approved the plan and Ross administrated the effort. The Cherokee were moved from removal forts to internment camps until travel resumed.

Although the last parties under Ross left in early fall and arrived in Oklahoma during the brutal winter of 1838-

---

195 Heiskell, S. G., 190-195
196 Burnett, John G. http://www.powersource.com/cherokee/burnett.html

39, he significantly reduced the loss of life among his people. Twelve detachments of the Principal People that left in November traveled to Indian Territory overland on existing roads across Tennessee, Kentucky, Illinois, and Missouri. One detachment was led by the Rev. Jesse Bushyhead and his Cherokee wife. He had been brought up within the culture of the Indians, and became a leader among Cherokee in their struggle against the white man's intrusion. [197]

These detachments also met many hardships on their twelve hundred-miles-long journey to the west. Heavy rains turned the primitive roads to mud, and the Cherokee were often forced to manually drag the wagons out of the mud. Supplies of food were of poor quality. Road conditions, illness, and the distress of winter made death a daily occurrence.

Two-thirds of the ill-equipped Cherokee that were trapped beside the frozen Mississippi River still remembered a half century later the hundreds of sick and dying in wagons, or lying on the frozen ground with only a single blanket provided by the government to each Cherokee for shelter from the cold wind. Falling temperatures caused the surface of the river to freeze before all the detachments could be ferried across. The ice prevented both boat and horses from moving. Besides the cold, there was starvation and malnutrition. Weakened by the hunger, the Cherokee became easy victims of disease, particularly cholera, smallpox, and dysentery. Many died on both sides of the river waiting for the journey to resume. Quatie Ross, Chief Ross' wife, gave her only blanket to a child and died of pneumonia.

A traveler who witnessed a passing mother holding her dying child wrote: "She could only carry her dying child in her arms a few miles farther, and then, she must stop in a stranger-land and consign her much loved babe to the cold ground, and in that without pomp or ceremony, and pass on with the multitude." [198]

Another survivor of the march remembered:

"Long time we travel on way to new land. People feel bad when they leave old nation. Women cry and make sad wails. Children cry and make men cry, and all look sad like when friends die, but they say nothing and just put heads down and keep go towards West. Many days pass and people die very much. We bury close by Trail." [199]

In March 1839, all survivors had arrived at the Indian Territory, now known as Arkansas and Oklahoma, a word that means "red people." It was estimated that of the sixteen thousand who started the dreary march westward, more than four thousand Cherokee (nearly a fifth of the Cherokee population) died as a result of the removal. The route they made, and the journey itself, which lasted nearly a year, became known as the Trail of Tears. And so a country formed fifty years earlier on the premise "… that all men are created equal, and that they are endowed by their Creator with certain unalienable rights, among these the right to life, liberty and the pursuit of happiness…" brutally closed the curtain on a culture that had done no wrong. [200]

---

[197] http://www.bradley.edu/las/eng/lotm/TrailofTears/trailtext.htm
[198] North Carolina Museum of History: A Smithsonian Affiliate (https://www.ncmuseumofhistory.org)
[199] Ibid.
[200] http://www.bradley.edu/las/eng/lotm/TrailofTears/trailtext.htm

> **WITHIN**
> These narrow walls are deposited the Mortal Remains of
> # JOHN WOODS,
> Who, at the tender age of Eighteen Years, was
> ## SHOT TO DEATH,
> At Fort Strother, by the Orders of
> ## GENERAL ANDREW JACKSON.
> ---
> ### Stop Traveller,
> Wouldst thou learn the cause of the untimely end of this youth, know that, although he was the stay and comfort of an aged mother, she suffered him to
> VOLUNTEER IN DEFENCE OF HIS COUNTRY,
> Against a Savage Foe, on the 22d Jan. 1814.
> Whilst on Guard, he was permitted to retire for a short time, to satisfy the cravings of hunger.
> When over his humble repast, he was rudely ordered to a menial duty.
> *Inconsistent with that in which he was engaged;*
> And by one having no authority.
> As a Soldier, he promptly refused obedience to an illegal command,
> And insisted on returning to his duty on Guard,
> From which his absence was only by temporary permission.
> A RASH VOW
> Previously made by the General, could only be satisfied by his DEATH.
> A Pardon was offered to him, if he would
> ENLIST IN THE REGULAR SERVICE:
> A fatal reliance on the strict justice of his cause induced him to decline the offer;
> And although the Court, and all the Officers petitioned for his reprieve,
> *His Doom had been Sealed,*
> And he was SHOT TO DEATH, for strict adherence to duty,
> And for refusing compliance with an order
> Which, if complied with, must have led to the same fatal End!
> ---
> *The Youths of the American Militia*
> Have Erected this Monument to his Memory, July 4, 1828.

*Hurja Campaign Literature written by Col. John Williams 1828*

# Chapter 10
# The Finale

John Williams conceded the loss of Cherokee lands to the government; he'd seen the inevitable and simply proposed another method of compensation that might avoid bloodshed and future conflict after removal. He felt so strongly that he attempted to make good his suggestion of a personal interview by attempting to return to Washington, D.C.

Family tradition holds that shortly after leaving his house on horseback, he stopped near the junction of the two rivers east of Knoxville to cut a switch with which to hasten his horse. When he reached for the branch he was bitten by a scorpion. He suffered a reaction to the poison and was found by "a friendly Indian" who brought him home unconscious. Before an Indian medicine man could be summoned, he died on August 10, 1837.

I don't believe that at all—he only made it about two miles and his enemies knew he was coming. He told Van Buren, who could have told others. Secondly, I asked an entomologist for the state of Tennessee if we had ever had scorpions whose sting would kill a human and he said, "No."

Many newspapers took note of his passing, and a large obituary extolling his virtues was printed in Knoxville and North Carolina. He was laid to rest in the graveyard at First Presbyterian Church, one block off of the main street of Knoxville and a straight two-mile procession from his home. He left everything to his wife, Melinda, and the part that was taxed was "531 acres 1 free pole of land, 17 slaves, and 1 carriage." [201]

Goodspeed said of him: "Associates characterized him as possessed of graceful, courtly, dignified manners. His complacent and benevolent countenance, however, made him accessible to his humblest acquaintans. These qualities endeared him to all classes of people." [202]

*"It was Judge White's wilderness journey to go to Gen. Jackson's relief and it was the gallant regiment under the brave Col. Williams that enabled Jackson to win the victory at Horse Shoe, in all probability there would have been no New Orleans for Jackson, and without the prestige of the glorious victory at New Orleans, who can say that Andrew Jackson would ever have been President of the United States."* [203]

We now know some of the psychological implications of ostracism. It is a means of punishment for the ostracizer and leads to low self-esteem in the victim. In the feud between her husband and Andrew Jackson, Melinda White Williams became the victim.

In the early morning hours of March 2, 1838, seven months after John died, Melinda White Williams crept down the steps of the house she had built in 1826. Charles, her ten-year-old youngest child, was at his Uncle Alexander's house in Greeneville. Melinda White, daughter of the Southwestern frontier and the founders of

---

201 Knox County Estate Book No. 6 (Knox County Courthouse, Knoxville) 162: Minutes of County Court of Knox County No. 16 (Knox County Courthouse, Knoxville) 42
202 *A History of Tennessee, Nashville*: Goodspeed Publishing Company, 1886
203 *The Chattanooga Times*, Sept. 17, 1899

Knoxville, suffered from the quick loss of her husband and youngest remaining ten-year-old child. She was found in the early morning hours at her kitchen hearth with mortal wounds to her neck. The family kept her perceived suicide secret for 156 years. I have been told by doctors that it is a difficult way to commit suicide.

We now understand that suicide is the last, desperate act of a confused and temporarily besieged mind. It is part of the psychology of depression; we have medicines and trained counselors to deal with the symptoms. It is an illness, just like cancer, heart disease, or alcoholism, and the reversal back to the beginning of the *grieving process* simply overwhelmed her. She could no longer stand the loss of love she had so cherished. Still, John and Melinda died mysteriously and quickly—a source of great grievance for the remaining generations of the White, Overton, and Williams families.

When the procession carrying Melinda to the churchyard left the house she had built, there were no crowds lining the roads. The field slaves, however, dropped their tools, removed their hats, walked to the side of the road, and bowed their heads in honor of the lady with and for whom they had worked. Her descendants would speak of her in nothing but the finest terms for many generations, and a line of Melinda-named descendants exists to the present.

Colonel Williams died virtually anonymously; few know of his exploits, achievements, reputation, nickname, service to the country and state, and the love with which he established his family and lived his life. Williams' comment that Jackson "never seized upon the ruin of any man without accomplishing it" was especially true for himself. Williams lost to Jackson three times—militarily, politically, and diplomatically, but he never gave up. It has been said that Jackson saw Williams in every action that opposed him, and he was partially correct. Williams in his political opposition did the only thing he could do: he *wrote*.

He wrote some of the anti-Jackson pamphlets of 1828. It is believed he conspired with Joseph Binns of Philadelphia to publish the famous coffin handbills showing the coffins of six militiamen. He wrote political columns anonymously in several newspapers. Most of what Williams wrote was true, and Jackson's claim that his enemies had killed Rachel was a diversion. Many times he used that excuse to draw attention away from other issues. Most convincingly he wrote and published a complete book on the events of his time: *The Political Mirror: or a Review Of Jacksonism*. Someone at the Library of Congress wrote upon the title page that it was "curious and suppressed by the party." It gained no notoriety and has yet to be recognized as John's work. It reads as if it were a legal brief...for 264 pages. Little of his writing remains, but the lessons he learned have served his descendants well for many generations.

We have a habit of convicting our heroes so that, after a penance period, we can then come back and forgive them. It is a self-serving sociological device. It cleanses us from the sins we propagate against others, and it makes us feel self-worth for being human enough to "forgive" them of their sins. That is the legacy these many years of the Native American Indians. In generations of defeat and acceptance of being conquered, *they* have learned to forgive *us*. They have taught us NOT to hate, and through persistence, character, and nobility, they have beaten their conquerors from within. We have reached a maturity as a country that allows us to admit our sins of how we treated the Native Americans. We can memorialize that, forgive ourselves, and move on. I asked a Creek chief if he would consider a lawsuit to get some of their land back and he replied, "We are happy where we are." [204]

The contempt between the Jacksons and Williamses is over. It was politics. Neither was right nor wrong, but we can learn from the past and seek wisdom for the future.

General Woodward gave a great summation of General Jackson in 1859:

> "I shall close this by giving you what I think was the true disposition and character of Gen. Jackson. If he was not the most sensible and best man that I have ever known, he was the greatest man, with a large portion of the American people, whom I have had any thing to do with. His mind was stronger and better cultivated than many have thought it to be; a man of bitter prejudices and unforgiving disposition, and a true friend when he really proposed it. He could not be corrupted with money, strictly honest in all monied transactions, despised flattery though he often had it heaped upon him by the quantity, in his latter days. The only ones who could flatter him were those whom he looked upon as being so low they could have no motive, and those who stood so high as not to be suspected. He preferred having his own judgment respected more than that of the balance of the world. If he bet ten dollars on a horse race, he would pay a hundred rather than lose the ten; for with the loss of the ten dollars would go his judgment. He would never, for a moment, suffer himself to think that those he placed in office would

[204] Personal conversation: Muskogee Chief to Alex Brandau III

act dishonest—he being honest in money manners himself—and that was the cause of there being some defaulters in office during his administration. He would admit of no superior, and was jealous of those the people looked upon as his equals and was not at all times a judge of his true friends. There were thousands who appreciated him properly and admired him for his good qualities, but opposed some of his arbitrary measures, and some had not voted for him. Those he looked upon as his enemies, and never missed an opportunity to deliver them a blow under the fifth rib. His popularity at one time, and for a long time, was almost irresistible. He would suffer it used in the support of a friend, regardless of every thing, when silence on his part would have placed him in a more enviable attitude with the more reflecting and intelligent portion of mankind. I will cite one instance among many to show how far he would go. It has been the custom, and is expected, that demagogues and politicians will use every means to carry their points in elections. But there has always been one rule observed among our army and naval officers, and it never should be violated; for they established the rule and take them according to number, they are and have been the most thorough gentlemen I have any knowledge of. That rule was never for one officer to speak disparagingly of another, unless it was well known that he had been guilty of a gross violation of duty, or something else, that had rendered him an unfit associate for the balance. Gen. Harrison had been a Major General in the army and resigned. Gen Jackson succeeded to the command which Gen. Harrison would have held had he continued in the service. Gen. Jackson did much. He achieved a victory that the history of wars seldom records. The American people thanked him, they rewarded him, placed him in the highest office known to civilized men. But not to their credit do I say they submitted to his iron will, and in some instances a gross violation of their rights. It is well known, in a country like ours, that in some instances too high an estimate has been placed on military fame. It has governed in some of the most important elections, and has resulted in but little good to the country. In 1840 Gen. Harrison was a candidate for the Presidency. His friends seized upon his military deeds, and other things, as had Gen. Jackson's friends done before. Instead of remaining quiet and letting the people, arrange their own matters, Gen. Jackson departed so far from what I think should have been his proper course as to write a letter, giving the people, and particularly his own friends, to understand that he never had looked upon Gen. Harrison as a military man. This was objectionable, coming from the source it did. The times and circumstances at the time, some men have lived, have had much to do in building or pulling down their fortunes. It is quite likely that if Oliver Cromwell lived in England at any other time than that in which he did live, from the reign of Egbert down to Victoria he would have been looked upon as what he really was—a base hypocrit. - Clay, Webster, Calhoun, and Gaston (if the latter had possessed more ambition) would have been great at any age of the world, and so would Gen. Jackson have been more than an ordinary man at any time. And had he been old enough and placed at the head of any army, in the revolution, no doubt he would have distinguished himself, but never would have been rated higher than many engaged in that service, and perhaps not as high as Green, Wayne, Stark, Daniel Morgan, or Ethan Allen. And had there, but chance or otherwise, been any one who was placed higher in the scale of greatness than himself, I think it quite likely that he would have evinced, or would have shown, to some extent, a kind of jealousy to Charles Lee or Horatio Gates. Those of the Revolution were a different people to those of Gen. Jackson's time. In the Revolution, men were willing to serve, and if by chance they were killed, it would answer for their friends to read and speak of their deeds and daring. But not so in Gen. Jackson's time. There were too many who chose to live and see their name puffed in the newspapers, whether they merited it or not. Gen. Jackson knew the people he lived amongst, and knew how to control them and did do it.

"The best evidence I can give of his being a great man is, that without money and friends he raised himself from an obscure Irish boy to the head of this nation, and was the most popular man that ever was and perhaps ever will be in it again. I have not said Irish boy from any invidious motive, or to detract any thing from his true merit. - For I think if his true origin were known, it would only add to his standing, and prove to the world that he descended from a race of the right blood to make great men. One thing can be said of a truth, that he made more would-be great-men, the last twenty years of his life, than God has made truly great ones for the last two centuries. And if his ambition, at times, caused him to err, his love of country made him a good patriot; and the American people will cherish his memory, particularly those living in his time, while he sleeps quietly where the laudations of psycophantic and hypocritical friends and the reproaches of his enemies cannot interrupt his repose.

Yours Truly.<br>T. S. WOODWARD" [205]

### ---!!!

In his lifetime, Colonel John Williams studied law and military history and educated himself highly above what was customary in his times while serving in the United States Army as a captain. He became an expert on the United States Constitution; his expertise was recognized by his colleagues in the United States Senate.

He immigrated to Tennessee and helped establish courts of law in East Tennessee. While doing so he remarked to Federal Judge John Overton that the federal government should "use the abundant energy in the many streams of East Tennessee." After the Creek massacre at Fort Mims, he recognized the danger to his frontier home in Knoxville and called for action by the citizens to deal with the Seminoles to their south crossing into Georgia from Florida; the men he led were known as the Tennessee Volunteers. He enlisted 850 men for service in that war. He served as attorney general of Tennessee before and during the War of 1812. He met with President James Madison, who asked him to inspect West Point.

Colonel Williams commanded, recruited, and trained the 39th Infantry Regiment. They had orders to report to General Flournoy at New Orleans where Flournoy hoped to be placed as Seventh District Military Commander by promoting Williams to brigadier general. On the way to New Orleans, Hugh Lawson White (his brother-in-law), Thomas Lanier Williams (his brother), and Luke Lea, all of whom had made the trek through the wilderness to Fort Strother, told Colonel Williams of the perilous condition of Jackson's troops; Jackson's force was down to "about 75 men and were eating roots and berries." It took them all night to convince Colonel Williams to *disobey* his orders from General Flournoy and proceed toward Fort Strother to General Jackson's rescue. While en route, Colonel Williams received a second set of orders from General Pinckney to go to Jackson's aid; the 39th Infantry Regiment's arrival at Fort Strother resupplied Jackson's forces and restored military discipline to that expedition.

At the Battle of Horseshoe Bend, the 39th Infantry was instrumental in attacking the Creek barricade, which turned the battle into a rout that broke the back of the Creek Nation, ended the Creek War, and gave General Jackson his first significant military victory. Colonel Williams gave the order to charge with his sword drawn and his unit flag aloft. News of said victory was known at the negotiations to end the War of 1812; it was significant in Britain's decision to negotiate the war's conclusion. It led to General Jackson's promotion to major general in the United States Army and made him a national military figure *within about two months*, which led to his command at New Orleans.

Seeing his military accomplishments claimed by General Jackson, Williams was appointed to the United States Senate in 1815. He consorted with the best minds in the country and supported William H. Crawford for president in 1824. This aroused the supporters of General Jackson, who defeated Williams for another term in the Senate in 1823.

Williams was sent as our first diplomat to Central America by President John Quincy Adams in 1825, and he met Simon Bolivar there. Bolivar referred to him as "the elegant gentleman." Chief Justice John Marshall even sent his son with John Williams to Guatemala to learn from him. He submitted a request that Central American countries join with the United States in outlawing slave ships. He also helped the English get a treaty for a canal across Guatemala more than seventy years before the Panama Canal was begun. Williams accurately predicted the Civil War and its result in defeat for the South and was an early advocate for the end of slavery.

After serving the federal government, he retired from public life. He wrote many campaign documents in his feud with Jackson in both 1824 and 1828. Jackson and his supporters ostracized the colonel in Knoxville, his hometown, and he considered himself persecuted. He continued to provide legal aid to the Cherokee through his friend, John Ross. He spent the last winter of his life with the Cherokee in New Echota and added many articles to their newspaper, The Phoenix. He proposed to President Van Buren that the Cherokee could be paid for their lands in railroad stock and thus avoid what became the Trail of Tears. Williams died mysteriously, being poisoned in some fashion two miles from his home.

These facts are documented, and Colonel Williams' suppression and omission from history books has too long been forgotten. We, his descendants, have never forgotten his and his wife Melinda's contribution to their times. He never gave up in attempting to tell the truth; we don't either!

---

[205] Woodward, T. S., , pp 163-165

HOUSTON PIERCED WITH AN ARROW.

*Later in his life, Houston was asked what he had in his hands at Horseshoe Bend and he said he could not remember. No combat veteran in US military history has ever forgotten what he carried into battle. The Williams family contends it was the flag of the 39th Infantry that he had tended as Ensign and that he dipped to give the order to charge.*

Texas State Library and Archives

*Mary McConnell White Overton*
Public domain

*John Williams Overton*
Public domain

*John Williams II*
Used with permission of Charles and Lesli Higgins, personal property

*Princeton Cadets*
personal property of Alex Brandau III

# Epilogue

**A**ndrew Jackson outlived John Williams by seven years even though he was thirteen years older. In his later years at the Hermitage, he and Rachel were surrounded by her family, where he was loved, cared for, and generally adored. He became an American icon honored by more statues, city namings, street namings, and namesakes than anyone since George Washington.

His face adorns our most common denominator, the $20 bill. Nothing will ever change his accomplishments or place in our country's history; his legend has persisted much too long to be recalled. His home is visited by many tourists every year and has been rehabbed several times with government grants. He and Rachel are buried in the garden, where they lived and loved so well and for so long.

Yet Cherokee chief Junaluska, late in his life said of Jackson, "I was with him at the horse shoe all day. If I had known then that Andrew Jackson would later drive us from our home, I would have killed him that day at Horseshoe Bend." [206]

---!!!

**Sam Houston** lived to become the only American to serve as senator/governor of a state after having previously been president of his own country. His victory at San Jacinto made Texas our second-largest state. He learned soldiering from John Williams.

**John Overton** married Melinda White's sister. Within the family he shared some of the blame for Melinda's demise. Two of John Overton's great-grandchildren were named John Williams Overton and Melinda White Overton.

**John Williams Overton** was on pace to perhaps become the first sub-four-minute miler when WWI came along. He enlisted and was sent to France. Arriving late in the day, he was told that his unit was several miles away, and in the darkness of night he ran to their site only to perish in his first few days, at twenty-four.

**John and Rhoda Campbell Williams II** built their home, Marbledale, just down the hill from Melinda's Williams House in 1848. His elder brother was named for his paternal grandfather, so his naming after his father denoted him as II, not Junior. He…

"…was three or four times honored by an election to the lower house of the Legislature of Tennessee, from Knox County. In 1861 he was serving in that capacity, when the question of secession came up for consideration in that body, during its two extra sessions, and he, with unfaltering courage, voted against every proposition looking to that end. His vote was recorded with the small minority of brave men who, amid the storm and delirium of the hour, voted against the ordinance of secession. No man in the state was more outspoken or more bitter in his denunciation of this movement. He was earnest and unequivocal in his course and made no compromise. The whole movement was absolutely wicked, in his estimation. He announced it everywhere, never concealing or withholding his sentiments. Even after the state had voted to secede, and Confederate armies had occupied the country, in the presence of soldiers and officers, both publicly and privately, and at all times proclaimed himself a Union man, but he was a gentleman of the highest type of the old school, frank, manly, open, noble. There was no deceit, nothing false in him. He was as true as the laws of nature. In consequence of these qualities, men could always trust him, and his influence in molding and shaping the opinions of neighbors and acquaintances, in the shifting, changing condition of public opinion in 1861 was considerable. He was no speaker, but a worker and fine talker, his name lending strength to any cause that he espoused. In an eminent degree he possessed the qualities most needed in the terrible times of 1861, determination and a courage that knew no retreat. His family has just cause of pride in his record as one of the best and truest Union men in the South." [207]

206 Alderman, Pat. *Cherokee Chieftaness/Cherokee-Chickamauga War Chief.* Johnson City, TN: The Overmountain Press, 1978
207 Oliver P. Temple, *Notable Men of Tennessee*, New York: Cosmopolitan Press, 1912, p. 152

*Elizabeth Williams Sneed*
Personal property of Alex Brandau III

*Linda Lanier Sneed Brandau Wolfenbarger 1891-1972*
Photo personal property of Alex F. Brandau III

*Alexander Fyffe Brandau Jr*
Personal property of Alex F. Braandau III

*Picture of Melinda White Williams' bootprint from 1826*
Personal property of Michael Lanier Brandau

When Andrew Johnson came home from Washington in 1869 after being impeached, the only person who met him at the train station was John Williams II, who rode home to Greenville with him.

**Rhoda Campbell Morgan** was the daughter of Rufus Morgan, brother of Gideon Morgan, who led the Cherokee at Horseshoe Bend and whose mother, Patience Cogswell, was of Puritan stock from Essex, Massachusetts. Her mother was Elizabeth Trigg. She was the epitome of a southern lady.

John and Rhoda Campbell Morgan lived through the Civil War as Union sympathizers in Confederate Tennessee. She birthed four sons and two daughters who lived to adulthood. They placed their sons in Princeton during the war and sneaked letters through the battle lines.

Their daughter, Elizabeth Trigg Williams, married her second cousin (grandson of Alexander Williams), Joseph Williams Sneed. Knowing the decline of our family fortune, my great-grandmother said on her deathbed, "Remember who you are and where you came from," and we *try* to do that every day, five generations later.

Her brother, **Thomas Lanier Williams II**, married Isabel Coffin, who died at age twenty-eight of tuberculosis. Lizzie and Joe, as they were known within the family, reared TL's children—Ella, Isabelle, and Cornelius Coffin "C. C." Williams. C. C. Williams married Edwina Dakin Williams.

C. C. and Edwina had three children. Their firstborn son was **Thomas Lanier Williams III**, who became known as the celebrated playwright, "Tennessee" Williams. Tom wrote, among many topics, about his ancestors and particularly Colonel John and Melinda Williams and their family homeplace. Many of his works were based upon family history.

It is somewhat alleged within the family that his secret collaborator was Lizzie and Joseph Sneed's youngest daughter, **Linda Lanier Sneed Brandau Wolfenbarger,** my grandmother. Linda and Tom were first cousins once removed. It was *she* who most preserved the stories of Colonel John and Melinda Williams and the Flag of the 39th Infantry. She single-handedly saved the flag and gave me the office of family historian; I gladly pass it along to my daughter, Mildred Lanier Brandau Day

Her son, **Alex F. Brandau Jr.**, my father, grew up to be a sole proprietor in business. In his youth he owned a neighborhood store in the Morningside Community of East Knoxville. He served onboard the *USS Arkansas* during WWII and founded a business machine company, Dixie Cash Register.

So it is that by verbal history the adventures and romance of the Horseshoe Colonel and his bride have passed through *seven* generations.

---!!!

One hundred eighty-two years after she built it, Melinda White Williams' house was restored by her descendants. Shortly before we rededicated the house, our story was once again told in the *Knoxville News Sentinel.*

---!!!

Our family's wish is that the people of the future can learn from the mistakes of the past. By not having to learn every mistake firsthand, we might be able to ease some of the defeats we are bound to encounter. If we know how to handle the mental process for dealing with conflict, perhaps we can do it without hurting ourselves or each other.

The goal-oriented society in which we now exist rewards different kinds of people for how they play whatever game they choose—business, politics, money, fame. Andrew Jackson was awarded more fame and glory than he could have ever wished to see. John Williams was rewarded on this Earth with good children; a wonderful, loving wife; and generations of descendants who yet cherish and honor their memory. He excelled and won at the game of life.

Life is about the love. It is not about whether you win or lose, but how you adhere to the conscience you carry around with you and wake up with every morning. Families come and go through the generations. Some things get passed down to the next and many get simply forgotten. But, some things learned by our ancestors of the past get passed along to the future.

Summarized Russell Baker in his book, *The Happy Years:* "So it is with families. We pass the dead generations on to the future aboard our children. This keeps the people of the past alive long after we have taken them to the church yard."

"After all, high station in life is earned by the gallantry with which appalling experiences are survived with grace. A man must live through his life's duration with his own little set of fears and angers, suspicions and vanities, and his appetites, spiritual and carnal. Life is built of them and he is built of life." — *Memoirs*, by Tennessee Williams

*MEMOIRS, copyright ©1975 by The University of the South. Reprinted by permission of New Directions Publishing Corp.*

# The End

The Author greatly thanks Lanier Brandau Day and
Linda Edwards Brandau for their valuable assistance;
without them this book would not have happened.

**AFB III**

*Four Alexander Brandaus: Alex F. III, Alex F. Sr., Alex F. Jr., Alexander Lawrence*
*Personal property of Michael Lanier Brandau*

www.ingramcontent.com/pod-product-compliance
Lightning Source LLC
Chambersburg PA
CBHW062132160426

43191CB00013B/2276